Basic Documents of International Organization

Revised Edition

**Edited with Notes and
an Introduction by**

Samuel Shih-Tsai Chen
Central Connecticut State College

KENDALL/HUNT PUBLISHING COMPANY
2460 Kerper Boulevard, Dubuque, Iowa 52001

B   401947   01

To
my students
far and near

Contents

Introduction

The dream of "One World," the yearning for universal peace, and the aspiration for bettering their lots, all drive men and women from every corner of the earth toward international organization. It is beyond any shade of doubt that international institutions are multiplying and international interactions are increasing at remarkable rates, and it is not surprising that popular interest in international organization is growing rapidly throughout the entire world.

In order to meet a common demand and as a companion to my book, *The Theory and Practice of International Organization,* this volume is designed to serve the purpose of ready reference to the basic documents relating to the various aspects of international organization. For the sake of convenience, the documents have been classified into two groups, namely, (1) documents for global application, and (2) documents for regional application. It is important to bear in mind that none of these documents is standing alone. On the contrary, they are interrelated one to another, and they have been woven into a complex fabric in the international community.

In the following pages, it is hoped that the readers will be able to see not only the static conditions of international organization, such as the constitutional foundation of the United Nations system, but also the dynamics of international organization, such as the progressive implementation of the principles concerning the protection of human rights. However, because of space limitation, the documents contained in this collection have been largely confined to those which are generally regarded as basic to the study of international organization. While all these documents are in current use, the Covenant of the League of Nations is included as an appendix because of its historical importance.

Part I
Documents for Global Application

1. Charter of the United Nations

Adopted by the United Nations Conference on International Organization at San Francisco on June 26, 1945, the Charter came into force on October 24, 1945. Amendments are printed in italics in substitution for the original text in brackets.

WE THE PEOPLES OF THE UNITED NATIONS DETERMINED

to save succeeding generations from the scourge of war, which twice in our lifetime has brought untold sorrow to mankind, and

to reaffirm faith in fundamental human rights, in the dignity and worth of the human person, in the equal rights of men and women and of nations large and small, and

to establish conditions under which justice and respect for the obligations arising from treaties and other sources of international law can be maintained, and

to promote social progress and better standards of life in larger freedom,

AND FOR THESE ENDS

to practice tolerance and live together in peace with one another as good neighbors, and

to unite our strength to maintain international peace and security, and

to ensure, by the acceptance of principles and the institution of methods, that armed force shall not be used, save in the common interest, and

to employ international machinery for the promotion of the economic and social advancement of all peoples,

HAVE RESOLVED TO COMBINE OUR EFFORTS TO ACCOMPLISH THESE AIMS

Accordingly, our respective Governments, through representatives assembled in the city of San Francisco, who have exhibited their full powers found to be in good and due form, have agreed to the present Charter of the United Nations and do hereby establish an international organization to be known as the United Nations.

I. PURPOSES AND PRINCIPLES

ARTICLE 1

The Purposes of the United Nations are:

1. To maintain international peace and security, and to that end: to take effective collective measures for the prevention and removal of threats to the peace, and for the suppression of acts of aggression or other breaches of the peace, and to bring about by peaceful means, and in conformity with the principles of justice and international law, adjustment or settlement of international disputes or situations which might lead to a breach of the peace;

2. To develop friendly relations among nations based on respect for the principle of equal rights and self-determination of peoples, and to take other appropriate measures to strengthen universal peace;

3. To achieve international cooperation in solving international problems of an economic, social, cultural, or humanitarian character, and in promoting and encouraging respect for human rights and for fundamental freedoms for all without distinction as to race, sex, language, or religion; and

4. To be a center for harmonizing the actions of nations in the attainment of these common ends.

ARTICLE 2

The Organization and its Members, in pursuit of the Purposes stated in Article 1, shall act in accordance with the following Principles.

1. The Organization is based on the principle of the sovereign equality of all its Members.

2. All Members, in order to ensure to all of them the rights and benefits resulting from membership, shall fulfill in good faith the obligations assumed by them in accordance with the present Charter.

3. All Members shall settle their international disputes by peaceful means in such a manner that international peace and security, and justice, are not endangered.

4. All Members shall refrain in their international relations from the threat or use of force against the territorial integrity or political independence of any state, or in any other manner inconsistent with the Purposes of the United Nations.

5. All Members shall give the United Nations every assistance in any action it takes in accordance with the present Charter, and shall refrain from giving assistance to any state against which the United Nations is taking preventive or enforcement action.

6. The Organization shall ensure that states which are not Members of the United Nations act in accordance with these principles so far as may be necessary for the maintenance of international peace and security.

7. Nothing contained in the present Charter shall authorize the United Nations to intervene in matters which are essentially within the domestic jurisdiction of any state or shall require the Members to submit such matters to settlement under the present Charter; but this principle shall not prejudice the application of enforcement measures under Chapter VII.

II. MEMBERSHIP

ARTICLE 3

The original Members of the United Nations shall be the states which, having participated in the United Nations Conference on International Organization at San Francisco, or having previously signed the Declaration by United Nations of January 1, 1942, sign the present Charter and ratify it in accordance with Article 110.

ARTICLE 4

1. Membership in the United Nations is open to all other peace-loving states which accept the obligations contained in the present Charter and, in the judgment of the Organization, are able and willing to carry out these obligations.

2. The admission of any such state to membership in the United Nations will be effected by a decision of the General Assembly upon the recommendation of the Security Council.

ARTICLE 5

A Member of the United Nations against which preventive or enforcement action has been taken by the Security Council may be suspended from the exercise of the rights and privileges of membership by the General Assembly upon the recommendation of the Security Council. The exercise of these rights and privileges may be restored by the Security Council.

ARTICLE 6

A Member of the United Nations which has persistently violated the Principles contained in the present Charter may be expelled from the Organization by the General Assembly upon the recommendation of the Security Council.

III. ORGANS

ARTICLE 7

1. There are established as the principal organs of the United Nations: a General Assembly, a Security Council, an Economic and Social Council, a Trusteeship Council, an International Court of Justice, and a Secretariat.

2. Such subsidiary organs as may be found necessary may be established in accordance with the present Charter.

ARTICLE 8

The United Nations shall place no restrictions on the eligibility of men and women to participate in any capacity and under conditions of equality in its principal and subsidiary organs.

IV. THE GENERAL ASSEMBLY

Composition

ARTICLE 9

1. The General Assembly shall consist of all the Members of the United Nations.

2. Each Member shall have not more than five representatives in the General Assembly.

Functions and Powers

ARTICLE 10

The General Assembly may discuss any questions or any matters within the scope of the present Charter or relating to the powers and functions of any organs provided for in the present Charter, and except as provided in Article 12, may make recommendations to the Members of the United Nations or to the Security Council or to both on any such questions or matters.

ARTICLE 11

1. The General Assembly may consider the general principles of cooperation in the maintenance of international peace and security, including the principles governing disarmament and the regulation of armaments, and may make recommendations with regard to such principles to the Members or to the Security Council or to both.

2. The General Assembly may discuss any questions relating to the maintenance of international peace and security brought before it by any Member of the United Nations, or by the Security Council, or by a state which is not a Member of the United Nations in accordance with Article 35, paragraph 2, and, except as provided in Article 12, may make recommendations with regard to any such questions to the state or states concerned or to the Security Council or to both. Any such question on which action is necessary shall be referred to the Security Council by the General Assembly either before or after discussion.

3. The General Assembly may call the attention of the Security Council to situations which are likely to endanger international peace and security.

4. The powers of the General Assembly set forth in this Article shall not limit the general scope of Article 10.

ARTICLE 12

1. While the Security Council is exercising in respect of any dispute or situation the functions assigned to it in the present Charter, the General Assembly shall not make any recommendation with regard to that dispute or situation unless the Security Council so requests.

2. The Secretary-General, with the consent of the Security Council, shall notify the General Assembly at each session of any matters relative to the maintenance of international peace and security which are being dealt with by the Security Council and shall similarly notify the General Assembly, or the Members of the United Nations if the General Assembly is not in session, immediately the Security Council ceases to deal with such matters.

ARTICLE 13

1. The General Assembly shall initiate studies and make recommendations for the purpose of:

a. promoting international cooperation in the political field and encouraging the progressive development of international law and its codification;

b. promoting international cooperation in the economic, social, cultural, educational, and health fields, and assisting in the realization of human rights and fundamental freedoms for all without distinction as to race, sex, language, or religion.

2. The further responsibilities, functions, and powers of the General Assembly with respect to matters mentioned in paragraph 1 (b) above are set forth in Chapters IX and X.

ARTICLE 14

Subject to the provisions of Article 12, the General Assembly may recommend measures for the peaceful adjustment of any situation, regardless of origin, which it deems likely to impair the general welfare or friendly relations among nations, including situations resulting from a violation of the provisions of the present Charter setting forth the Purposes and Principles of the United Nations.

ARTICLE 15

1. The General Assembly shall receive and consider annual and special reports from the Security Council; these reports shall include an account of the measures that the Security Council has decided upon or taken to maintain international peace and security.

2. The General Assembly shall receive and consider reports from the other organs of the United Nations.

ARTICLE 16

The General Assembly shall perform such functions with respect to the international trusteeship system as are assigned to it under Chapters XII and XIII, including the approval of the trusteeship agreements for areas not designated as strategic.

ARTICLE 17

1. The General Assembly shall consider and approve the budget of the Organization.

2. The expenses of the Organization shall be borne by the Members as apportioned by the General Assembly.

3. The General Assembly shall consider and approve any financial and budgetary arrangements with specialized agencies referred to in Article 57 and shall examine the administrative budgets of such specialized agencies with a view to making recommendations to the agencies concerned.

Voting
ARTICLE 18

1. Each member of the General Assembly shall have one vote.

2. Decisions of the General Assembly on important questions shall be made by a two-thirds majority of the members present and voting. These questions shall include: recommendations with respect to the maintenance of international peace and security, the election of the nonpermanent members of the Security Council, the election of the members of the Economic and Social Council, the election of members of the Trusteeship Council in accordance with paragraph 1 (c) of Article 86, the admission of new Members to the United Nations, the suspension of the rights and privileges of membership, the expulsion of Members, questions relating to the operation of the trusteeship system, and budgetary questions.

3. Decisions on other questions, including the determination of additional categories of questions to be decided by a two-thirds majority, shall be made by a majority of the members present and voting.

ARTICLE 19

A Member of the United Nations which is in arrears in the payment of its financial contributions to the Organization shall have no vote in the General Assembly if the amount of its arrears equals or exceeds the amount of the contributions due from it for the preceding two full years. The General Assembly may, nevertheless, permit such a Member to vote if it is satisfied that the failure to pay is due to conditions beyond the control of the Member.

Procedure
ARTICLE 20
The General Assembly shall meet in regular annual sessions and in such special sessions as occasion may require. Special sessions shall be convoked by the Secretary-General at the request of the Security Council or of a majority of the Members of the United Nations.

ARTICLE 21
The General Assembly shall adopt its own rules of procedure. It shall elect its President for each session.

ARTICLE 22
The General Assembly may establish such subsidiary organs as it deems necessary for the performance of its functions.

V. THE SECURITY COUNCIL
Composition
ARTICLE 23
1. The Security Council shall consist of [eleven] *fifteen* Members of the United Nations. The Republic of China, France, the Union of Soviet Socialist Republics, the United Kingdom of Great Britain and Northern Ireland, and the United States of America shall be permanent members of the Security Council. The General Assembly shall elect [six] *ten* other Members of the United Nations to be nonpermanent members of the Security Council, due regard being specially paid, in the first instance to the contribution of Members of the United Nations to the maintenance of international peace and security and to the other purposes of the Organization, and also to equitable geographical distribution.

2. The nonpermanent members of the Security Council shall be elected for a term of two years. In the first election of the nonpermanent members [however, three shall be chosen for a term of one year] *after the increase of the membership of the Security Council from eleven to fifteen, two of the four additional members shall be chosen for a term of one year.* A retiring member shall not be eligible for immediate reelection.

3. Each member of the Security Council shall have one representative.

Functions and Powers
ARTICLE 24
1. In order to ensure prompt and effective action by the United Nations, its Members confer on the Security Council primary responsibility for

the maintenance of international peace and security, and agree that in carrying out its duties under this responsibility the Security Council acts on their behalf.

2. In discharging these duties the Security Council shall act in accordance with the Purposes and Principles of the United Nations. The specific powers granted to the Security Council for the discharge of these duties are laid down in Chapters VI, VII, VIII, and XII.

3. The Security Council shall submit annual and, when necessary, special reports to the General Assembly for its consideration.

ARTICLE 25

The Members of the United Nations agree to accept and carry out the decisions of the Security Council in accordance with the present Charter.

ARTICLE 26

In order to promote the establishment and maintenance of international peace and security with the least diversion for armaments of the world's human and economic resources, the Security Council shall be responsible for formulating, with the assistance of the Military Staff Committee referred to in Article 47, plans to be submitted to the Members of the United Nations for the establishment of a system for the regulation of armaments.

Voting
ARTICLE 27

1. Each member of the Security Council shall have one vote.

2. Decisions of the Security Council on procedural matters shall be made by an affirmative vote of [seven] *nine* members.

3. Decisions of the Security Council on all other matters shall be made by an affirmative vote of [seven] *nine* members including the concurring votes of the permanent members; provided that, in decisions under Chapter VI, and under paragraph 3 of Article 52, a party to a dispute shall abstain from voting.

Procedure
ARTICLE 28

1. The Security Council shall be so organized as to be able to function continuously. Each member of the Security Council shall for this purpose be represented at all times at the seat of the Organization.

2. The Security Council shall hold periodic meetings at which each of its members may, if it so desires, be represented by a member of the government or by some other specially designated representative.

3. The Security Council may hold meetings at such places other than the seat of the Organization as in its judgment will best facilitate its work.

ARTICLE 29
The Security Council may establish such subsidiary organs as it deems necessary for the performance of its functions.

ARTICLE 30
The Security Council shall adopt its own rules of procedure, including the method of selecting its President.

ARTICLE 31
Any Member of the United Nations which is not a member of the Security Council may participate, without vote, in the discussion of any question brought before the Security Council whenever the latter considers that the interests of that Member are specially affected.

ARTICLE 32
Any Member of the United Nations which is not a member of the Security Council or any state which is not a Member of the United Nations, if it is a party to a dispute under consideration by the Security Council, shall be invited to participate, without vote, in the discussion relating to the dispute. The Security Council shall lay down such conditions as it deems just for the participation of a state which is not a Member of the United Nations.

VI. PACIFIC SETTLEMENT OF DISPUTES

ARTICLE 33
1. The parties to any dispute, the continuance of which is likely to endanger the maintenance of international peace and security, shall, first of all, seek a solution by negotiation, enquiry, mediation, conciliation, arbitration, judicial settlement, resort to regional agencies or arrangements, or other peaceful means of their own choice.

2. The Security Council shall, when it deems necessary, call upon the parties to settle their dispute by such means.

ARTICLE 34
The Security Council may investigate any dispute, or any situation which might lead to international friction or give rise to a dispute, in order to determine whether the continuance of the dispute or situation is likely to endanger the maintenance of international peace and security.

ARTICLE 35
1. Any Member of the United Nations may bring any dispute, or any situation of the nature referred to in Article 34, to the attention of the Security Council or of the General Assembly.

2. A state which is not a Member of the United Nations may bring to the attention of the Security Council or of the General Assembly any dispute to which it is a party if it accepts in advance, for the purposes of the dispute, the obligations of pacific settlement provided in the present Charter.

3. The proceedings of the General Assembly in respect of matters brought to its attention under this Article will be subject to the provisions of Articles 11 and 12.

ARTICLE 36

1. The Security Council may, at any stage of a dispute of the nature referred to in Article 33 or of a situation of like nature, recommend appropriate procedures or methods of adjustment.

2. The Security Council should take into consideration any procedures for the settlement of the dispute which have already been adopted by the parties.

3. In making recommendations under this Article the Security Council should also take into consideration that legal disputes should as a general rule be referred by the parties to the International Court of Justice in accordance with the provisions of the Statute of the Court.

ARTICLE 37

1. Should the parties to a dispute of the nature referred to in Article 33 fail to settle it by the means indicated in that Article, they shall refer it to the Security Council.

2. If the Security Council deems that the continuance of the dispute is in fact likely to endanger the maintenance of international peace and security, it shall decide whether to take action under Article 36 or to recommend such terms of settlement as it may consider appropriate.

ARTICLE 38

Without prejudice to the provisions of Articles 33 to 37, the Security Council may, if all the parties to any dispute so request, make recommendations to the parties with a view to a pacific settlement of the dispute.

VII. ACTION WITH RESPECT TO THREATS THE PEACE, BREACHES OF THE PEACE, AND ACTS OF AGGRESSION

ARTICLE 39

The Security Council shall determine the existence of any threat to the peace, breach of the peace, or act of aggression and shall make recommendations, or decide what measures shall be taken in accordance with Articles 41 and 42, to maintain or restore international peace and security.

ARTICLE 40

In order to prevent an aggravation of the situation, the Security Council may, before making the recommendations or deciding upon the measures provided for in Article 39, call upon the parties concerned to comply with such provisional measures as it deems necessary or desirable. Such provisional measures shall be without prejudice to the rights, claims, or position of the parties concerned. The Security Council shall duly take account of failure to comply with such provisional measures.

ARTICLE 41

The Security Council may decide what measures not involving the use of armed force are to be employed to give effect to its decisions, and it may call upon the Members of the United Nations to apply such measures. These may include complete or partial interruption of economic relations and of rail, sea, air, postal, telegraphic, radio, and other means of communication, and the severance of diplomatic relations.

ARTICLE 42

Should the Security Council consider that measures provided for in Article 41 would be inadequate or have proved to be inadequate, it may take such action by air, sea, or land forces as may be necessary to maintain or restore international peace and security. Such action may include demonstrations, blockade, and other operations by air, sea, or land forces of Members of the United Nations.

ARTICLE 43

1. All Members of the United Nations, in order to contribute to the maintenance of international peace and security, undertake to make available to the Security Council, on its call and in accordance with a special agreement or agreements, armed forces, assistance, and facilities, including rights of passage, necessary for the purpose of maintaining international peace and security.

2. Such agreement or agreements shall govern the numbers and types of forces, their degree of readiness and general location, and the nature of the facilities and assistance to be provided.

3. The agreement or agreements shall be negotiated as soon as possible on the initiative of the Security Council. They shall be concluded between the Security Council and Members or between the Security Council and groups of Members and shall be subject to ratification by the signatory states in accordance with their respective constitutional processes.

ARTICLE 44

When the Security Council has decided to use force it shall, before calling upon a Member not represented on it to provide armed forces in fulfillment of the obligations assumed under Article 43, invite that Member, if the Member so desires, to participate in the decisions of the Security Council concerning the employment of contingents of that Member's armed forces.

ARTICLE 45

In order to enable the United Nations to take urgent military measures, Members shall hold immediately available national air-force contingents for combined international enforcement action. The strength and degree of readiness of these contingents and plans for their combined action shall be determined, within the limits laid down in the special agreement or agreements referred to in Article 43, by the Security Council with the assistance of the Military Staff Committee.

ARTICLE 46

Plans for the application of armed force shall be made by the Security Council with the assistance of the Military Staff Committee.

ARTICLE 47

1. There shall be established a Military Staff Committee to advise and assist the Security Council on all questions relating to the Security Council's military requirements for the maintenance of international peace and security, the employment and command of forces placed at its disposal, the regulation of armaments, and possible disarmament.

2. The Military Staff Committee shall consist of the Chiefs of Staff of the permanent members of the Security Council or their representatives. Any Member of the United Nations not permanently represented on the Committee shall be invited by the Committee to be associated with it when the efficient discharge of the Committee's responsibilities requires the participation of that Member in its work.

3. The Military Staff Committee shall be responsible under the Security Council for the strategic direction of any armed forces placed at the disposal of the Security Council. Questions relating to the command of such forces shall be worked out subsequently.

4. The Military Staff Committee, with the authorization of the Security Council and after consultation with appropriate regional agencies, may establish regional subcommittees.

ARTICLE 48

1. The action required to carry out the decisions of the Security Council for the maintenance of international peace and security shall be taken by

all the Members of the United Nations or by some of them, as the Security Council may determine.

2. Such decisions shall be carried out by the Members of the United Nations directly and through their action in the appropriate international agencies of which they are members.

ARTICLE 49

The Members of the United Nations shall join in affording mutual assistance in carrying out the measures decided upon by the Security Council.

ARTICLE 50

If preventive or enforcement measures against any state are taken by the Security Council, any other state, whether a Member of the United Nations or not, which finds itself confronted with special economic problems arising from the carrying out of those measures shall have the right to consult the Security Council with regard to a solution of those problems.

ARTICLE 51

Nothing in the present Charter shall impair the inherent right of individual or collective self-defense if an armed attack occurs against a Member of the United Nations, until the Security Council has taken the measures necessary to maintain international peace and security. Measures taken by Members in the exercise of this right of self-defense shall be immediately reported to the Security Council and shall not in any way affect the authority and responsibility of the Security Council under the present Charter to take at any time such action as it deems necessary in order to maintain or restore international peace and security.

VIII. REGIONAL ARRANGEMENTS

ARTICLE 52

1. Nothing in the present Charter precludes the existence of regional arrangements or agencies for dealing with such matters relating to the maintenance of international peace and security as are appropriate for regional action, provided that such arrangements or agencies and their activities are consistent with the Purposes and Principles of the United Nations.

2. The Members of the United Nations entering into such arrangements or constituting such agencies shall make every effort to achieve pacific settlement of local disputes through such regional arrangements or by such regional agencies before referring them to the Security Council.

3. The Security Council shall encourage the development of pacific settlement of local disputes through such regional arrangements or by such regional agencies either on the initiative of the states concerned or by reference from the Security Council.

4. This Article in no way impairs the application of Articles 34 and 35.

ARTICLE 53

1. The Security Council shall, where appropriate, utilize such regional arrangements or agencies for enforcement action under its authority. But no enforcement action shall be taken under regional arrangements or by regional agencies without the authorization of the Security Council, with the exception of measures against any enemy state, as defined in paragraph 2 of this Article, provided for pursuant to.Article 107 or in regional arrangements directed against renewal of aggressive policy on the part of any such state, until such time as the Organization may, on request of the Governments concerned, be charged with the responsibility for preventing further aggression by such a state.

2. The term enemy state as used in paragraph 1 of this Article applies to any state which during the Second World War has been an enemy of any signatory of the Present Charter.

ARTICLE 54

The Security Council shall at all times be kept fully informed of activities undertaken or in contemplation under regional arrangements or by regional agencies for the maintenance of international peace and security.

IX. INTERNATIONAL ECONOMIC AND SOCIAL COOPERATION

ARTICLE 55

With a view to the creation of conditions of stability and well-being which are necessary for peaceful and friendly relations among nations based on respect for the principle of equal rights and self-determination of peoples, the United Nations shall promote:

a. higher standards of living, full employment, and conditions of economic and social progress and development;

b. solutions of international economic, social, health, and related problems; and international cultural and educational cooperation; and

c. universal respect for, and observance of, human rights and fundamental freedoms for all without distinction as to race, sex, language, or religion.

ARTICLE 56

All Members pledge themselves to take joint and separate action in cooperation with the Organization for the achievement of the purposes set forth in Article 55.

ARTICLE 57

1. The various specialized agencies, established by intergovernmental agreement and having wide international responsibilities, as defined in their basic instruments, in economic, social, cultural, educational, health, and related fields, shall be brought into relationship with the United Nations in accordance with the provisions of Article 63.

2. Such agencies thus brought into relationship with the United Nations are hereinafter referred to as specialized agencies.

ARTICLE 58

The Organization shall make recommendations for the coordination of the policies and activities of the specialized agencies.

ARTICLE 59

The Organization shall, where appropriate, initiate negotiations among the states concerned for the creation of any new specialized agencies required for the accomplishment of the purposes set forth in Article 55.

ARTICLE 60

Responsibility for the discharge of the functions of the Organization set forth in this Chapter shall be vested in the General Assembly and, under the authority of the General Assembly, in the Economic and Social Council, which shall have for this purpose the powers set forth in Chapter X.

X. THE ECONOMIC AND SOCIAL COUNCIL

Composition

ARTICLE 61

1. The Economic and Social Council shall consist of [eighteen] *twenty-seven* Members of the United Nations elected by the General Assembly.

2. Subject to the provisions of paragraph 3, [six] *nine* members of the Economic and Social Council shall be elected each year for a term of three years. A retiring member shall be eligible for immediate reelection.

3. At the first election [eighteen members of the Economic and Social Council shall be chosen. The term of office of six members so chosen shall expire at the end of one year, and of six other members at the end of two

years,] *after the increase in the membership of the Economic and Social Council from eighteen to twenty-seven members, in addition to the members elected in place of the six members whose term of office expires at the end of that year, nine additional members shall be elected. Of these nine additional members, the term of office of three members so elected shall expire at the end of one year, and of three other members at the end of two years,* in accordance with arrangements made by the General Assembly.

4. Each member of the Economic and Social Council shall have one representative.

Functions and Powers
ARTICLE 62

1. The Economic and Social Council may make or initiate studies and reports with respect to international economic, social, cultural, educational, health, and related matters and may make recommendations with respect to any such matters to the General Assembly, to the Members of the United Nations, and to the specialized agencies concerned.

2. It may make recommendations for the purpose of promoting respect for, and observance of, human rights and fundamental freedoms for all.

3. It may prepare draft conventions for submission to the General Assembly, with respect to matters falling within its competence.

4. It may call, in accordance with the rules prescribed by the United Nations, international conferences on matters falling within its competence.

ARTICLE 63

1. The Economic and Social Council may enter into agreements with any of the agencies referred to in Article 57, defining the terms on which the agency concerned shall be brought into relationship with the United Nations. Such agreements shall be subject to approval by the General Assembly.

2. It may coordinate the activities of the specialized agencies through consultation with and recommendations to such agencies and through recommendations to the General Assembly and to the Members of the United Nations.

ARTICLE 64

1. The Economic and Social Council may take appropriate steps to obtain regular reports from the specialized agencies. It may make arrangements with the Members of the United Nations and with the specialized agencies to obtain reports on the steps taken to give effect to its

own recommendations and to recommendations on matters falling within its competence made by the General Assembly.

2. It may communicate its observations on these reports to the General Assembly.

ARTICLE 65

The Economic and Social Council may furnish information to the Security Council and shall assist the Security Council upon its request.

ARTICLE 66

1. The Economic and Social Council shall perform such functions as fall within its competence in connection with the carrying out of the recommendations of the General Assembly.

2. It may, with the approval of the General Assembly, perform services at the request of Members of the United Nations and at the request of specialized agencies.

3. It shall perform such other functions as are specified elsewhere in the present Charter or as may be assigned to it by the General Assembly.

Voting
ARTICLE 67

1. Each member of the Economic and Social Council shall have one vote.

2. Decisions of the Economic and Social Council shall be made by a majority of the members present and voting.

Procedure
ARTICLE 68

The Economic and Social Council shall set up commissions in economic and social fields and for the promotion of human rights, and such other commissions as may be required for the performance of its functions.

ARTICLE 69

The Economic and Social Council shall invite any Member of the United Nations to participate, without vote, in its deliberations on any matter of particular concern to that Member.

ARTICLE 70

The Economic and Social Council may make arrangements for representatives of the specialized agencies to participate, without vote, in its deliberations and in those of the commissions established by it, and for its representatives to participate in the deliberations of the specialized agencies.

ARTICLE 71

The Economic and Social Council may make suitable arrangements for consultation with nongovernmental organizations which are concerned with matters within its competence. Such arrangements may be made with international organizations and, where appropriate, with national organizations after consultation with the Member of the United Nations concerned.

ARTICLE 72

1. The Economic and Social Council shall adopt its own rules of procedure including the method of selecting its President.

2. The Economic and Social Council shall meet as required in accordance with its rules, which shall include provision for the convening of meetings on the request of a majority of its members.

XI. DECLARATION REGARDING NON—SELF—GOVERNING-TERRITORIES

ARTICLE 73

Members of the United Nations which have or assume responsibilities for the admisistration of territories whose peoples have not yet attained a full measure of self-government recognize the principle that the interests of the inhabitants of these territories are paramount, and accept as a sacred trust the obligation to promote to the utmost, within the system of international peace and security established by the present Charter, the well-being of the inhabitants of these territories, and, to this end:

a. to ensure, with the due respect for the culture of the peoples concerned, their political, economic, social, and educational advancement, their just treatment, and their protection against abuses;

b. to develop self-government, to take due account of the political aspirations of the peoples, and to assist them in the progressive development of their free political institutions, according to the particular circumstances of each territory and its peoples and their varying stages of advancement;

c. to further international peace and security;

d. to promote constructive measures of development, to encourage research, and to cooperate with one another and, when and where appropriate, with specialized international bodies with a view to the practical achievement of the social, economic, and scientific purposes set forth in this Article, and

e. to transmit regularly to the Secretary-General for information purposes, subject to such limitation as security and constitutional considerations may require, statistical and other information of a technical nature relating to economic, social, and educational conditions in the territories for which they are respectively responsible other than those territories to which Chapters XII and XIII apply.

ARTICLE 74

Members of the United Nations also agree that their policy in respect of the territories to which this Chapter applies, no less than in respect of their metropolitan areas, must be based on the general principle of good-neighborliness, due account being taken of the interests and well-being of the rest of the world, in social, economic, and commercial matters.

XII. INTERNATIONAL TRUSTEESHIP SYSTEM

ARTICLE 75

The United Nations shall establish under its authority an international trusteeship system for the administration and supervision of such territories as may be placed thereunder by subsequent individual agreements. These territories are hereinafter referred to as trust territories.

ARTICLE 76

The basic objectives of the trusteeship system, in accordance with the Purposes of the United Nations laid down in Article 1 of the present Charter, shall be:

a. to further international peace and security;

b. to promote the political, economic, social, and educational advancement of the inhabitants of the trust territories, and their progressive development towards self-government or independence as may be appropriate to the particular circumstances of each territory and its peoples and the freely expressed wishes of the peoples concerned, and as may be provided by the terms of each trusteeship agreement;

c. to encourage respect for human rights and for fundamental freedoms for all without distinction as to race, sex, language, or religion, and to encourage recognition of the interdependence of the peoples of the world; and

d. to ensure equal treatment in social, economic, and commercial matters for all Members of the United Nations and their nationals, and also equal treatment for the latter in the administration of justice, without prejudice to the attainment of the foregoing objectives and subject to the provisions of Article 80.

ARTICLE 77

1. The trusteeship system shall apply to such territories in the following categories as may be placed thereafter by means of trusteeship agreements:

a. territories now held under mandate;

b. territories which may be detached from enemy states as a result of the Second World War, and

c. territories voluntarily placed under the system by states responsible for their administration.

2. It will be a matter for subsequent agreement as to which territories in the foregoing categoires will be brought under the trusteeship system and upon what terms.

ARTICLE 78

The trusteeship system shall not apply to territories which have become Members of the United Nations, relationship among which shall be based on respect for the principle of sovereign equality.

ARTICLE 79

The terms of trusteeship for each territory to be placed under the trusteeship system, including any alteration or amendment, shall be agreed upon by the states directly concerned, including the mandatory power in the case of territories held under mandate by a Member of the United Nations, and shall be approved as provided for in Articles 83 and 85.

ARTICLE 80

1. Except as may be agreed upon in individual trusteeship agreements, made under Articles 77, 79, and 81, placing each territory under the trusteeship system, and until such agreements have been concluded, nothing in this Chapter shall be construed in or of itself to alter in any manner the rights whatsoever of any states or any peoples or the terms of existing international instruments to which Members of the United Nations may respectively be parties.

2. Paragraph 1 of this Article shall not be interpreted as giving grounds for delay or postponement of the negotiation and conclusion of agreements for placing mandated and other territories under the trusteeship system as provided for in Article 77.

ARTICLE 81

The trusteeship agreement shall in each case include the terms under which the trust territory will be administered and designate the authority which will exercise the administration of the trust territory. Such authority, hereinafter called the administering authority, may be one or more states or the Organization itself.

ARTICLE 82

There may be designated, in any trusteeship agreement, a strategic area or areas which may include part or all of the trust territory to which the agreement applies, without prejudice to any special agreement or agreements made under Article 43.

ARTICLE 83

1. All functions of the United Nations relating to strategic areas, including the approval of the terms of the trusteeship agreements and of their alteration or amendment, shall be exercised by the Security Council.

2. The basic objectives set forth in Article 76 shall be applicable to the people of each strategic area.

3. The Security Council shall, subject to the provisions of the trusteeship agreements and without prejudice to security considerations, avail itself of the assistance of the Trusteeship Council to perform those functions of the United Nations under the trusteeship system relating to political, economic, social, and educational matters in the strategic areas.

ARTICLE 84

It shall be the duty of the administering authority to ensure that the trust territory shall play its part in the maintenance of international peace and security. To this end the administering authority may make use of volunteer forces, facilities, and assistance from the trust territory in carrying out the obligations towards the Security Council undertaken in this regard by the administering authority, as well as for local defense and the maintenance of law and order within the trust territory.

ARTICLE 85

1. The functions of the United Nations with regard to trusteeship agreements for all areas not designated as strategic, including the approval of the terms of the trusteeship agreements and of their alteration or amendment, shall be exercised by the General Assembly.

2. The Trusteeship Council, operating under the authority of the General Assembly, shall assist the General Assembly in carrying out these functions.

XIII. THE TRUSTEESHIP COUNCIL

Composition
ARTICLE 86

1. The Trusteeship Council shall consist of the following Members of the United Nations:

a. those Members administering trust territories;

b. such of those Members mentioned by name in Article 23 as are not administering trust territories; and

c. as many other Members elected for three-year terms by the General Assembly as may be necessary to ensure that the total number of members of the Trusteeship Council is equally divided between those Members of the United Nations which administer trust territories and those which do not.

2. Each member of the Trusteeship Council shall designate one specially qualified person to represent it therein.

Functions and Powers
ARTICLE 87

The General Assembly and, under its authority, the Trusteeship Council, is carrying out their functions, may:

a. consider reports submitted by the administering authority;

b. accept petitions and examine them in consultation with the administering authority;

c. provide for periodic visits to the respective trust territories at times agreed upon with the administering authority; and

d. take these and other actions in conformity with the terms of the trusteeship agreements.

ARTICLE 88

The Trusteeship Council shall formulate a questionnaire on the political, economic, social, and educational advancement of the inhabitants of each trust territory, and the administering authority for each trust territory within the competence of the General Assembly shall make an annual report to the General Assembly upon the basis of such questionnaire.

Voting
ARTICLE 89

1. Each member of the Trusteeship Council shall have one vote.

2. Decisions of the Trusteeship Council shall be made by a majority of the members present and voting.

Procedure
ARTICLE 90
1. The Trusteeship Council shall adopt its own rules of procedure, including the method of selecting its President.
2. The Trusteeship Council shall meet as required in accordance with its rules, which shall include provision for the convening of meetings on the request of a majority of its members.

ARTICLE 91
The Trusteeship Council shall, when appropriate, avail itself of the assistance of the Economic and Social Council and of the specialized agencies in regard to matters with which they are respectively concerned.

XIV. THE INTERNATIONAL COURT OF JUSTICE
ARTICLE 92
The International Court of Justice shall be the principal judicial organ of the United Nations. It shall function in accordance with the annexed Statute, which is based upon the Statue of the Permanent Court of International Justice and forms an integral part of the present Charter.

ARTICLE 93
1. All Members of the United Nations are *ipso facto* parties to the Statute of the International Court of Justice.
2. A state which is not a Member of the United Nations may become a party to the Statute of the International Court of Justice on conditions to be determined in each case by the General Assembly upon the recommendation of the Security Council.

ARTICLE 94
1. Each Member of the United Nations undertakes to comply with the decision of the International Court of Justice in any case to which it is a party.
2. If any party to a case fails to perform the obligations incumbent upon it under a judgment rendered by the Court, the other party may have recourse to the Security Council, which may, if it deems necessary, make recommendations or decide upon measures to be taken to give effect to the judgment.

ARTICLE 95
Nothing in the present Charter shall prevent Members of the United Nations from entrusting the solution of their differences to other tribunals

by virtue of agreements already in existence or which may be concluded in the future.

ARTICLE 96

1. The General Assembly or the Security Council may request the International Court of Justice to give an advisory opinion on any legal question.

2. Other organs of the United Nations and specialized agencies, which may at any time be so authorized by the General Assembly, may also request advisory opinions of the Court on legal questions arising within the scope of their activities.

XV. THE SECRETARIAT

ARTICLE 97

The Secretariat shall comprise a Secretary-General and such staff as the Organization may require. The Secretary-General shall be appointed by the General Assembly upon the recommendation of the Security Council. He shall be the chief administrative officer of the Organization.

ARTICLE 98

The Secretary-General shall act in that capacity in all meetings of the General Assembly, of the Security Council, of the Economic and Social Council, and of the Trusteeship Council, and shall perform such other functions as are entrusted to him by these organs. The Secretary-General shall make an annual report to the General Assembly on the work of the Organization.

ARTICLE 99

The Secretary-General may bring to the attention of the Security Council any matter which in his opinion may threaten the maintenance of international peace and security.

ARTICLE 100

1. In the performance of their duties the Secretary-General and the staff shall not seek or receive instructions from any government or from any other authority external to the Organization. They shall refrain from any action which might reflect on their position as international officials responsible only to the Organization.

2. Each Member of the United Nations undertakes to respect the exclusively international character of the responsibilities of the Secretary-General and the staff and not to seek to influence them in the discharge of their responsibilities.

ARTICLE 101

1. The staff shall be appointed by the Secretary-General under regulations established by the General Assembly.

2. Appropriate staffs shall be permanently assigned to the Economic and Social Council, the Trusteeship Council, and, as required, to other organs of the United Nations. These staffs shall form a part of the Secretariat.

3. The paramount consideration in the employment of the staff and in the determination of the conditions of service shall be the necessity of securing the highest standards of efficiency, competence, and integrity. Due regard shall be paid to the importance of recruiting the staff on as wide a geographical basis as possible.

XVI. MISCELLANEOUS PROVISIONS

ARTICLE 102

1. Every treaty and every international agreement entered into by any Member of the United Nations after the present Charter comes into force shall as soon as possible be registered with the Secretariat and published by it.

2. No party to any such treaty or international agreement which has not been registered in accordance with the provisions of paragraph 1 of this Article may invoke that treaty or agreement before any organ of the United Nations.

ARTICLE 103

In the event of a conflict between the obligations of the Members of the United Nations under the present Charter and their obligations under any other international agreement, their obligations under the present Charter shall prevail.

ARTICLE 104

The Organization shall enjoy in the territory of each of its Members such legal capacity as may be necessary for the exercise of its functions and the fulfillment of its purposes.

ARTICLE 105

1. The Organization shall enjoy in the territory of each of its Members such privileges and immunities as are necessary for the fulfillment of its purposes.

2. Representatives of the Members of the United Nations and officials of the Organization shall similarly enjoy such privileges and immunities as

are necessary for the independent exercise of their functions in connection with the Organization.

3. The General Assembly may make recommendations with a view to determining the details of the application of paragraphs 1 and 2 of this Article or may propose conventions to the Members of the United Nations for this purpose.

XVII. TRANSITIONAL SECURITY ARRANGEMENTS
ARTICLE 106
Pending the coming into force of such special agreements referred to in Article 43 as in the opinion of the Security Council enable it to begin the exercise of its responsibilities under Article 42, the parties to the Four-Nation Declaration, signed at Moscow, October 30, 1943, and France, shall, in accordance with the provisions of paragraph 5 of that Declaration, consult with one another and as occasion requires with other Members of the United Nations with a view to such joint action on behalf of the Organization as may be necessary for the purpose of maintaining international peace and security.

ARTICLE 107
Nothing in the present Charter shall invalidate or preclude action, in relation to any state which during the Second World War has been an enemy of any signatory of the present Charter, taken or authorized as a result of that war by the Governments having responsibility for such action.

XVIII. AMENDMENTS
ARTICLE 108
Amendments to the present Charter shall come into force for all Members of the United Nations when they have been adopted by a vote of two-thirds of the members of the General Assembly and ratified in accordance with their respective constitutional processes by two-thirds of the Members of the United Nations, including all the permanent members of the Security Council.

ARTICLE 109
1. A General Conference of the Members of the United Nations for the purpose of reviewing the present Charter may be held at a date and place to be fixed by a two-thirds vote of the members of the General Assembly and by a vote of any [seven] *nine* members of the Security Council. Each Member of the United Nations shall have one vote in the conference.

2. Any alteration of the present Charter recommended by a two-thirds vote of the conference shall take effect when ratified in accordance with their respective constitutional processes by two-thirds of the Members of the United Nations including all the permanent members of the Security Council.

3. If such a conference has not been held before the tenth annual session of the General Assembly following the coming into force of the present Charter, the proposal to call such a conference shall be placed on the agenda of that session of the General Assembly, and the conference shall be held if so decided by a majority vote of the members of the General Assembly and by a vote of any [seven] *nine* members of the Security Council.

XIX. RATIFICATION AND SIGNATURE
ARTICLE 110

1. The present Charter shall be ratified by the signatory states in accordance with their respective constitutional processes.

2. The ratification shall be deposited with the Government of the United States of America, which shall notify all the signatory states of each deposit as well as the Secretary-General of the Organization when he has been appointed.

3. The present Charter shall come into force upon the deposit of ratifications by the Republic of China, France, the Union of Soviet Socialist Republics, the United Kingdom of Great Britain and Northern Ireland, and the United States of America, and by a majority of the other signatory states. A protocol of the ratifications deposited shall thereupon be drawn up by the Government of the United States of America which shall communicate copies thereof to all the signatory states.

4. The states signatory to the present Charter which ratify it after it has come into force will become original Members of the United Nations on the date of the deposit of their respective ratifications.

ARTICLE 111

The present Charter of which the Chinese, French, Russian, English, and Spanish texts are equally authentic, shall remain deposited in the archives of the Government of the United States of America. Duly certified copies thereof shall be transmitted by that Government to the Governments of the other signatory states.

In faith whereof the representatives of the Governments of the United Nations have signed the present Charter.

Done at the city of San Francisco the twenty-sixth day of June, one thousand nine hundred and forty-five.

2. Statute of the International Court of Justice

As an integral part of the Chapter of the United Nations, the Statute was adopted on June 26, 1945, and it came into force on October 24, 1945, just the same as that of the Charter. Parties to the Statute include, but are not limited to, all members of the United Nations.

ARTICLE 1

The International Court of Justice established by the Charter of the United Nations as the principal judicial organ of the United Nations shall be constituted and shall function in accordance with the provisions of the present Statute.

I. ORGANIZATION OF THE COURT

ARTICLE 2

The Court shall be composed of a body of independent judges, elected regardless of their nationality from among persons of high moral character, who possess the qualifications required in their respective countries for appointment to the highest judicial offices, or are jurisconsults of recognized competence in international law.

ARTICLE 3

1. The Court shall consist of fifteen members, no two of whom may be nationals of the same state.

2. A person who for the purposes of membership in the Court could be regarded as a national of more than one state shall be deemed to be a national of the one in which he ordinarily exercises civil and political rights.

ARTICLE 4

1. The members of the Court shall be elected by the General Assembly and by the Security Council from a list of persons nominated by the national groups in the Permanent Court of Arbitration, in accordance with the following provisions.

2. In the case of Members of the United Nations not represented in the Permanent Court of Arbitration, candidates shall be nominated by national groups appointed for this purpose by their governments under the same conditions as those prescribed for members of the Permanent Court of Arbitration by Article 44 of the Convention of The Hague of 1907 for the pacific settlement of international disputes.

3. The conditions under which a state which is a party to the present Statute but is not a Member of the United Nations may participate in electing the members of the Court shall, in the absence of a special agreement, be laid down by the General Assembly upon recommendation of the Security Council.

ARTICLE 5

1. At least three months before the date of the election, the Secretary-General of the United Nations shall address a written request to the members of the Permanent Court of Arbitration belonging to the states which are parties to the present Statute, and to the members of the national groups appointed under Article 4, paragraph 2, inviting them to undertake, within a given time, by national groups, the nomination of persons in a position to accept the duties of a member of the Court.

2. No group may nominate more than four persons, not more than two of whom shall be of their own nationality. In no case may the number of candidates nominated by a group be more than double the number of seats to be filled.

ARTICLE 6

Before making these nominations, each national group is recommended to consult its highest court of justice, its legal faculties and schools of law, and its national academics and national sections of international academies devoted to the study of law.

ARTICLE 7

1. The Secretary-General shall prepare a list in alphabetical order of all the persons thus nominated. Save as provided in Article 12, Paragraph 2, these shall be the only persons eligible.

2. The Secretary-General shall submit this list to the General Assembly and to the Security Council.

ARTICLE 8

The General Assembly and the Security Council shall proceed independently of one another to elect the members of the Court.

ARTICLE 9

At every election, the electors shall bear in mind not only that the persons to be elected should individually possess the qualifications required, but also that in the body as a whole the representation of the main forms of civilization and of the principal legal systems of the world should be assured.

ARTICLE 10

1. Those candidates who obtain an absolute majority of votes in the General Assembly and in the Security Council shall be considered as elected.

2. Any vote of the Security Council, whether for the election of judges or for the appointment of members of the conference envisaged in Article 12, shall be taken without any distinction between permanent and nonpermanent members of the Security Council.

3. In the event of more than one national of the same state obtaining an absolute majority of the votes both of the General Assembly and of the Security Council, the eldest of these only shall be considered as elected.

ARTICLE 11

If, after the first meeting held for the purpose of the election, one or more seats remain to be filled, a second and, if necessary, a third meeting shall take place.

ARTICLE 12

1. If, after the third meeting, one or more seats still remain unfilled, a joint conference consisting of six members, three appointed by the General Assembly and three by the Security Council, may be formed at any time at the request of either the General Assembly or the Security Council, for the purpose of choosing by the vote of an absolute majority one name for each seat still vacant, to submit to the General Assembly and the Security Council for their respective acceptance.

2. If the joint conference is unanimously agreed upon any person who fulfils the required conditions, he may be included in its list, even though he was not included in the list of nominations referred to in Article 7.

3. If the joint conference is satisfied that it will not be successful in procuring an election, those members of the Court who have already been elected shall, within a period to be fixed by the Security Council, proceed to fill the vacant seats by selection from among those candidates who have obtained votes either in the General Assembly or in the Security Council.

4. In the event of an equality of votes among the judges, the eldest judge shall have a casting vote.

ARTICLE 13

1. The members of the Court shall be elected for nine years and may be reelected; provided, however, that of the judges elected at the first election, the terms of five judges shall expire at the end of three years and the terms of five more judges shall expire at the end of six years.

2. The judges whose terms are to expire at the end of the above-mentioned initial periods of three and six years shall be chosen by lot to be drawn by the Secretary-General immediately after the first election has been completed.

3. The members of the Court shall continue to discharge their duties until their places have been filled. Though replaced, they shall finish any cases which they may have begun.

4. In the case of the resignation of a member of the Court, the resignation shall be addressed to the President of the Court for transmission to the Secretary-General. This last notification makes the place vacant.

ARTICLE 14

Vacancies shall be filled by the same method as that laid down for the first election, subject to the following provision; the Secretary-General shall, within one month of the occurrence of the vacancy, proceed to issue the invitations provided for in Article 5, and the date of the election shall be fixed by the Security Council.

ARTICLE 15

A member of the Court elected to replace a member whose term of office has not expired shall hold office for the remainder of his predecessor's term.

ARTICLE 16

1. No member of the Court may exercise any political or administrative function, or engage in any other occupation of a professional nature.

2. Any doubt on this point shall be settled by the decision of the Court.

ARTICLE 17

1. No member of the Court may act as agent, counsel, or advocate in any case.

2. No member may participate in the decision of any case in which he has previously taken part as agent, counsel, or advocate for one of the parties, or as a member of a national or international court, or of a commission of enquiry, or in any other capacity.

3. Any doubt on this point shall be settled by the decision of the Court.

ARTICLE 18

1. No member of the Court can be dismissed unless, in the unanimous opinion of the other members, he has ceased to fulfill the required conditions.

2. Formal notification thereof shall be made to the Secretary-General by the Registrar.

3. This notification makes the place vacant.

ARTICLE 19

The members of the Court, when engaged on the business of the Court, shall enjoy diplomatic privileges and immunities.

ARTICLE 20

Every member of the Court shall, before taking up his duties, make a solemn declaration in open court that he will exercise his powers impartially and conscientiously.

ARTICLE 21

1. The Court shall elect its President and Vice-President for three years; they may be reelected.

2. The Court shall appoint its Registrar and may provide for the appointment of such other officers as may be necessary.

ARTICLE 22

1. The seat of the Court shall be established at The Hague. This, however, shall not prevent the Court from sitting and exercising its functions elsewhere whenever the Court considers it desirable.

2. The President and the Registrar shall reside at the seat of the Court.

ARTICLE 23

1. The Court shall remain permanently in session, except during the judicial vacations, the dates and duration of which shall be fixed by the Court.

2. Members of the Court are entitled to periodic leave, the dates and duration of which shall be fixed by the Court, having in mind the distance between The Hague and the home of each judge.

3. Members of the Court shall be bound, unless they are on leave or prevented from attending by illness or other serious reasons duly explained to the President, to hold themselves permanently at the disposal of the Court.

ARTICLE 24

1. If, for some special reason, a member of the Court considers that he should not take part in the decision of a particular case, he shall so inform the President.

2. If the President considers that for some special reason one of the members of the Court should not sit in a particular case, he shall give him notice accordingly.

3. If in any such case the member of the Court and the President disagree, the matter shall be settled by the decision of the Court.

ARTICLE 25

1. The full Court shall sit except when it is expressly provided otherwise in the present Statute.

2. Subject to the condition that the number of judges available to constitute the Court is not thereby reduced below eleven, the Rules of the Court may provide for allowing one or more judges, according to circumstances and in rotation, to be dispensed from sitting.

3. A quorum of nine judges shall suffice to constitute the Court.

ARTICLE 26

1. The Court may from time to time form one or more chambers, composed of three or more judges as the Court may determine, for dealing with particular categories of cases; for example, labor cases and cases relating to transit and communications.

2. The Court may at any time form a chamber for dealing with a particular case. The number of judges to constitute such a chamber shall be determined by the Court with the approval of the parties.

3. Cases shall be heard and determined by the chambers provided for in this Article if the parties so request.

ARTICLE 27

A judgment given by any of the chambers provided for in Articles 26 and 29 shall be considered as rendered by the Court.

ARTICLE 28

The chambers provided for in Articles 26 and 29 may, with the consent of the parties, sit and exercise their functions elsewhere than at The Hague.

ARTICLE 29

With a view to the speedy dispatch of business, the Court shall form annually a chamber composed of five judges which, at the request of the parties, may hear and determine cases by summary procedure. In addition, two judges shall be selected for the purpose of replacing judges who find it impossible to sit.

ARTICLE 30

1. The Court shall frame rules for carrying out its functions. In particular, it shall lay down rules of procedure.

2. The Rules of the Court may provide for assessors to sit with the Court or with any of its chambers, without the right to vote.

ARTICLE 31

1. Judges of the nationality of each of the parties shall retain their right to sit in the case before the Court.

2. If the Court includes upon the Bench a judge of the nationality of one of the parties, any other party may choose a person to sit as judge. Such person shall be chosen preferably from among those persons who have been nominated as candidates as provided in Articles 4 and 5.

3. If the Court includes upon the Bench no judge of the nationality of the parties, each of these parties may proceed to choose a judge as provided in paragraph 2 of this Article.

4. The provisions of this Article shall apply to the case of Articles 26 and 29. In such cases, the President shall request one or, if necessary, two of the members of the Court forming the chamber to give place to the members of the Court of the nationality of the parties concerned, and, failing such, or if they are unable to be present, to the judges specially chosen by the parties.

5. Should there be several parties in the same interest, they shall, for the purpose of the preceding provisions, be reckoned as one party only. Any doubt upon this point shall be settled by the decision of the Court.

6. Judges chosen as laid down in paragraphs 2, 3, and 4 of this Article shall fulfil the conditions required by Articles 2, 17 (paragraph 2), 20, and 24 of the present Statute. They shall take part in the decision on terms of complete equality with their colleagues.

ARTICLE 32

1. Each member of the Court shall receive an annual salary.

2. The President shall receive a special annual allowance.

3. The Vice-President shall receive a special allowance for every day on which he acts as President.

4. The judges chosen under Article 31, other than members of the Court, shall receive compensation for each day on which they exercise their functions.

5. These salaries, allowances, and compensation shall be fixed by the General Assembly. They may not be decreased during the term of office.

6. The salary of the Registrar shall be fixed by the General Assembly on the proposal of the Court.

7. Regulations made by the General Assembly shall fix the conditions under which retirement pensions may be given to members of the Court and the Registrar, and the conditions under which members of the Court and the Registrar shall have their traveling expenses refunded.

8. The above salaries, allowances, and compensation shall be free of all taxation.

ARTICLE 33

The expenses of the Court shall be borne by the United Nations in such a manner as shall be decided by the General Assembly.

II. COMPETENCE OF THE COURT

ARTICLE 34

1. Only states may be parties in cases before the Court.

2. The Court, subject to and in conformity with its Rules, may request of the public international organizations information relevant to cases before it, and shall receive such information presented by such organizations on their own initiative.

3. Whenever the construction of the constituent instrument of a public international organization or of an international convention adopted thereunder is in question in a case before the Court, the Registrar shall so notify the public international organization concerned and shall communicate to it copies of all the written proceedings.

ARTICLE 35

1. The Court shall be open to the states parties to the present Statute.

2. The conditions under which the Court shall be open in other states shall, subject to the special provisions contained in treaties in force, be laid down by the Security Council, but in no case shall such conditions place the parties in a position of inequality before the Court.

3. When a state which is not a Member of the United Nations is a party to a case, the Court shall fix the amount which that party is to contribute towards the expenses of the Court. This provision shall not apply if such state is bearing a share of the expenses of the Court.

ARTICLE 36

1. The jurisdiction of the Court comprises all cases which the parties refer to it and all matters specially provided for in the Charter of the United Nations or in treaties and conventions in force.

2. The states parties to the present Statute may at any time declare that they recognize as compulsory *impo facto* and without special agreement, in relation to any other state accepting the same obligation, the jurisdiction of the Court in all legal disputes concerning.

    a. the interpretation of a treaty;

    b. any question of international law;

    c. the existence of any fact which, if established, would constitute a breach of an international obligation;

    d. the nature or extent of the reparation to be made for the breach of an international obligation.

    3. The declarations referred to above may be made unconditionally or on condition of reciprocity on the part of several or certain states, on for a certain time.

    4. Such declarations shall be deposited with the Secretary-General of the United Nations, who shall transmit copies thereof to the parties to the Statute and to the Registrar of the Court.

    5. Declarations made under Article 36 of the Statute of the Permanent Court of International Justice and which are still in force shall be deemed, as between the parties to the present Statute, to be acceptances of the compulsory jurisdiction of the International Court of Justice for the period which they still have to run and in accordance with their terms.

    6. In the event of a dispute as to whether the Court has jurisdiction, the matter shall be settled by the decision of the Court.

ARTICLE 37

    Whenever a treaty or convention in force provides for reference of a matter to a tribunal to have been instituted by the League of Nations, or to the Permanent Court of International Justice, the matter shall, as between the parties to the present Statute, be referred to the International Court of Justice.

ARTICLE 38

    1. The Court, whose function is to decide in accordance with international law such disputes as re submitted to it, shall apply:

    a. international conventions, whether general or particular, establishing rules expressly recognized by the contesting states;

    b. international custom, as evidence of a general practice accepted as law;

    c. the general principles of law recognized by civilized nations;

    d. subject to the provisions of Article 59, judicial decisions and the teachings of the most highly qualified publicists of the various nations, as subsidiary means for the determination of rules of law.

    2. This provision shall not prejudice the power of the Court to decide a case *ex aequo et bono,* if the parties agree thereto.

III. PROCEDURE

ARTICLE 39

    1. The official languages of the Court shall be French and English. If the parties agree that the case shall be conducted in French, the judgment shall be delivered in French. If the parties agree that the case shall be con-

ducted in English, the judgment shall be conducted in English, the judgment shall be delivered in English.

2. In the absence of an agreement as to which language shall be employed, each party may, in the pleadings, use the language which it prefers; the decision of the Court shall be given in French and English. In this case the Court shall at the same time determine which of the two texts shall be considered as authoritative.

3. The Court shall, at the request of any party, authorize a language other than French or English to be used by that party.

ARTICLE 40

1. Cases are brought before the Court, as the case may be, either by the notification of the special agreement or by a written application addressed to the Registrar. In either case the subject of the dispute and the parties shall be indicated.

2. The Registrar shall forthwith communicate the application to all concerned.

3. He shall also notify the Members of the United Nations through the Secretary-General, and also any other states entitled to appear before the Court.

ARTICLE 41

1. The Court shall have the power to indicate, if it considers that circumstances to require, any provisional measures which ought to be taken to preserve the respective rights of either party.

2. Pending the final decision, notice of the measures suggested shall forthwith be given to the parties and to the Security Council.

ARTICLE 42

1. The parties shall be represented by agents.

2. They may have the assistance of counsel or advocates before the Court.

3. The agents, counsel, and advocates of parties before the Court shall enjoy the privileges and immunities necessary to the independent exercise of their duties.

ARTICLE 43

1. The procedure shall consist of two parts: written and oral.

2. The written proceedings shall consist of the communication to the Court and to the parties of memorials, counter-memorials and, if necessary, replies; also all papers and documents in support.

3. These communications shall be made through the Registrar, in the order and within the time fixed by the Court.

4. A certified copy of every document produced by one party shall be communicated to the other party.

5. The oral proceedings shall consist of the hearing by the Court of witnesses, experts, agents, counsel, and advocates.

ARTICLE 44
1. For the service of all notices upon persons other than the agents, counsel, and advocates, the Court shall apply direct to the government of the state upon whose territory the notice has to be served.

2. The same provision shall apply whenever steps are to be taken to procure evidence on the spot.

ARTICLE 45
The hearing shall be under the control of the President or, if he is unable to preside, of the Vice-President; if neither is able to preside, the senior judge present shall preside.

ARTICLE 46
The hearing in Court shall be public, unless the Court shall decide otherwise, or unless the parties demand that the public be not admitted.

ARTICLE 47
1. Minutes shall be made at each hearing and signed by the Registrar and the President.

2. These minutes alone shall be authentic.

ARTICLE 48
The Court shall make orders for the conduct of the case, shall decide the form and time in which each party must conclude its arguments, and make all arrangements connected with the taking of evidence.

ARTICLE 49
The Court may, even before the hearing begins, call upon the agents to produce any document or to supply any explanations. Formal note shall be taken of any refusal.

ARTICLE 50
The Court may, at any time, entrust any individual, body, bureau, commission, or other organization that it may select, with the task of carrying out an enquiry or giving an expert opinion.

ARTICLE 51
During the hearing any relevant questions are to be put to the witnesses and experts under the conditions laid down by the Court in the rules of procedure referred to in Article 30.

ARTICLE 52

After the Court has received the proofs and evidence within the time specified for the purpose, it may refuse to accept any further oral or written evidence that one party may desire to present unless the other side consents.

ARTICLE 53

1. Whenever one of the parties does not appear before the Court, or fails to defend its case, the other party may call upon the Court to decide in favor of its claim.

2. The Court must, before doing so, satisfy itself, not only that it has jurisdiction in accordance with Articles 36 and 37, but also that the claim is well founded in fact and law.

ARTICLE 54

1. When, subject to the control of the Court, the agents, counsel, and advocates have completed their presentation of the case, the President shall declare the hearing closed.

2. The Court shall withdraw to consider the judgment.

3. The deliberations of the Court shall take place in private and remain secret.

ARTICLE 55

1. All questions shall be decided by a majority of the judges present.

2. In the event of an equality of votes, the President or the judge who acts in his place shall have a casting vote.

ARTICLE 56

1. The judgment shall state the reasons on which it is based.

2. It shall contain the names of the judges who have taken part in the decision.

ARTICLE 57

If the judgment does not represent in whole or in part the unanimous opinion of the judges, any judge shall be entitled to deliver a separate opinion.

ARTICLE 58

The judgment shall be signed by the President and by the Registrar. It shall be read in open court, due notice having been given to the agents.

ARTICLE 59

The decision of the Court has no binding force except between the parties and in respect of that particular case.

ARTICLE 60

The judgment is final and without appeal. In the event of dispute as to the meaning or scope of the judgment, the Court shall construe it upon the request of any party.

ARTICLE 61

1. An application for revision of a judgment may be made only when it is based upon the discovery of some fact of such a nature as to be a decisive factor, which fact was, when the judgment was given, unknown to the Court and also to the party claiming revision, always provided that such ignorance was not due to negligence.

2. The proceedings for revision shall be opened by a judgment of the Court expressly recording the existence of the new fact, recognizing that it has such a character as to lay the case open to revision, and declaring the application admissible on this ground.

3. The Court may require previous compliance with the terms of the judgment before it admits proceedings in revision.

4. The application for revision must be made at latest within six months of the discovery of the new fact.

5. No application for revision may be made after the lapse of ten years from the date of the judgment.

ARTICLE 62

1. Should a state consider that it has an interest of a legal nature which may be affected by the decision in the case, it may submit a request to the Court to be permitted to intervene.

2. It shall be for the Court to decide upon this request.

ARTICLE 63

1. Whenever the construction of a convention to which states other than those concerned in the case are parties is in question, the Registrar shall notify all such states forthwith.

2. Every state so notified has the right to intervene in the proceedings; but if it uses this right, the construction given by the judgment will be equally binding upon it.

ARTICLE 64

Unless otherwise decided by the Court, each party shall bear its own costs.

IV. ADVISORY OPINIONS

ARTICLE 65

1. The Court may give an advisory opinion on any legal question at the request of whatever body may be authorized by or in accordance with the Charter of the United Nations to make such a request.

2. Questions upon which the advisory opinion of the Court is asked shall be laid before the Court by means of a written request containing an exact statement of the question upon which an opinion is required, and accompanied by all documents likely to throw light upon the question.

ARTICLE 66

1. The Registrar shall forthwith give notice of the request for an advisory opinion to all states entitled to appear before the Court.

2. The Registrar shall also, by means of a special and direct communication, notify any state entitled to appear before the Court or international organization considered by the Court, or, should it not be sitting, by the President, as likely to be able to furnish information on the question, that the Court will be prepared to receive, within a time limit to be fixed by the President, written statements, or to hear, at a public sitting to be held for the purpose, oral statements relating to the question.

3. Should any such state entitled to appear before the Court have failed to receive the special communication referred to in paragraph 2 of this Article, such state may express a desire to submit a written statement or to be heard; and the Court will decide.

4. States and organizations having presented written or oral statements or both shall be permitted to comment on the statements made by other states or organizations in the form, to the extent, and within the time limits which the Court, or, should it not be sitting, the President, shall decide in each particular case. Accordingly, the Registrar shall in due time communicate any such written statements to states and organizations having submitted similar statements.

ARTICLE 67

The Court shall deliver its advisory opinions in open court, notice having been given to the Secretary-General and to the representatives of Members of the United Nations, of other states and of international organizations immediately concerned.

ARTICLE 68

In the exercise of its advisory functions the Court shall further be guided by the provisions of the present Statute which apply in contentious cases to the extent to which it recognizes them to be applicable.

V. AMENDMENT

ARTICLE 69

Amendments to the present Statute shall be effected by the same procedure as is provided by the Charter of the United Nations for amendments to that Charter, subject however to any provisions which the General Assembly upon recommendation of the Security Council may adopt concerning the participation of states which are parties to the present Statute but are not Members of the United Nations.

ARTICLE 70

The Court shall have power to propose such amendments to the present Statute as it may deem necessary, through written communications to the Secretary-General, for consideration with the provisions of Article 69.

3. Statement of Interpretation by the Sponsoring Governments of San Francisco Conference

The Sponsoring Governments were the Republic of China, the Union of Soviet Socialist Republics, the United Kingdom of Great Britain and Northern Ireland, and the United States of America. France, although not a Sponsoring Government, subscribed to this Statement. UNCIO Doc. 852,III/1/37(1).

Specific questions covering the voting procedure in the Security Council have been submitted by a Sub-Committee of the Conference Committee on Structure and Procedures of the Security Council to the Delegations of the four Governments sponsoring the Conference—the United States of America, the United Kingdom of Great Britain and Northern Ireland, the Union of Soviet Socialist Republics, and the Republic of China. In dealing with these questions, the four Delegations desire to make the following statement of their general attitude towards the whole question of unanimity of permanent members in the decision of the Security Council.

I

1. The Yalta voting formula recognizes that the Security Council, in discharging its responsibilities for the maintenance of international peace and security, will have two broad groups of functions. Under Chapter VIII, the Council will have to make decisions which involve its taking direct measures in connection with settlement of disputes, adjustment of situations likely to lead to disputes, determination of threats to the peace, removal of threats to the peace, and suppression of breaches of the peace. It will also have to make decisions which do not involve the taking of such measures. The Yalta formula provides that the second of these two groups of decisions will be governed by a procedural vote—that is, the vote of any seven members. The first group of decisions will be governed by a qualified vote—that is, the vote of seven members, including the concurring votes of the five permanent members, subject to the proviso that in decisions under Section A and a part of Section C of Chapter VIII parties to a dispute shall abstain from voting.

2. For example, under the Yalta formula a procedural vote will govern the decisions made under the entire Section D of Chapter VI. This means that the Council will, by a vote of any seven of its members, adopt or alter its rules of procedure; determine the method of selecting its President; organize itself in such a way as to be able to function continuously; select the times and places of its regular and special meetings; establish such bodies or agencies as it may deem necessary for the performance of its functions; invite a member of the Organization not represented on the Council to participate in its discussions when that member's interests are specially affected; and invite any state when it is a party to a dispute being considered by the Council to participate in the discussion relating to that dispute.

3. Further, no individual member of the Council can alone prevent consideration and discussion by the Council of a dispute or situation brought to its attention under paragraph 2, Section A, Chapter VIII. Nor can parties to such dispute be prevented by these means from being heard by the Council. Likewise, the requirements for unanimity of the permanent members cannot prevent any member of the Council from reminding the members of the Organization of their general obligations assumed under the Charter as regards peaceful settlement of international disputes.

4. Beyond this point, decisions and actions by the Security Council may well have major political consequences and may even initiate a chain of events which might, in the end, require the Council under its responsibilities to invoke measures of enforcement under Section B, Chapter VIII. This chain of events begins when the Council decides to make an investigation, or determines that the time has come to call upon states to settle their differences, or makes recommendations to the parties. It is to such decisions and actions that unanimity of the permanent members applies, with the important proviso, referred to above, for abstention from voting by parties to a dispute.

5. To illustrate: in ordering an investigation, the Council has to consider whether the investigation—which may involve calling for reports, hearing witnesses, dispatching a commission of inquiry, or other means— might not further aggravate the situation. After investigation, the Council must determine whether the continuance of the situation or dispute would be likely to endanger international peace and security. If it so determines, the Council would be under obligation to take further steps. Similarly, the decision to make recommendations, even when all parties request it to do so, or to call upon parties to a dispute to fulfill their obligations under the Charter, might be the first step on a course of action from which the Security Council could withdraw only at the risk of failing to discharge its responsibilities.

6. In appraising the significance of the vote required to take such decisions or actions, it is useful to make comparison with the requirements of the League Covenant with reference to decisions of the League Council. Substantive decisions of the League of Nations Council could be taken only by the unanimous vote of all its members, whether permanent or not, with the exception of parties to a dispute under Article XV of the League Covenant. Under Article XI, under which most of the disputes brought before the League were dealt with and decisions to make investigations taken, the unanimity rule was invariably interpreted to include even the votes of the parties to a dispute.

7. The Yalta voting formula substitutes for the rule of complete unanimity of the League Council a system of qualified majority voting in the Security Council. Under this system nonpermanent members of the Security Council individually would have no "veto." As regards the permanent members, there is no question under the Yalta formula of investing them with a new right, namely, the right to veto, a right which the permanent members of the League Council always had. The formula proposed for the taking of action in the Security Council by a majority of seven would make the operation of the Council less subject to obstruction, than was the case under the League of Nations rule of complete unanimity.

8. It should also be remembered that under the Yalta formula the five major powers could not act by themselves, since even under the unanimity requirement any decisions of the Council would have to include the concurring votes of at least two of the nonpermanent members. In other words, it would be possible for five nonpermanent members as a group to exercise a "veto." It is not to be assumed however, that the permanent members, any more than the nonpermanent members, would use their "veto" power willfully to obstruct the operation of the Council.

9. In view of the primary responsibilities of the permanent members, they could not be expected, in the present condition of the world, to assume the obligation to act in so serious a matter as the maintenance of international peace and security in consequence of a decision in which they had not concurred. Therefore, if a majority voting in the Security Council is to be made possible, the only practicable method is to provide, in respect of nonprocedural decisions, for unanimity of the permanent members plus the concurring votes of at least two of the nonpermanent members.

10. For all these reasons, the four sponsoring Governments agreed on the Yalta formula and have presented it to this Conference as essential if an international organization is to be created through which all peace-loving nations can effectively discharge their common responsibilities for the maintenance of international peace and security.

II

In the light of the considerations set forth in Part I of this statement, it is clear what the answers to the questions submitted by the Sub-committee should be, with the exception of Question 19. The answer to that questions is as follows:

1. In the opinion of the Delegations of the Sponsoring Governments, the Draft Charter itself contains an indication of the application of the voting procedures to the various functions of the Council.

2. In this case, it will be unlikely that there will arise in the future any matters of great importance on which a decision will have to be made as to whether a procedural vote would apply. Should, however, such a matter arise, the decision regarding the preliminary question as to whether or not such a matter is procedural must be taken by a vote of seven members of the Security Council, including the concurring votes of the permanent members.

4. Rules of Procedure of the General Assembly of the United Nations

Adopted by Resolution 173(II) of the General Assembly on November 17, 1947, these Rules have been amended many times. The present text embodies all amendments and additions now in effect. See also Explanatory Note below. A/520/Rev.10.

I. SESSIONS

Regular Sessions

Date of Meeting

RULE 1[1]

The General Assembly shall meet every year in regular session commencing on the third Tuesday in September.

Duration of Session

RULE 2

On the recommendation of the General Committee, the General Assembly shall, at the beginning of each session, fix a closing date for the session.

EXPLANATORY NOTE

Rules 49, 84, 85, 87, 145, 147 and 162, which reproduce textually provisions of the Charter, are printed in bold type and are, in addition, provided with a footnote. A footnote has also been added in the case of other rules which, while based directly on provisions of the Charter, do not reproduce those provisions textually.

Figures indicated between square brackets in sections dealing with rules for plenary meetings refer to identical or corresponding rules for committee meetings, and *vice versa*.

Attention is drawn to rule 163, which provides: "The description of the rules in the table of contents and the notes in italics to these rules shall be disregarded in the interpretation of the rules."

Place of Meeting
RULE 3
Sessions shall be held at the Headquarters of the United Nations unless convened elsewhere in pursuance of a decision of the General Assembly at a previous session or at the request of a majority of the Members of the United Nations.

RULE 4
Any Member of the United Nations may, at least one hundred and twenty days before the date fixed for the opening of a regular session, request that the session be held elsewhere than at the Headquarters of the United Nations. The Secretary-General shall immediately communicate the request, together with his recommendations, to the other Members of the United Nations. If within thirty days of the date of this communication a majority of the Members concur in the request, the session shall be held accordingly.

Notification of Session
RULE 5
The Secretary-General shall notify the Members of the United Nations, at least sixty days in advance, of the opening of a regular session.

Adjournment of Session
RULE 6
The General Assembly may decide at any session to adjourn temporarily and resume its meetings at a later date.

Special Sessions
Summoning by the General Assembly
RULE 7[2]
The General Assembly may fix a date for a special session.

Summoning on Request from the Security Council or Members
RULE 8
(*a*) Special sessions of the General Assembly shall be held within fifteen days of the receipt by the Secretary-General of a request for such a session from the Security Council, or of a request from a majority of the Members of the United Nations, or of the concurrence of a majority of Members as provided in rule 9.

(*b*) Emergency special sessions pursuant to General Assembly resolution 377 A (V) shall be convened within twenty-four hours of the receipt by the Secretary-General of a request for such a session from the Security Council, on the vote of any nine mbmers thereof, or of a request from a majority of the Members of the United Nations expressed by vote in the Interim Committee or otherwise, or of the concurrence of a majority of Members as provided in rule 9.

Request by Members

RULE 9

(*a*) Any Member of the United Nations may request the Secretary-General to summon a special session. The Secretary-General shall immediately inform the other Members of the United Nations of the request and inquire whether they concur in it. If within thirty days of the date of the communication of the Secretary-General a majority of the Members concur in the request, a special session of the General Assembly shall be summoned in accordance with rule 8.

(*b*) This rule shall apply also to a request by any Member for an emergency special session pursuant to resolution 377 A (V). In such a case the Secretary-General shall communicate with the other Members by the most expeditious means of communication available.

Notification of Session

RULE 10

The Secretary-General shall notify the Members of the United Nations, at least fourteen days in advance, of the opening of a special session summoned at the request of the Security Council, and, at least ten days in advance, in the case of a request by a majority of the Members or the concurrence of a majority in the request of any Member. In the case of an emergency special session convened pursuant to rule 8 (*b*), the Secretary-General shall notify the Members of the United Nations at least twelve hours in advance of the opening of the session.

Regular and Special Sessions
Notification to Other Bodies

RULE 11

Copies of the notice summoning each session shall be addressed to all other principal organs of the United Nations and to the specialized agencies referred to in Article 57, paragraph 2, of the Charter.

II. AGENDA

Regular Sessions

Provisional Agenda

RULE 12

The provisional agenda for a regular session shall be drawn up by the Secretary-General and communicated to the Members of the United Nations at least sixty days before the opening of the session.

RULE 13

The provisional agenda of a regular session shall include:

(*a*) The report of the Secretary-General on the work of the Organization;

(*b*) Reports from the Security Council, the Economic and Social Council, the Trusteeship Council, the International Court of Justice, the subsidiary organs of the General Assembly, specialized agencies (where such reports are called for under agreements entered into);

(*c*) All items the inclusion of which has been ordered by the General Assembly at a previous session;

(*d*) All items proposed by the other principal organs of the United Nations;

(*e*) All items proposed by any Member of the United Nations;

(*f*) All items pertaining to the budget for the next financial year and the report on the accounts for the last financial year;

(*g*) All items which the Secretary-General deems it necessary to put before the General Assembly;

(*h*) All items proposed under Article 35, paragraph 2, of the Charter by States not Members of the United Nations.

Supplementary Items

RULE 14

Any Member or principal organ of the United Nations or the Secretary-General may, at least thirty days before the date fixed for the opening of a regular session, request the inclusion of supplementary items in the agenda. These items shall be placed on a supplementary list, which shall be communicated to the Members of the United Nations at least twenty days before the date fixed for the opening of the session.

Additional Items

RULE 15

Additional items of an important and urgent character, proposed for inclusion in the agenda less than thirty days before the opening of a regular session or during a regular session, may be placed on the agenda, if the General Assembly so decides by a majority of the Members present and voting. No additional items may be considered until seven days have elapsed since it was placed on the agenda, unless the General Assembly, by a two-thirds majority of the Members present and voting, decides otherwise, and until a committee has reported upon the question concerned.

Special Sessions

Provisional Agenda

RULE 16

The provisional agenda of a special session summoned at the request of the Security Council shall be communicated to the Members of the United Nations at least fourteen days before the opening of the session. The provisional agenda of a special session summoned at the request of a majority of the Members, or the concurrence of a majority in the request of any Member, shall be communicated at least ten days before the opening of the session. The provisional agenda of an emergency special session shall be communicated to the Members of the United Nations simultaneously with the communication summoning the session.

RULE 17

The provisional agenda for a special session shall consist only of those items proposed for consideration in the request for the holding of the session.

Supplementary Items

RULE 18

Any Member or principal organ of the United Nations or the Secretary-General may, at least four days before the date fixed for the opening of a special session, request the inclusion of supplementary items in the agenda. Such items shall be placed on a supplementary list which shall be communicated to the Members of the United Nations as soon as possible.

Additional Items

RULE 19

During a special session items on the supplementary list and additional items may be added to the agenda by a two-thirds majority of the Members present and voting. During an emergency special session additional items concerning the matters dealt with in resolution 377 A (V) may be added to the agenda by a two-thirds majority of the Members present and voting.

Regular and Special Sessions

Explanatory Memoranda

RULE 20

All items proposed for inclusion in the agenda shall be accompanied by an explanatory memorandum and, if possible, by basic documents or by a draft resolution.

Approval of the Agenda

RULE 21

At each session the provisional agenda and the supplementary list, together with the report of the General Committee theron, shall be submitted to the General Assembly for approval as soon as possible after the opening of the session.

Amendment and Deletion of Items

RULE 22

Items on the agenda may be amended or deleted by the General Assembly by a majority of the Members present and voting.

Debate on Inclusion of Items

RULE 23

Debate on the inclusion of an item in the agenda, when that item has been recommended for inclusion by the General Committee, shall be limited to three speakers in favour of and three against the inclusion. The President may limit the time to be allowed to speakers under this rule.

Modification of the Allocation of Expenses

RULE 24

No proposal for a modification of the allocation of expenses for the time being in force shall be placed on the agenda unless it has been communicated to the Members of the United Nations at least ninety days before the date fixed for the opening of the session.

III. DELEGATIONS

Composition

RULE 25[3]

The delegation of a Member shall consist of not more than five representatives and five alternate representatives, and as many advisers, technical advisers, experts and persons of similar status as may be required by the delegation.

Alternates

RULE 26

An alternate representative may act as a representative upon designation by the Chairman of the delegation.

IV. CREDENTIALS

Submission of Credentials

RULE 27

The credentials of representatives and the names of members of a delegation shall be submitted to the Secretary-General if possible not less than one week before the date fixed for the opening of the session. The credentials shall be issued either by the Head of the State or Government or by the Minister for Foreign Affairs.

Credentials Committee

RULE 28

A Credentials Committee shall be appointed at the beginning of each session. It shall consist of nine members, who shall be appointed by the General Assembly on the proposal of the President. The Committee shall elect its own officers. It shall examine the credentials of representatives and report without delay.

Provisional Admission to a Session

RULE 29

Any representative to whose admission a Member has made objection shall be seated provisionally with the same rights as other representatives, until the Credentials Committee has reported and the General Assembly has given its decision.

V. PRESIDENT AND VICE-PRESIDENTS

Temporary President

RULE 30

At the opening of each session of the General Assembly, the Chairman of that delegation from which the President of the previous session was elected shall preside until the General Assembly has elected a President for the session.

Elections
RULE 31
The General Assembly shall elect a President and seventeen Vice-Presidents,[4] who shall hold office until the close of the session at which they are elected.[5] The Vice-Presidents shall be elected, after the election of the Chairmen of the seven Main Committees referred to in rule 101, on the basis of ensuring the representative character of the General Committee.

Acting President
RULE 32 [107]
If the President finds it necessary to be absent during a meeting or any part thereof, he shall appoint one of the Vice-Presidents to take his place.

RULE 33 [107]
A Vice-President acting as President shall have the same powers and duties as the President.

Replacement of the President
RULE 34 [107]
If the President is unable to perform his functions, a new President shall be elected for the unexpired term.

General Powers of the President
RULE 35 [108]
In addition to exercising the powers which are conferred upon him elsewhere by these rules, the President shall declare the opening and closing of each plenary meeting of the session, shall direct the discussions in plenary meeting, ensure observance of these rules, accord the right to speak, put questions and announce decisions. He shall rule on points of order, and, subject to those rules, shall have complete control of the proceedings at any meeting and over the maintenance of order thereat. The President may, in the course of the discussion of an item, propose to the General Assembly the limitation of the time to be allowed to speakers, the limitation of the number of times each representative may speak on any question, the closure of the list of speakers or the closure of the debate. He may also propose the suspension or the adjournment of the meeting or the adjournment of the debate on the item under discussion.

RULE 36 [109]
The President, in the exercise of his functions, remains under the authority of the General Assembly.

The President Shall Not Vote

RULE 37 [106]

The President, or Vice-President acting as President, shall not vote but shall appoint another member of his delegation to vote in his place.

VI. GENERAL COMMITTEE

Composition

RULE 38

The General Committee shall comprise the President of the General Assembly, who shall preside, the seventeen Vice-Presidents and the Chairmen of the seven Main Committees. No two members of the General Committee shall be members of the same delegation, and it shall be so constituted as to ensure its representative character. Chairmen of other committees upon which all Members have the right to be represented and which are established by the General Assembly to meet during the session shall be entitled to attend meetings of the General Committee and may participate without vote in the discussions.

Substitute Members

RULE 39

If a Vice-President of the General Assembly finds it necessary to be absent during a meeting of the General Committee he may designate a member of his delegation as his substitute. The Chairman of a Main Committee shall, in case of absence, designate the Vice-Chairman of the Committee as his substitute. A Vice-Chairman shall not have the right to vote if he is of the same delegation as another member of the Committee.

Functions

RULE 40

The General Committee shall, at the beginning of each session, consider the provisional agenda, together with the supplementary list, and shall make recommendations to the General Assembly with regard to each item proposed, concerning its inclusion in the agenda, the rejection of the request for inclusion, or the inclusion of the item in the provisional agenda of a future session. It shall, in the same manner, examine requests for the inclusion of additional items in the agenda, and shall make recommendations thereon to the General Assembly. In considering matters relating to the agenda of the General Assembly, the General Committee shall not discuss the substance of any item, except in so far as this bears upon the question whether the General Committee should recommend the inclusion of the item in the agenda, the rejection of the request for inclusion, or the inclusion of the item in the provisional agenda of a future session, and what priority should be accorded to an item the inclusion of which has been recommended.

RULE 41

The General Committee shall make recommendations to the General Assembly concerning the closing date of the session. It shall assist the President and the General Assembly in drawing up the agenda for each plenary meeting, in determining the priority of its items, and in the coordination of the proceedings of all committees of the General Assembly. It shall assist the President in the general conduct of the work of the General Assembly which falls within the competence of the President. It shall not, however, decide any political question.

RULE 42

The General Committee shall meet periodically throughout each session to review the progress of the General Assembly and its committees and to make recommendations for furthering such progress. It shall also meet at such other times as the President deems necessary or upon the request of any other of its members.

Participation by Representatives of Members Requesting the Inclusion of Items in the Agenda

RULE 43

A Member of the General Assembly which has no representative on the General Committee and which has requested the inclusion of an item in the agenda shall be entitled to attend any meeting of the General Committee at which its request is discussed, and may participate, without vote, in the discussion of that item.

Formal Revision of Resolutions of the General Assembly

RULE 44

The General Committee may revise the resolutions adopted by the General Assembly, changing their form but not their substance. Any such changes shall be reported to the General Assembly for its consideration.

VII. SECRETARIAT

Duties of the Secretary-General

RULE 45

The Secretary-General shall act in that capacity in all meetings of the General Assembly,[6] its committees and subcommittees. He may designate a member of the staff to act in his place at these meetings.

RULE 46

The Secretary-General shall provide and direct the staff required by the General Assembly and any committees or subsidiary organs which it may establish.

Duties of the Secretariat

RULE 47

The Secretariat shall receive, translate, print and distribute documents, reports and resolutions of the General Assembly, its committees and organs; interpret speeches made at the meetings; prepare, print and circulate the summary records of the session; have the custody and proper preservation of the documents in the archives of the General Assembly; publish the report of the meetings; distribute all documents of the General Assembly to the Members of the United Nations, and, generally, perform all other work which the General Assembly may require.

Annual Report of the Secretary-General

RULE 48

The Secretary-General shall make an annual report, and such supplementary reports as are required, to the General Assembly on the work of the Organization.[6] He shall communicate the annual report to the Members of the United Nations at least forty-five days before the opening of the session.

Notification Under Article 12 of the Charter

RULE 49[7]

The Secretary-General, with the consent of the Security-Council, shall notify the General Assembly at each session of any matters relative to the maintenance of international peace and security which are being dealt with by the Security Council, and shall similarly notify the General Assembly, or the Members of the United Nations if the General Assembly is not in session, immediately the Security Council ceases to deal with such matters.

Regulations Concerning the Secretariat

RULE 50[8]

The General Assembly shall establish regulations concerning the staff of the Secretariat.

VIII. LANGUAGES

Official and Working Languages

RULE 51

Chinese, English, French, Russian and Spanish shall be the official languages of the General Assembly, its committees and subcommittees. English, French, Russian and Spanish shall be the working languages.

Interpretation from a Working Language

RULE 52

Speeches made in any of the working languages shall be interpreted into the other three working languages.

Interpretation from an Official Language

RULE 53

Speeches made in the other official language shall be interpreted into the four working languages.

Interpretation from Other Languages

RULE 54

Any representative may make a speech in a language other than the official languages. In this case, he shall himself provide for interpretation into one of the working languages. Interpretation into the other working languages by the interpreters of the Secretariat may be based on the interpretation given in the first working language.

Language of Verbatim Records

RULE 55

Verbatim records shall be drawn up in the working languages. A translation of the whole or part of any verbatim record into the other official language shall be furnished if requested by any delegation.

Language of Summary Records

RULE 56

Summary records shall be drawn up as soon as possible in the official languages.

Language of Journal
RULE 57
The Journal of the General Assembly shall be issued in the working languages.

Language of Resolutions and Important Documents
RULE 58
All resolutions and other important documents shall be made available in the official languages. Upon the request of any representative, any other document shall be made available in any or all of the official languages.

Publications in Languages Other than the Official Languages
RULE 59
Documents of the General Assembly, its committees and subcommittees shall, if the General Assembly so decides, be published in any languages other than the official languages.

IX. RECORDS

Verbatim Records
RULE 60
Verbatim records of all plenary meetings shall be drawn up by the Secretariat and submitted to the General Assembly after approval by the President. Verbatim records shall also be made of the proceedings of the Main Committees established by the General Assembly. Other committees or subcommittees may decide upon the form of their records.

Resolutions
RULE 61
Resolutions adopted by the General Assembly shall be communicated by the Secretary-General to the Members of the United Nations within fifteen days after the termination of the session.

X. PUBLIC AND PRIVATE MEETINGS OF THE GENERAL ASSEMBLY, ITS COMMITTEES AND SUBCOMMITTEES

General Principles
RULE 62
The meetings of the General Assembly and its Main Committees shall be held in public unless the body concerned decides that exceptional circumstances require that the meeting be held in private. Meetings of other

committees and subcommittees shall also be held in public unless the body concerned decides otherwise.

Private Meetings

RULE 63

All decisions of the General Assembly taken at a private meeting shall be announced at an early public meeting of the General Assembly. At the close of each private meeting of the Main Committees, other committees and subcommittees, the Chairman may issue a *communiqué* through the Secretary-General.

XI. MINUTE OF SILENT PRAYER OR MEDITATION

Invitation to Silent Prayer or Meditation

RULE 64

Immediately after the opening of the first plenary meeting and immediately preceeding the closing of the final plenary meeting of each session of the General Assembly, the President shall invite the representatives to observe one minute of silence dedicated to prayer or meditation.

XII. PLENARY MEETINGS

Conduct of Business

Emergency Special Sessions

RULE 65

Notwithstanding the provisions of any other rule and unless the General Assembly decides otherwise, the Assembly, in case of an emergency special session, shall convene in plenary session only and proceed directly to consider the item proposed for consideration in the request for the holding of the session, without previous reference to the General Committee or to any other committee; the President and Vice-Presidents for such emergency special sessions shall be, respectively, the Chairmen of those delegations from which were elected the President and Vice-Presidents of the previous session.

Report of the Secretary-General

RULE 66

Proposals to refer any portion of the report of the Secretary-General to one of the Main Committees without debate shall be decided upon by the General Assembly without previous reference to the General Committee.

Reference to Committees

RULE 67

The General Assembly shall not, unless it decides otherwise, make a final decision upon any item on the agenda until it has received the report of a committee on that item.

Discussion of Committee Reports

RULE 68

Discussion of a report of a Main Committee in a plenary meeting of the General Assembly shall take place if at least one third of the Members present and voting at the plenary meeting consider such a discussion to be necessary. Any proposal to this effect shall not be debated, but shall be immediately put to the vote.

Quorum

RULE 69 [110]

A majority of the Members of the General Assembly shall constitute a quorum.

Speeches

RULE 70 [111]

No representative may address the General Assembly without having previously obtained the permission of the President. The President shall call upon speakers in the order in which they signify their desire to speak. The President may call a speaker to order if his remarks are not relevant to the subject under discussion.

Precedence

RULE 71 [112]

The Chairman and the Rapporteur of a committee may be accorded precedence for the purpose of explaining the conclusions arrived at by their committee.

Statements by the Secretariat

RULE 72 [113]

The Secretary-General, or a member of the Secretariat designated by him as his representative, may, at any time, make either oral or written statements to the General Assembly concerning any question under consideration by it.

Points of Order

RULE 73 [114]

During the discussion of any matter, a representative may rise to a point of order, and the point of order shall be immediately decided by the President in accordance with the rules of procedure. A representative may appeal against the ruling of the President. The appeal shall be immediately put to the vote and the President's ruling shall stand unless overruled by a majority of the Members present and voting. A representative rising to a point of order may not speak on the substance of the matter under discussion.

Time Limit on Speeches

RULE 74 [115]

The General Assembly may limit the time to be allowed to each speaker and the number of times each representative may speak on any question. When debate is limited and a representative has spoken his allotted time, the President shall call him to order without delay.

Closing of List of Speakers

RULE 75 [116]

During the course of a debate the President may announce the list of speakers and, with the consent of the General Assembly, declare the list closed. He may, however, accord the right of reply to any Member if a speech delivered after he has declared the list closed makes this desirable.

Adjournment of Debate

RULE 76 [117]

During the discussion of any matter, a representative may move the adjournment of the debate on the item under discussion. In addition to the proposer of the motion, two representatives may speak in favour of, and two against, the motion, after which the motion shall be immediately put to the vote. The President may limit the time to be allowed to speakers under this rule.

Closure of Debate

RULE 77 [118]

A representative may at any time move the closure of the debate on the item under discussion, whether or not any other representative has signified his wish to speak. Permission to speak on the closure of the debate shall be accorded only to two speakers opposing the closure, after which the motion shall be immediately put to the vote. If the General Assembly is in favour of the closure, the President shall declare the closure of the debate. The President may limit the time to be allowed to speakers under this rule.

Suspension or Adjournment of the Meeting
RULE 78 [119]
During the discussion of any matter, a representative may move the suspension or the adjournment of the meeting. Such motions shall not be debated, but shall be immediately put to the vote. The President may limit the time to be allowed to the speaker moving the suspension or adjournment of the meeting.

Order of Procedural Motions
RULE 79 [120]
Subject to rule 73, the following motions shall have precedence in the following order over all other proposals or motions before the meeting:
(*a*) To suspend the meeting;
(*b*) To adjourn the meeting;
(*c*) To adjourn the debate on the item under discussion;
(*d*) For the closure of the debate on the item under discussion.

Proposals and Amendments
RULE 80 [121]
Proposals and amendments shall normally be introduced in writing and handed to the Secretary-General, who shall circulate copies to the delegations. As a general rule, no proposal shall be discussed or put to the vote at any meeting of the General Assembly unless copies of it have been circulated to all delegations not later than the day preceding the meeting. The President may, however, permit the discussion and consideration of amendments, or of motions as to procedure, even though these amendments and motions have not been circulated or have only been circulated the same day.

Decisions on Competence
RULE 81 [122]
Subject to rule 79, any motion calling for a decision on the competence of the General Assembly to adopt a proposal submitted to it shall be put to the vote before a vote is taken on the proposal in question.

Withdrawal of Motions
RULE 82 [123]
A motion may be withdrawn by its proposer at any time before voting on it has commenced, provided that the motion has not been amended. A motion which has thus been withdrawn may be reintroduced by any Member.

Reconsideration of Proposals

RULE 83 [124]

When a proposal has been adopted or rejected it may not be reconsidered at the same session unless the General Assembly, by a two-thirds majority of the Members present and voting, so decides. Permission to speak on a motion to reconsider shall be accorded only to two speakers opposing the motion, after which it shall be immediately put to the vote.

Voting

Voting Rights

RULE 84⁹ [125]

Each Member of the General Assembly shall have one vote.

Two-Thirds Majority

RULE 85⁹

Decisions of the General Assembly on important questions shall be made by a two-thirds majority of the Members present and voting. These questions shall include: recommendations with respect to the maintenance of international peace and security, the election of the nonpermanent members of the Security Council, the election of the members of the Economic and Social Council, the election of members of the Trusteeship Council in accordance with paragraph 1 c of Article 86 of the Charter, the admission of new Members to the United Nations, the suspension of the rights and privileges of membership, the expulsion of Members, questions relating to the operation of the Trusteeship System, and budgetary questions.

RULE 86

Decisions of the General Assembly on amendments to proposals relating to important questions, and on parts of such proposals put to the vote separately, shall be made by a two-thirds majority of the Members present and voting.

Simple Majority

RULE 87⁹ [126]

Decisions of the General Assembly on questions other than those provided for in rule 85, including the determination of additional categories of questions to be decided by a two-thirds majority, shall be made by a majority of the Members present and voting.

Meaning of the Expression "Members Present and Voting"
RULE 88 [127]
For the purposes of these rules, the phrase "Members present and voting" means Members casting an affirmative or negative vote. Members which abstain from voting are considered as not voting.

Method of Voting
RULE 89 [128]
(*a*) The General Assembly shall normally vote by show of hands or by standing, but any representative may request a roll-call. The roll-call shall be taken in the English alphabetical order of the names of the Members, beginning with the Member whose name is drawn by lot by the President. The name of each Member shall be called in any roll-call and one of its representatives shall reply "yes," "no" or "abstention." The result of the voting shall be inserted in the record in the English alphabetical order of the names of the Members.

(*b*) When the General Assembly votes by mechanical means, a nonrecorded vote shall replace a vote by show of hands or by standing and a recorded vote shall replace a roll-call vote. Any representative may request a recorded vote. In the case of a recorded vote, the General Assembly shall, unless a representative requests otherwise, dispense with the procedure of calling out the names of the Members; nevertheless, the result of the voting shall be inserted in the record in the same manner as that of a roll-call vote.

Conduct During Voting
RULE 90 [129]
After the President has announced the beginning of voting, no representative shall interrupt the voting except on a point of order in connexion with the actual conduct of the voting. The President may permit Members to explain their votes, either before or after the voting, except when the vote is taken by secret ballot. The President may limit the time to be allowed for such explanations. The President shall not permit the proposer of a proposal or of an amendment to explain his vote on his own proposal or amendment.

Division of Proposals and Amendments
RULE 91 [130]
A representative may move that parts of a proposal or of an amendment shall be voted on separately. If objection is made to the request for division, the motion for division shall be voted upon. Permission to speak

on the motion for division shall be given only to two speakers in favour and two speakers against. If the motion for division is carried, those parts of the proposal or of the amendment which are subsequently approved shall be put to the vote as a whole. If all operative parts of the proposal or of the amendment have been rejected, the proposal or the amendment shall be considered to have been rejected as a whole.

Voting on Amendments

RULE 92 [131]

When an amendment is móved to a proposal, the amendment shall be voted on first. When two or more amendments are moved to a proposal, the General Assembly shall first vote on the amendment furthest removed in substance from the original proposal and then on the amendment next furthest removed therefrom, and so on, until all the amendments have been put to the vote. Where, however, the adoption of one amendment necessarily implies the rejection of another amendment, the latter amendment shall not be put to the vote. If one or more amendments are adopted, the amended proposal shall then be voted upon. A motion is considered an amendment to a proposal if it merely adds to, deletes from or revises part of the proposal.

Voting on Proposals

RULE 93 [132]

If two or more proposals relate to the same question, the General Assembly shall, unless it decides otherwise, vote on the proposals in the order in which they have been submitted. The General Assembly may, after each vote on a proposal, decide whether to vote on the next proposal.

Elections

RULE 94 [195]

All elections shall be held by secret ballot. There shall be no nominations.

RULE 95 [133]

When only one person or Member is to be elected and no candidate obtains in the first ballot the majority required, a second ballot shall be taken, which shall be restricted to the two candidates obtaining the largest number of votes. If in the second ballot the votes are equally divided, and a majority is required, the President shall decide between the candidates by drawing lots. If a two-thirds majority is required, the balloting shall be continued until one candidate secures two-thirds of the votes cast; provided that, after the third inconclusive ballot, votes may be cast for any eligible person or Member. If three such unrestricted ballots are inconclusive, the next three ballots shall be restricted to the two candidates who obtained the greatest number of votes in the third of the unrestricted ballots, and the following three ballots thereafter shall be unrestricted, and so on until a person or Member is elected. These provisions shall not prejudice the application of rules 144, 145, 147 and 149.

RULE 96

When two or more elective places are to be filled at one time under the same conditions, those candidates obtaining in the first ballot the majority required shall be elected. If the number of candidates obtaining such majority is less than the number of persons or Members to be elected, there shall be additional ballots to fill the remaining places, the voting being restricted to the candidates obtaining the greatest number of votes in the previous ballot, to a number not more than twice the places remaining to be filled; provided that, after the third inconclusive ballot, votes may be cast for any eligible person or Member. If three such unrestricted ballots are inconclusive, the next three ballots shall be restricted to the candidates who obtained the greatest number of votes in the third of the unrestricted ballots, to a number not more than twice the places remaining to be filled, and the following three ballots thereafter shall be unrestricted, and so on until all the places have been filled. These provisions shall not prejudice the application of rules 144, 145, 147 and 149.

Equally Divided Votes

RULE 97 [134]

If a vote is equally divided on matters other than elections, a second vote shall be taken at a subsequent meeting which shall be held within forty-eight hours of the first vote, and it shall be expressly mentioned in the agenda that a second vote will be taken on the matter in question. If this vote also results in equality, the proposal shall be regarded as rejected.

XIII. COMMITTEES

Creation, Officers, Etc.

Creation

RULE 98

The General Assembly may set up such committees as it deems necessary for the performance of its functions.

Categories of Subjects

RULE 99

Items relating to the same category of subjects shall be referred to the committee or committees dealing with that category of subjects. Committees shall not introduce new items on their own initiative.

Priorities

RULE 100

Each Main Committee, taking into account the closing date for the session fixed by the General Assembly on the recommendation of the General Committee, shall adopt its own priorities and meet as may be necessary to complete the consideration of the items referred to it.

Main Committees

RULE 101

The Main Committees of the General Assembly are:

(*a*) Political and Security Committee (including the regulation of armaments) (First Committee);

(*b*) Special Political Committee;

(*c*) Economic and Financial Committee (Second Committee);

(*d*) Social, Humanitarian and Cultural Committee (Third Committee);

(*e*) Trusteeship Committee (including Non-Self-Governing Territories) (Fourth Committee);

(*f*) Administrative and Budgetary Committee (Fifth Committee);

(*g*) Legal Committee (Sixth Committee).

Representation of Members

RULE 102

Each Member may be represented by one person on each Main Committee and on any other committee that may be constituted upon which all Members have the right to be represented. It may also assign to these committees advisers, technical advisers, experts or persons of similar status.

RULE 103

Upon designation by the Chairman of the delegation, advisers, technical advisers, experts or persons of similar status may act as members of committees. Persons of this status shall not, however, unless designated as alternate representatives, be eligible for appointment as Chairmen, Vice-Chairmen or Rapporteurs of committees or for seats in the General Assembly.

Subcommittees

RULE 104

Each committee may set up subcommittees, which shall elect their own officers.

Officers

RULE 105 [94]

Each committee shall elect its own Chairman, Vice-Chairman and Rapporteur. These officers shall be elected on the basis of equitable geographical distribution, experience and personal competence. These elections shall be held by secret ballot.

The Chairman of a Main Committee Shall Not Vote

RULE 106 [37]

The Chairman of a Main Committee shall not vote but another member of his delegation may vote in his place.

Absence of Officers

RULE 107 [32–34]

If the Chairman finds it necessary to be absent during a meeting or any part thereof, the Vice-Chairman shall take his place. A Vice-Chairman acting as Chairman shall have the same powers and duties as the Chairman. If any officer of the committee is unable to perform his functions, a new officer shall be elected for the unexpired term.

Functions of the Chairman

RULE 108 [35]

The Chairman shall declare the opening and closing of each meeting of the committee, shall direct its discussions, ensure observance of these rules, accord the right to speak, put questions and announce decisions. He shall rule on points of order and, subject to these rules, shall have complete control of the proceedings of the committee and over the maintenance of order at its meetings. The Chairman may, in the course of the discussion of an item, propose to the committee the limitation of the time to be allowed to speakers, the limitation of the number of times each representative may speak on any question, the closure of the list of speakers or the closure of the debate. He may also propose the suspension or the adjournment of the meeting or the adjournment of the debate on the item under discussion.

RULE 109 [36]

The Chairman, in the exercise of his functions, remains under the authority of the committee.

Conduct of Business

Quorum

RULE 110 [69]

One-third of the members of a committee shall constitute a quorum. The presence of a majority of the members of the committee is, however, required for a question to be put to the vote.

Speeches

RULE 111 [70]

No represenatative may address the committee without having previously obtained the permission of the Chairman. The Chairman shall call upon speakers in the order in which they signify their desire to speak. The Chairman may call a speaker to order if his remarks are not relevant to the subject under discussion.

Precedence

RULE 112 [71]

The Chairman and the Rapporteur of a committee or subcommittee may be accorded precedence for the purpose of explaining the conclusion arrived at by their committee or subcommittee.

Statements by the Secretariat

RULE 113 [72]

The Secretary-General, or a member of the Secretariat designated by him as his representative, may, at any time, make either oral or written statements to any committee or subcommittee concerning any question under consideration by it.

Points of Order

RULE 114 [73]

During the discussion of any matter, a representative may rise to a point of order, and the point of order shall be immediately decided by the Chairman in accordance with the rules of procedure. A representative may appeal against the ruling of the Chairman. The appeal shall be immediately put to the vote and the Chairman's ruling shall stand unless overruled by a majority of the members present and voting. A representative rising to a point of order may not speak on the substance of the matter under discussion.

Time Limit on Speeches
RULE 115 [74]
The committee may limit the time to be allowed to each speaker and the number of times each representative may speak on any question. When the debate is limited and a representative has spoken his allotted time, the Chairman shall call him to order without delay.

Closing of List of Speakers
RULE 116 [75]
During the course of a debate the Chairman may announce the list of speakers and, with the consent of the committee, declare the list closed. He may, however, accord the right of reply to any member if a speech delivered after he has declared the list closed makes this desirable.

Adjournment of Debate
RULE 117 [76]
During the discussion of any matter, a representative may move the adjournment of the debate on the item under discussion. In addition to the proposer of the motion, two representatives may speak in favour of, and two against, the motion, after which the motion shall be immediately put to the vote. The Chairman may limit the time to be allowed to speakers under this rule.

Closure of Debate
RULE 118 [77]
A representative may at any time move the closure of the debate on the item under discussion, whether or not any other representative has signified his wish to speak. Permission to speak on the closure of the debate shall be accorded only to two speakers opposing the closure, after which the motion shall be immediately put to the vote. If the committee is in favour of the closure, the Chairman shall declare the closure of the debate. The Chairman may limit the time to be allowed to speakers under this rule.

Suspension or Adjournment of the Meeting
RULE 119 [78]
During the discussion of any matter, a representative may move the suspension or the adjournment of the meeting. Such motions shall not be debated, but shall be immediately put to the vote. The Chairman may limit the time to be allowed to the speaker moving the suspension or adjournment of the meeting.

Order of Procedural Motions

RULE 120 [79]

Subject to rule 114, the following motions shall have precedence in the following order over all other proposals or motions before the meeting:

(*a*) To suspend the meeting;

(*b*) To adjourn the meeting;

(*c*) To adjourn the debate on the item under discussion;

(*d*) For the closure of the debate on the item under discussion.

Proposals and Amendments

RULE 121 [80]

Proposals and amendments shall normally be introduced in writing and handed to the Secretary-General, who shall circulate copies to the delegations. As a general rule, no proposal shall be discussed or put to the vote at any meeting of the committee unless copies of it have been circulated to all delegations not later than the day preceding the meeting. The Chairman may, however, permit the discussion and consideration of amendements, or of motions as to procedure, even though these amendments and motions have not been circulated or have only been circulated the same day.

Decisions on Competence

RULE 122 [81]

Subject to rule 120, any motion calling for a decision on the competence of the General Assembly or the committee to adopt a proposal submitted to it shall be put to the vote before a vote is taken on the proposal in question.

Withdrawal of Motions

RULE 123 [82]

A motion may be withdrawn by its proposer at any time before voting on it has commenced, provided that the motion has not been amended. A motion which has thus been withdrawn may be reintroduced by any member.

Reconsideration of Proposals

RULE 124 [83]

When a proposal has been adopted or rejected it may not be reconsidered at the same session unless the committee, by a two-thirds majority of the members present and voting, so decides. Permission to speak on a motion to reconsider shall be accorded only to two speakers opposing the motion, after which it shall be immediately put to the vote.

Voting

Voting Rights

RULE 125 [84]

Each member of the committee shall have one vote.

Majority Required

RULE 126 [87]

Decisions in the committees of the General Assembly shall be made by a majority of the members present and voting.

Meaning of the Expression "Members Present and Voting"

RULE 127 [88]

For the purposes of these rules, the phrase "members present and voting" means members casting an affirmative or negative vote. Members which abstain from voting are considered as not voting.

Method of Voting

RULE 128 [89]

(*a*) The committee shall normally vote by show of hands or by standing, but any representative may request a roll-call. The roll-call shall be taken in the English alphabetical order of the names of the members, beginning with the member whose name is drawn by lot by the Chairman. The name of each member shall be called in any roll-call and he shall reply "yes," "no" or "abstention." The result of the voting shall be inserted in the record in the English alphabetical order of the names of the members.

(*b*) When the committee votes by mechanical means, a nonrecorded vote shall replace a vote by show of hands or by standing and a recorded vote shall replace a roll-call vote. Any representative may request a recorded vote. In the case of a recorded vote, the committee shall, unless a representative requests otherwise, dispense with the procedure of calling out the names of the members; nevertheless, the result of the voting shall be inserted in the record in the same manner as that of a roll-call vote.

Conduct During Voting

RULE 129 [90]

After the Chairman has announced the beginning of voting, no representative shall interrupt the voting except on a point of order in connexion with the actual conduct of the voting. The Chairman may permit members to explain their votes, either before or after the voting, except when the vote is taken by secret ballot. The Chairman may limit the time to be allowed for such explanations. The Chairman shall not permit the proposer of a proposal or of an amendment to explain his vote on his own proposal or amendment.

Division of Posposals and Amendments

RULE 130 [91]

A representative may move that parts of a proposal or of an amendment shall be voted on separately. If objection is made to the request for division, the motion for division shall be voted upon. Permission to speak on the motion for division shall be given only to two speakers in favour and two speakers against. If the motion for division is carried, those parts of the proposal or of the amendment which are subsequently approved shall be put to the vote as a whole. If all operative parts of the proposal or of the amendment have been rejected, the proposal or the amendment shall be considered to have been rejected as a whole.

Voting on Amendments

RULE 131 [192]

When an amendment is moved to a proposal, the amendment shall be voted on first. When two or more amendments are moved to a proposal, the committee shall first vote on the amendment furthest removed in substance from the original proposal and then on the amendment next furthest removed therefrom, and so on, until all the amendments have been put to the vote. Where, however, the adoption of one amendment necessarily implies the rejection of another amendment, the latter amendment shall not be put to the vote. If one or more amendments are adopted, the amended proposal shall then be voted upon. A motion is considered an amendment to a proposal if it merely adds to, deletes from or revises part of that proposal.

Voting on Proposals

RULE 132 [93]

If two or more proposals relate to the same question, a committee shall, unless it decides otherwise, vote on the proposals in the order in which they have been submitted. A committee may, after each vote on a proposal, decide whether to vote on the next proposal.

Elections

RULE 133 [95]

When only one person or Member is to be elected and no candidate obtains in the first ballot the majority required, a second ballot shall be taken, which shall be restricted to the two candidates obtaining the largest number of votes. If in the second ballot the votes are equally divided, and a majority is required, the Chairman shall decide between the candidates by drawing lots.

Equally Divided Votes
RULE 134 [97]
If a vote is equally divided on matters other than elections, the proposal shall be regarded as rejected.

XIV. ADMISSION OF NEW MEMBERS TO THE UNITED NATIONS

Applications
RULE 135
Any State which desires to become a Member of the United Nations shall submit an application to the Secretary-General. This application shall contain a declaration, made in a formal instrument, that it accepts the obligations contained in the Charter.

Notification of Applications
RULE 136
The Secretary-General shall send for information a copy of the application to the General Assembly, or to the Members of the United Nations if the General Assembly is not in session.

Consideration and Decision by the General Assembly
RULE 137
If the Security Council recommends the applicant State for membership the General Assembly shall consider whether the applicant is a peace-loving State and is able and willing to carry out the obligations contained in the Charter, and shall decide, by a two-thirds majority of the Members present and voting, upon its application for membership.
RULE 138
If the Security Council does not recommend the applicant State for membership or postpones the consideration of the application, the General Assembly may, after full consideration of the special report of the Security Council, send back the application to the Security Council, together with a full record of the discussion in the General Assembly, for further consideration and recommendation or report.

Notification of Decision and Effective Date of Membership
RULE 139
The Secretary-General shall inform the applicant State of the decision of the General Assembly. If the application is approved, membership will become effective on the date on which the General Assembly takes its decision on the application.

XV. ELECTIONS TO PRINCIPAL ORGANS

General Provisions

Terms of Office

RULE 140

Except as provided in rule 148, the term of office of members of Councils shall begin on 1 January following their election by the General Assembly, and shall end on 31 December following the election of their successors.

By-elections

RULE 141

Should a member cease to belong to a Council before its term of office expires, a by-election shall be held separately at the next session of the General Assembly to elect a member for the unexpired term.

Appointment of the Secretary-General

Appointment of the Secretary-General

RULE 142

When the Security Council has submitted its recommendation on the appointment of the Secretary-General, the General Assembly shall consider the recommendation and vote upon it by secret ballot in private meeting.

Security Council

Annual Elections

RULE 143[10]

The General Assembly shall each year, in the course of its regular session, elect five nonpermanent members of the Security Council for a term of two years.[11]

Qualifications for Membership

RULE 144[12]

In the election of nonpermanent members of the Security Council, in accordance with Article 23, paragraph 1, of the Charter due regard shall be specially paid, in the first instance, to the contribution of Members of the United Nations to the maintenance of international peace and security and to the other purposes of the Organization, and also to equitable geographical distribution.

Reeligibility

RULE 145[13]

A retiring member of the Security Council shall not be eligible for immediate reelection.

Economic and Social Council

Annual Elections

RULE 146[14]

The General Assembly shall each year, in the course of its regular session, elect nine members of the Economic and Social Council for a term of three years.[15]

Reeligibility

RULE 147[16]

A retiring member of the Economic and Social Council shall be eligible for immediate reelection.

Trusteeship Council

Occasions for Elections

RULE 148

When a Trusteeship Agreement has been approved and a Member of the United Nations has become an Administering Authority of a Trust Territory in accordance with Article 83 or 85 of the Charter, the General Assembly shall proceed to such election or elections to the Trusteeship Council as may be necessary, in accordance with Article 86. A Member of Members elected at any such election at a regular session shall take office immediately upon their election and shall complete their terms in accordance with the provisions of rule 140, as if they had begun their terms of office on 1 January following their election.

Term of Office and Reeligibility

RULE 149[17]

A nonadministering member of the Trusteeship Council shall be elected for a term of three years and shall be eligible for immediate reelection.

Vacancies

RULE 150

At each session the General Assembly shall, in accordance with Article 86 of the Charter, elect members to fill any vacancies.

International Court of Justice

Method of Election

RULE 151

The election of the members of the International Court of Justice shall take place in accordance with the Statute of the Court.

RULE 152

Any meeting of the General Assembly held in pursuance of the Statute of the International Court of Justice for the purpose of the election of members of the Court shall continue until as many candidates as are required for all the seats to be filled have obtained in one or more ballots an absolute majority of votes.

XVI. ADMINISTRATIVE AND BUDGETARY QUESTIONS

Regulations for Financial Administration

RULE 153

The General Assembly shall establish regulations for the financial administration of the United Nations.

Estimates of Expenditures

RULE 154

No resolution involving expenditure shall be recommended by a committee for approval by the General Assembly unless it is accompanied by an estimate of expenditures prepared by the Secretary-General. No resolution in respect of which expenditures are anticipated by the Secretary-General shall be voted by the General Assembly until the Administrative and Budgetary Committee has had an opportunity of stating the effect of the proposal upon the budget estimates of the United Nations.

Information on the Cost of Resolutions

RULE 155

The Secretary-General shall keep all committees informed of the detailed estimated cost of all resolutions which have been recommended by the committees for approval by the General Assembly.

Advisory Committee on Administrative and Budgetary Questions

Appointment

RULE 156

The General Assembly shall appoint an Advisory Committee on Administrative and Budgetary Questions (hereinafter called the "Advisory Committee"), with a membership of twelve, including at least three financial experts of recognized standing.

Composition

RULE 157

The members of the Advisory Committee, no two of whom shall be nationals of the same State, shall be selected on the basis of broad geographical representation, personal qualifications and experience, and shall serve for three years corresponding to three financial years, as defined in the regulations for the financial administration of the United Nations. Members shall retire by rotation and shall be eligible for reappointment. The three financial experts shall not retire simultaneously. The General Assembly shall appoint the members of the Advisory Committee at the regular session immediately preceding the expiration of the term of office of the members, or, in case of vacancies, at the next session.

Functions

RULE 158

The Advisory Committee shall be responsible for expert examination of the budget of the United Nations and shall assist the Administrative and Budgetary Committee of the General Assembly. At the commencement of each regular session, it shall submit to the General Assembly a detailed report on the budget for the next financial year and on the accounts of the last financial year. It shall also examine on behalf of the General Assembly the administrative budgets or specialized agencies and proposals for financial and budgetary arrangements with such agencies. It shall perform such other duties as may be assigned to it under the regulations for the financial administration of the United Nations.

Committee on Contributions

Appointment

RULE 159

The General Assembly shall appoint an expert Committee on Contributions, consisting of twelve members.

Composition

RULE 160

The members of the Committee on Contributions, no two of whom shall be nationals of the same State, shall be selected on the basis of broad geographical representation, personal qualifications and experience, and shall serve for a period of three years corresponding to three financial years, as defined in the regulations for the financial administration of the United Nations. Members shall retire by rotation and shall be eligible for reappointment. The General Assembly shall appoint the members of the Committee on Contributions at the regular session immediately preceding the expiration of the term of office of the members, or, in case of vacancies, at the next session.

Functions

RULE 161

The Committee on Contributions shall advise the General Assembly concerning the apportionment, under Article 17, paragraph 2, of the Charter, of the expenses of the Organization among Members, broadly according to capacity to pay. The scale of assessments, when once fixed by the General Assembly, shall not be subject to a general revision for at least three years, unless it is clear that there have been substantial changes in relative capacities to pay. The Committee shall also advise the General Assembly on the assessments to be fixed for new Members, on appeals by Members for a change of assessments, and on the action to be taken with regard to the application of Article 19 of the Charter.

XVII. SUBSIDIARY ORGANS OF THE GENERAL ASSEMBLY

Creation and Rules of Procedure

RULE 162

The General Assembly may establish such subsidiary organs as it deems necessary for the performance of its functions.[18] The rules relating to the procedure of committees of the General Assembly, as well as rules 45 and 62, shall apply to the procedure of any subsidiary organ, unless the General Assembly or the subsidiary organ decides otherwise.

XVII. INTERPRETATION AND AMENDMENTS

Notes in Italics

RULE 163

The description of the rules in the table of contents and the notes in italics to these rules shall be disregarded in the interpretation of the rules.

Method of Amendment

RULE 164

These rules of procedure may be amended by a decision of the General Assembly taken by a majority of the Members present and voting, after a committee has reported on the proposed amendment.

NOTES

1. Rule based directly on a provision of the Charter (Article 20).
2. Rule based directly on a provision of the Charter (Article 20).
3. Rule based directly on a provision of the Charter (Article 9, paragraph 2).
4. In the annex to resolution 1990 (XVIII) of 17 December 1963, the General Assembly decided as follows:

"1.   In the election of the President of the General Assembly, regard shall be had for equitable geographical rotation of this office among the regions mentioned in paragraph 4 below.

"2.   The seventeen Vice-Presidents of the General Assembly shall be elected according to the following pattern, subject to paragraph 3 below:

"(a)   Seven representatives from African and Asian States;

"(b)   One representative from an Eastern European State;

"(c)   Three representatives from Latin American States;

"(d)   Two representatives from Western European and other States;

"(e)   Five representatives from the permanent members of the Security Council.

"3.   The election of the President of the General Assembly will, however, have the effect of reducing by one the number of vice-presidencies allocated to the region from which the President is elected in accordance with paragraph 2 above.

"4.   The seven Chairmen of the Main Committees shall be elected according to the following pattern:

"(a)   Three representatives from African and Asian States;

"(b)   One representative from an Eastern European State;

"(c)   One representative from a Latin American State;

"(d)   One representative from a Western European or other State;

"(e)   The seventh chairmanship shall rotate every alternate year among representatives of States mentioned in subparagraphs (c) and (d) above.

5. Rule based directly on a provision of the Charter (Article 21, second sentence).

6. Rule based directly on a provision of the Charter (Article 98).

7. Rule reproducing textually a provision of the Charter (Article 12, paragraph 2).

8. Rule based directly on a provision of the Charter (Article 101, paragraph 1).

9. Rules 84, 85 and 87 reproduce the three paragraphs of Article 18 of the Charter

10. Rule based directly on a provision of the Charter (Article 23, paragraph 2, as amended under General Assembly resolution 1991 A (XVIII)).

11. Under paragraph 3 of resolution 1991 A (XVIII) of 17 December 1963, the General Assembly decided that:

"the ten nonpermanent members of the Security Council shall be elected according to the following pattern:

"(a)   Five from African and Asian States;

"(b)   One from Eastern European States;

"(c)   Two from Latin American States;

"(d)   Two from Western European and other States."

12. Rule based directly on a provision of the Charter (Article 23, paragraph 1).

13. Rule reproducing textually a provision of the Charter (Article 23, paragraph 2, last sentence).

14. Rule based directly on a provision of the Charter (Article 61, paragraph 2, as amended under General Assembly resolution 1991 B (XVIII)).

15. Under paragraph 3 of resolution 1991 B (XVIII) of 17 December 1963, the General Assembly decided that, "without prejudice to the present distribution of seats in the Economic and Social Council, the nine additional members shall be elected according to the following pattern: (a) seven from African and Asian States; (b) one from Latin American States; (c) one from Western European and other States." In the light of the effect given to that paragraph by the General Assembly at its twentieth session, the members of the Economic and Social Council are elected according to the following pattern:

(a)   Twelve from African and Asian States;

(b)   Three from Eastern European States;

(c)   Five from Latin American States;

(d)   Seven from Western European and other States.

16. Rule reproducing textually a provision of the Charter (Article 61, paragraph 2, last sentence).

17. Rule based directly on a provision of the Charter (Article 86, paragraph 1 c).

18. Rule reproducing textually a provision of the Charter (Article 22).

5. Provisional Rules of Procedure of the Security Council

Adopted by the Security Council at its first meeting, these Provisional Rules have been amended many times, the last time being at the 1463rd meeting on Jan. 24, 1969. S/96/Rev.5.

I. MEETINGS

RULE 1

Meetings of the Security Council shall, with the exception of the periodic meetings referred to in rule 4, be held at the call of the President at any time he deems necessary, but the interval between meetings shall not exceed fourteen days.

RULE 2

The President shall call a meeting of the Security Council at the request of any member of the Security Council.

RULE 3

The President shall call a meeting of the Security Council if a dispute or situation is brought to the attention of the Security Council under Article 35 or under Article 11 (3) of the Charter, or if the General Assembly makes recommendations or refers any question to the Security Council under Article 11 (2), or if the Secretary-General brings to the attention of the Security Council any matter under Article 99.

RULE 4

Periodic meetings of the Security Council called for in Article 28 (2) of the Charter shall be held twice a year, at such times as the Security Council may decide.

RULE 5

Meetings of the Security Council shall normally be held at the seat of the United Nations.

Any member of the Security Council or the Secretary-General may propose that the Security Council should meet at another place. Should the

Security Council accept any such proposal, it shall decide upon the place, and the period during which the Council shall meet at such place.

II. AGENDA

RULE 6

The Secretary-General shall immediately bring to the attention of all representatives on the Security Council all communications from States, organs of the United Nations, or the Secretary-General concerning any matter for the consideration of the Security Council in accordance with the provisions of the Charter.

RULE 7

The provisional agenda for each meeting of the Security Council shall be drawn up by the Secretary-General and approved by the President of the Security Council.

Only items which have been brought to the attention of the representatives on the Security Council in accordance with rule 6, items covered by rule 10, or matters which the Security Council has previously decided to defer, may be included in the provisional agenda.

RULE 8

The provisional agenda for a meeting shall be communicated by the Secretary-General to the representatives on the Security Council at least three days before the meeting, but in urgent circumstances it may be communicated simultaneously with the notice of the meeting.

RULE 9

The first item of the provisional agenda for each meeting of the Security Council shall be the adoption of the agenda.

RULE 10

Any item of the agenda of a meeting of the Security Council, consideration of which has not been completed at that meeting, shall, unless the Security Council otherwise decides, automatically be included in the agenda of the next meeting.

RULE 11

The Secretary-General shall communicate each week to the representatives on the Security Council a summary statement of matters of which the Security Council is seized and of the stage reached in their consideration.

RULE 12

The provisional agenda for each periodic meeting shall be circulated to the members of the Security Council at least twenty-one days before the opening of the meeting. Any subsequent change in or addition to the provisional agenda shall be brought to the notice of the members at least five days before the meeting. The Security Council may, however, in urgent circumstances, make additions to the agenda at any time during a periodic meeting.

The provisions of rule 7, paragraph 1, and of rule 9, shall apply also to periodic meetings.

III. REPRESENTATION AND CREDENTIALS

RULE 13

Each member of the Security Council shall be represented at the meetings of the Security Council by an accredited representative. The credentials of a representative on the Security Council shall be communicated to the Secretary-General not less than twenty-four hours before he takes his seat on the Security Council. The credentials shall be issued either by the Head of the State or of the Government concerned or by its Minister of Foreign Affairs. The Head of Government or Minister of Foreign Affairs of each member of the Security Council shall be entitled to sit on the Security Council without submitting credentials.

RULE 14

Any Member of the United Nations not a member of the Security Council and any State not a Member of the United Nations, if invited to participate in a meeting or meetings of the Security Council, shall submit credentials for the representative appointed by it for this purpose. The credentials of such a representative shall be communicated to the Secretary-General not less than twenty-four hours before the first meeting which he is invited to attend.

RULE 15

The credentials of representatives on the Security Council and of any representative appointed in accordance with rule 14 shall be examined by the Secretary-General who shall submit a report to the Security Council for approval.

RULE 16

Pending the approval of the credentials of a representative on the Security Council in accordance with rule 15, such representative shall be seated provisionally with the same rights as other representatives.

RULE 17

Any representative on the Security Council, to whose credentials objection has been made within the Security Council, shall continue to sit with the same rights as other representatives until the Security Council has decided the matter.

IV. PRESIDENCY

RULE 18

The presidency of the Security Council shall be held in turn by the members of the Security Council in the English alphabetical order of their names. Each President shall hold office for one calendar month.

RULE 19

The President shall preside over the meetings of the Security Council and, under the authority of the Security Council, shall represent it in its capacity as an organ of the United Nations.

RULE 20

Whenever the President of the Security Council deems that for the proper fulfillment of the responsibilities of the presidency he should not preside over the Council during the consideration of a particular question with which the member he represents is directly connected, he shall indicate his decision to the Council. The presidential chair shall then devolve, for the purpose of the consideration of that question, on the representative of the member next in English alphabetical order, it being understood that the provisions of this rule shall apply to the representatives on the Security Council called upon successively to preside. This rule shall not affect the representative capacity of the President as stated in rule 19, or his duties under rule 7.

V. SECRETARIAT

RULE 21

The Secretary-General shall act in that capacity in all meetings of the Security Council. The Secretary-General may authorize a deputy to act in his place at meetings of the Security Council.

RULE 22

The Secretary-General, or his deputy acting on his behalf, may make either oral or written statements to the Security Council concerning any question under consideration by it.

RULE 23
The Secretary-General may be appointed by the Security Council, in accordance with rule 28, as rapporteur for a specified question.

RULE 24
The Secretary-General shall provide the staff required by the Security Council. This staff shall form a part of the Secretariat.

RULE 25
The Secretary-General shall give to representatives on the Security Council notice of meetings of the Security Council and of its commissions and committees.

RULE 26
The Secretary-General shall be responsible for the preparation of documents required by the Security Council and shall, except in urgent circumstances, distribute them at least forty-eight hours in advance of the meeting at which they are to be considered.

VI. CONDUCT OF BUSINESS

RULE 27
The President shall call upon representatives in the order in which they signify their desire to speak.

RULE 28
The Security Council may appoint a commission or committee or a rapporteur for a specified question.

RULE 29
The President may accord precedence to any rapporteur appointed by the Security Council.

The Chairman of a commission or committee, or the rapporteur appointed by the commission or committee to present its report, may be accorded precedence for the purpose of explaining the report.

RULE 30
If a representative raises a point of order, the President shall immediately state his ruling. If it is challenged, the President shall submit his ruling to the Security Council for immediate decision and it shall stand unless overruled.

RULE 31

Proposed resolutions, amendments and substantive motions shall normally be placed before the representatives in writing.

RULE 32

Principal motions and draft resolutions shall have precedence in the order of their submission.

Parts of a motion or of a draft resolution shall be voted on separately at the request of any representative, unless the original mover objects.

RULE 33

The following motions shall have precedence in the order named over all principal motions and draft resolutions relative to the subject before the meeting:

1. To suspend the meeting;
2. To adjourn the meeting;
3. To adjourn the meeting to a certain day or hour;
4. To refer any matter to a committee, to the Secretary-General or to a rapporteur;
5. To postpone discussion of the question to a certain day or indefinitely; or
6. To introduce an amendment.

Any motion for the suspension or for the simple adjournment of the meeting shall be decided without debate.

RULE 34

It shall not be necessary for any motion or draft resolution proposed by a representative on the Security Council to be seconded before being put to a vote.

RULE 35

A motion or draft resolution can at any time be withdrawn so long as no vote has been taken with respect to it.

If the motion or draft resolution has been seconded, the representative on the Security Council who has seconded it may require that it be put to the vote as his motion or draft resolution with the same right of precedence as if the original mover had not withdrawn it.

RULE 36

If two or more amendments to a motion or draft resolution are proposed, the President shall rule on the order in which they are to be voted upon. Ordinarily, the Security Council shall first vote on the amendment furthest removed in substance from the original proposal and then on the amendment next furthest removed until all amendments have been put to the vote, but when an amendment adds to or deletes from the text of a motion or draft resolution, that amendment shall be voted on first.

RULE 37

Any Member of the United Nations which is not a member of the Security Council may be invited, as the result of a decision of the Security Council, to participate, without vote, in the discussion of any question brought before the Security Council when the Security Council considers that the interests of that Member are specially affected, or when a Member brings a matter to the attention of the Security Council in accordance with Article 35 (1) of the Charter.

RULE 38

Any Member of the United Nations invited in accordance with the preceding rule, or in application of Article 32 of the Charter, to participate in the discussions of the Security Council may submit proposals and draft resolutions. These proposals and draft resolutions may be put to a vote only at the request of a representative on the Security Council.

RULE 39

The Security Council may invite members of the Secretariat or other persons, whom it considers competent for the purpose, to supply it with information or to give other assistance in examining matters within its competence.

VII. VOTING

RULE 40

Voting in the Security Council shall be in accordance with the relevant Articles of the Charter and of the Statute of the International Court of Justice.

VIII. LANGUAGES

RULE 41

Chinese, English, French, Russian, and Spanish shall be the official languages of the Security Council, and English, French, Russian, and Spanish the working languages.

RULE 42

Speeches made in one of the working languages shall be interpreted into the other working languages.

RULE 43

Speeches made in the official languages shall be interpreted into the working languages.

RULE 44

Any representative may make a speech in a language other than the official languages. In this case he shall himself provide for interpretation into one of the working languages. Interpretation into the other working languages by an interpreter of the Secretariat may be based on the interpretation given in the first working language.

RULE 45

Verbatim records of meetings of the Security Council shall be drawn up in the working languages. At the request of any representative a verbatim record of any speech made in an official language other than the working languages shall be drawn up in the original language.

RULE 46

All resolutions and other important documents shall forthwith be made available in the official languages. Upon the request of any representative any other document shall be made available in any or all of the official languages.

RULE 47

Documents of the Security Council shall, if the Security Council so decides, be published in any language other than the official languages.

IX. PUBLICITY OF MEETINGS, RECORDS

RULE 48

Unless it decides otherwise, the Security Council shall meet in public. Any recommendation to the General Assembly regarding the appointment of the Secretary-General shall be discussed and decided at a private meeting.

RULE 49

Subject to the provisions of rule 51, the verbatim record of each meeting of the Security Council shall be made available in the working languages to the representatives on the Security Council and to the representatives of any other States which have participated in the meeting not later than 10 A.M. of the first working day following the meeting. The verbatim record of any speech made in any other of the official languages, which is drawn up in accordance with the provisions of rule 45, shall be made available in the same manner to any of the above-mentioned representatives at his request.

RULE 50
The representatives of the States which have participated in the meeting shall, within two working days after the time indicated in rule 49, inform the Secretary-General of any corrections they wish to have made in the verbatim record.

RULE 51
The Security Council may decide that for a private meeting the record shall be made in a single copy alone. This record shall be kept by the Secretary-General. The representatives of the States which have participated in the meeting shall, within a period of ten days, inform the Secretary-General of any corrections they wish to have made in this record.

RULE 52
Corrections that have been requested shall be considered approved unless the President is of the opinion that they are sufficiently important to be submitted to the representatives on the Security Council. In the latter case, the representatives on the Security Council shall submit within two working days any comments they may wish to make. In the absence of objections in this period of time, the record shall be corrected as requested.

RULE 53
The verbatim record referred to in rule 49 or the record referred to in rule 51, in which no corrections have been requested in the period of time required by rules 50 and 51, respectively, or which has been corrected in accordance with the provisions of rule 52, shall be considered as approved. It shall be signed by the President and shall become the official record of the Security Council.

RULE 54
The official record of public meetings of the Security Council, as well as the documents annexed thereto, shall be published in the official languages as soon as possible.

RULE 55
At the close of each private meeting the Security Council shall issue a *communiqué* through the Secretary-General.

RULE 56

The representatives of the Members of the United Nations which have taken part in a private meeting shall at all times have the right to consult the record of that meeting in the office of the Secretary-General. The Security Council may at any time grant access to this record to authorized representatives of other Members of the United Nations.

RULE 57

The Secretary-General shall, once each year, submit to the Security Council a list of the records and documents which up to that time have been considered confidential. The Security Council shall decide which of these shall be made available to other Members of the United Nations, which shall be made public, and which shall continue to remain confidential.

X. ADMISSION OF NEW MEMBERS

RULE 58

Any State which desires to become a Member of the United Nations shall submit an application to the Secretary-General. This application shall contain a declaration made in a formal instrument that it accepts the obligations contained in the Charter.

RULE 59

The Secretary-General shall immediately place the application for membership before the representatives on the Security Council. Unless the Security Council decides otherwise, the application shall be referred by the President to a committee of the Security Council upon which each member of the Security Council shall be represented. The committee shall examine any application referred to it and report its conclusions thereon to the Council not less than thirty-five days in advance of a regular session of the General Assembly or, if a special session of the General Assembly is called, not less than fourteen days in advance of such session.

RULE 60

The Security Council shall decide whether in its judgment the applicant is a peace-loving State and is able and willing to carry out the obligations contained in the Charter and, accordingly, whether to recommend the applicant State for membership.

If the Security Council recommends the applicant State for membership, it shall forward to the General Assembly the recommendation with a complete record of the discussion.

If the Security Council does not recommend the applicant State for membership or postpones the consideration of the application, it shall submit a special report to the General Assembly with a complete record of the discussion.

In order to ensure the consideration of its recommendation at the next session of the General Assembly following the receipt of the application, the Security Council shall make its recommendation not less than twenty-five days in advance of a regular session of the General Assembly, nor less than four days in advance of a special session.

In special circumstances, the Security Council may decide to make a recommendation to the General Assembly concerning an application for membership subsequent to the expiration of the time limits set forth in the preceding paragraph.

XI. RELATIONS WITH OTHER UNITED NATIONS ORGANS

RULE 61

Any meeting of the Security Council held in pursuance of the Statute of the International Court of Justice for the purpose of the election of members of the Court shall continue until as many candidates as are required for all the seats to be filled have obtained in one or more ballots an absolute majority of votes.

APPENDIX

Provisional procedure for dealing with communications from private individuals and nongovernmental bodies

A. A list of all communications from private individuals and nongovernmental bodies relating to matters of which the Security Council is seized shall be circulated to all representatives on the Security Council.

B. A copy of any communication on the list shall be given by the Secretariat to any representative on the Security Council at his request.

6. Uniting for Peace Resolution

Adopted as Resolution 377(V) by the General Assembly on November 3, 1950. General Assembly, Official Records, V, Supp. 20 (A/1775), pp. 10–12. Annex omitted.

The General Assembly,

Recognizing that the first two stated Purposes of the United Nations are:

"To maintain international peace and security, and to that end: to take effective collective measures for the prevention and removal of threats to the peace, and for the suppression of acts of aggression or other breaches of the peace, and to bring about by peaceful means, and in conformity with the principles of justice and international law, adjustment or settlement of international disputes or situations which might lead to a breach of the peace," and

"To develop friendly relations among nations based on respect for the principle of equal rights and self-determination of peoples, and to take other appropriate measures to strengthen universal peace,"

Reaffirming that it remains the primary duty of all Members of the United Nations, when involved in an international dispute, to seek settlement of such a dispute by peaceful means through the procedures laid down in Chapter VI of the Charter, and recalling the successful achievements of the United Nations in this regard on a number of previous occasions.

Finding that international tension exists on a dangerous scale,

Recalling its resolution 290 (IV) entitled "Essentials of Peace," which states that disregard of the Principles of the Charter of the United Nations is primarily responsible for the continuance of international tension, and desiring to contribute further to the objectives of that resolution.

Reaffirming the importance of the exercise by the Security Council of its primary responsibility for the maintenance of international peace and security, and the duty of the permanent members to seek unanimity and to exercise restraint in the use of the veto.

Reaffirming that the initiative in negotiating the agreements for armed forces provided for in Article 43 of the Charter belongs to the Security Council, and desiring to ensure that, pedding the conclusion of such agreements, the United Nations has at its disposal means for maintaining international peace and security.

Conscious that failure of the Security Council to discharge its responsibilities on behalf of all the Member States, particularly those responsibilities referred to in the two preceding paragraphs, does not relieve Member States of their obligations or the United Nations of its responsibility under the Charter to maintain international peace and security.

Recognizing in particular that such failure does not deprive the General Assembly of its rights or relieve it of its responsibilities under the Charter in regard to the maintenance of international peace and security.

Recognizing that discharge by the General Assembly of its responsibilities in these respects calls for possibilities of observation which would ascertain the facts and expose aggressors; for the existence of armed forces which could be used collectively; and for the possibility of timely recommendation by the General Assembly to Members of the United Nations for collective action which, to be effective, should be prompt,

A

1. Resolves that if the Security Council, because of lack of unanimity of the permanent members, fails to exercise its primary responsibility for the maintenance of international peace and security in any case where there appears to be a threat to the peace, breach of the peace or act of aggression, the General Assembly shall consider the matter immediately with a view to making appropriate recommendations to Members for collective measures, including in the case of a breach of the peace or act of aggression the use of armed force when necessary, to maintain or restore international peace and security. If not in session at the time, the General Assembly may meet in an emergency special session within twenty-four hours of the request therefor. Such emergency special session shall be called if requested by the Security Council on the vote of any seven members, or by a majority of the Members of the United Nations;

2. Adopts for this purpose the amendments to its rules of procedure set forth in the annex to this resolution;

B

3. Establishes a Peace Observation Commission, which for the calendar years 1951 and 1952 shall be composed of fourteen Members, namely: China, Colombia, Czechoslovakia, France, India, Iraq, Israel, New Zealand, Pakistan, Sweden, the Union of Soviet Socialist Republics, the United Kingdom of Great Britain and Northern Ireland, the United States of America and Uruguay, and which could observe and report on the situation in any area where there exists international tension the continuance of

which is likely to endanger the maintenance of international peace and security. Upon the invitation or with the consent of the State into whose territory the Commission would go, the General Assembly, or the Interim Committee when the Assembly is not in session, may utilize the Commission if the Security Council is not exercising the functions assigned to it by the Charter with respect to the matter in question. Decisions to utilize the Commission shall be made on the affirmative vote of two-thirds of the members present and voting. The Security Council may also utilize the Commission in accordance with its authority under the Charter;

4. Decides that the Commission shall have authority in its discretion to appoint subcommissions and to utilize the services of observers to assist it in the performance of its functions;

5. Recommends to all governments and authorities that they cooperate with the Commission and assist it in the performance of its functions;

6. Requests the Secretary-General to provide the necessary staff and facilities, utilizing, where directed by the Commission, the United Nations Panel of Field Observers envisaged in resolution 297 B (IV);

C

7. Invites each Member of the United Nations to survey its resources in order to determine the nature and scope of the assistance it may be in a position to render in support of any recommendations of the Security Council or of the General Assembly for the restoration of international peace and security;

8. Recommends to the Members of the United Nations that each Member maintain within its national armed forces elements so trained, organized and equipped that they could promptly be made available, in accordance with its constitutional processes, for service as a United Nations unit or units, upon recommendation by the Security Council or General Assembly, without prejudice to the use of such elsments in exercise of the right of individual or collective self-defense recognized in Article 51 of the Charter;

9. Invites the Members of the United Nations to inform the Collective Measures Committee provided for in paragraph 11 as soon as possible of the measures taken in implementation of the preceding paragraph;

10. Requests the Secretary-General to appoint, with the approval of the Committee provided for in paragraph 11, a panel of military experts who could be made available, on request, to Member States wishing to obtain technical advice regarding the organization, training, and equipment for prompt service as United Nations units of the elements referred to in paragraph 8;

D

11. Establishes a Collective Measures Committee consisting of fourteen Members, namely: Australia, Belgium, Brazil, Burma, Canada, Egypt, France, Mexico, Phillippines, Turkey, the United Kingdom of Great Britain and Northern Ireland, the United States of America, Venezuela and Yugoslavia, and directs the Committee, in consultation with the Secretary-General and with such Member States as the Committee finds appropriate, to study and make a report to the Security Council and the General Assembly, not later than 1 September 1951, on methods, including those of section C of the present resolution, which might be used to maintain and strengthen international peace and security in accordance with the Purposes and Principles of the Charter, taking account of collective self-defense and regional arrangements (Articles 51 and 52 of the Charter);

12. Recommends to all Member States that they cooperate with the Committee and assist it in the performance of its functions;

13. Requests the Secretary-General to furnish the staff and facilities necessary for the effective accomplishment of the purposes set forth in sections C and D of the present resolution;

E.

14. Is fully conscious that, in adopting the proposals set forth above, enduring peace will not be secured solely by collective security arrangements against breaches of international peace and acts of aggression, but that a genuine and lasting peace depends also upon the observance of all the Principles and Purposes established in the Charter of the United Nations, upon the implementation of the resolutions of the Security Council, the General Assembly and other principal organs of the United Nations intended to achieve the maintenance of international peace and security, and especially upon respect for and observance of human rights and fundamental freedoms for all and on the establishment and maintenance of conditions of economic and social well-being in all countries; and accordingly;

15. Urges Member States to respect fully, and to intensify, joint action, in cooperation with the United Nations, to develop and stimulate universal respect for an observance of human rights and fundamental freedoms, and to intensify individual and collective efforts to achieve conditions of economic stability and social progress, particularly through the development of underdeveloped countries and areas.

7. Declaration on Principles of International Law Concerning Friendly Relations and Cooperation Among States in Accordance with the Charter of the United Nations

Adopted by Resolution 2625 (XXV) of the General Assembly on October 24, 1970. U.N. General Assembly, 25th Sess., Doc. A/RES/2625 (XXV), U.N. Press Release GA/4355 (Dec. 17, 1970).

PREAMBLE

The General Assembly,

Reaffirming in the terms of the Charter of the United Nations that the maintenance of international peace and security and the development of friendly relations and cooperation between nations are among the fundamental purposes of the United Nations,

Recalling that the peoples of the United Nations are determined to practise tolerance and live together in peace with one another as good neighbours,

Bearing in mind the importance of maintaining and strengthening international peace founded upon freedom, equality, justice, and respect for fundamental human rights and of developing friendly relations among nations irrespective of their political, economic, and social systems or the levels of their development,

Bearing in mind also the paramount importance of the Charter of the United Nations in the promotion of the rule of law among nations,

Considering that the faithful observance of the principles of international law concerning friendly relations and cooperation among states and the fulfilment in good faith of the obligations assumed by states, in accordance with the Charter, is of the greatest importance for the maintenance of international peace and security and for the implementation of the other purposes of the United Nations,

Noting that the great political, economic and social changes and scientific progress which have taken place in the world since the adoption of the Charter give increased importance to these principles and to the need for their more effective application in the conduct of states wherever carried on,

Recalling the established principle that outer space, including the Moon and other celestial bodies, is not subject to national appropriation by claim of sovereignty, by means of use or occupation, or by any other means, and mindful of the fact that consideration is being given in the United Nations to the question of establishing other appropriate provisions similarly inspired,

Convinced that the strict observance by states of the obligation not to intervene in the affairs of any other state is an essential condition to ensure that nations live together in peace with one another, since the practice of any form of intervention not only violates the spirit and letter of the Charter, but also leads to the creation of situations which threaten international peace and security,

Recalling the duty of states to refrain in their international relations from military, political, economic, or any other form of coercion aimed against the political independence or territorial integrity of any state,

Considering it essential that all states shall refrain in their international relations from the threat or use of force against the territorial integrity or political independence of any state, or in any other manner inconsistent with the purposes of the United Nations,

Considering it equally essential that all states shall settle their international disputes by peaceful means in accordance with the Charter,

Reaffirming, in accordance with the Charter, the basic importance of sovereign equality and stressing that the purposes of the United Nations can be implemented only if states enjoy sovereign equality and comply fully with the requirements of this principle in their international relations,

Convinced that the subjection of peoples to alien subjugation, domination and exploitation constitutes a major obstacle to the promotion of international peace and security,

Convinced that the principle of equal rights and self-determination of peoples constitutes a significant contribution to contemporary international law, and that its effective application is of paramount importance for the promotion of friendly relations among states, based on respect for the principle of sovereign equality,

Convinced in consequence that any attempt aimed at the partial or total disruption of the national unity and territorial integrity of a state or country or at its political independence is incompatible with the purposes and principles of the Charter,

Considering the provisions of the Charter as a whole and taking into account the role of relevant resolutions adopted by the competent organs of the United Nations relating to the content of the principles,

Considering that the progressive development and codification of the following principles:

(a) The principle that states shall refrain in their international relations from the threat or use of force against the territorial integrity or political independence of any state, or in any other manner inconsistent with the purposes of the United Nations,
(b) The principle that states shall settle their international disputes by peaceful means in such a manner that international peace and security and justice are not endangered,
(c) The duty not to intervene in matters within the domestic jurisdiction of any state, in accordance with the Charter,
(d) The duty of states to cooperate with one another in accordance with the Charter,
(e) The principle of equal rights and self-determination of peoples,
(f) The principle of sovereign equality of states,
(g) The principle that states shall fulfil in good faith the obligations assumed by them in accordance with the Charter,

so as to secure their more effective application within the international community, would promote the realization of the purposes of the United Nations,

Having considered the principles of international law relating to friendly relations and cooperation among states,

1. *Solemnly proclaims* the following principles:

The principle that states shall refrain in their international relations from the threat or use of force against the territorial integrity or political independence of any state, or in any other manner inconsistent with the purposes of the United Nations

Every state has the duty to refrain in its international relations from the threat or use of force against the territorial integrity or political independence of any state, or in any other manner inconsistent with the purposes of the United Nations. Such a threat or use of force constitutes a violation of international law and the Charter of the United Nations and shall never be employed as a means of settling international issues.

A war of aggression constitutes a crime against the peace, for which there is responsibility under international law.

In accordance with the purposes and principles of the United Nations, states have the duty to refrain from propaganda for wars of aggression.

Every state has the duty to refrain from the threat or use of force to violate the existing international boundaries of another state or as a means of solving international disputes, including territorial disputes and problems concerning frontiers of states.

Every state likewise has the duty to refrain from the threat or use of force to violate international lines of demarcation, such as armistice lines, established by or pursuant to an international agreement to which it is a party or which it is otherwise bound to respect. Nothing in the foregoing shall be construed as prejudicing the positions of the parties concerned with regard to the status and effects of such lines under their special regimes or as affecting their temporary character.

States have a duty to refrain from acts of reprisal involving the use of force.

Every state has the duty to refrain from any forcible action which deprives peoples referred to in the elaboration of the principle of equal rights and self-determination of their right to self-determination and freedom and independence.

Every state has the duty to refrain from organizing or encouraging the organization of irregular forces or armed bands, including mercenaries, for incursion into the territory of another state.

Every state has the duty to refrain from organizing, instigating, assisting or participating in acts of civil strife or terrorist acts in another state or acquiescing in organized activities within its territory directed towards the commission of such acts, when the acts referred to in the present paragraph involve a threat or use of force.

The territory of a state shall not be the object of military occupation resulting from the use of force in contravention of the provisions of the Charter. The territory of a state shall not be the object of acquisition by another state resulting from the threat or use of force. No territorial acquisition resulting from the threat or use of force shall be recognized as legal. Nothing in the foregoing shall be construed as affecting:

(a) Provisions of the Charter or any international agreement prior to the Charter regime and valid under international law; or

(b) The powers of the Security Council under the Charter.

All states shall pursue in good faith negotiations for the early conclusion of a universal treaty on general and complete disarmament under effective international control and strive to adopt appropriate measures to reduce international tensions and strengthen confidence among states.

All states shall comply in good faith with their obligations under the generally recognized principles and rules of international law with respect to the maintenance of international peace and security, and shall endeavour to make the United Nations security system based upon the Charter more effective.

Nothing in the foregoing paragraphs shall be construed as enlarging or diminishing in any way the scope of the provisions of the Charter concerning cases in which the use of force is lawful.

The principle that states shall settle their international disputes by peaceful means in such a manner that international peace and security and justice are not endangered

Every state shall settle its international disputes with other states by peaceful means, in such a manner that international peace and security and justice are not endangered.

States shall accordingly seek early and just settlement of their international disputes by negotiation, inquiry, mediation, conciliation, arbitration, judicial settlement, resort to regional agencies or arrangements or other peaceful means of their choice. In seeking such a settlement the parties shall agree upon such peaceful means as may be appropriate to the circumstances and nature of the dispute.

The parties to a dispute have the duty, in the event of failure to reach a solution by any one of the above peaceful means, to continue to seek a settlement of the dispute by other peaceful means agreed upon by them.

States parties to an international dispute, as well as other states, shall refrain from any action which may aggravate the situation so as to endanger the maintenance of international peace and security, and shall act in accordance with the purposes and principles of the United Nations.

International disputes shall be settled on the basis of the sovereign equality of states and in accordance with the principle of free choice of means. Recourse to, or acceptance of, a settlement procedure freely agreed to by states with regard to existing or future disputes to which they are parties shall not be regarded as incompatible with sovereign equality.

Nothing in the foregoing paragraphs prejudices or derogates from the applicable provisions of the Charter, in particular those relating to the pacific settlement of international disputes.

The principle concerning the duty not to intervene in matters within the domestic jurisdiction of any state, in accordance with the Charter

No state or group of states has the right to intervene, directly or indirectly, for any reason whatever, in the internal or external affairs of any other state. Consequently, armed intervention and all other forms of interference or attempted threats against the personality of the state or against its political, economic and cultural elements, are in violation of international law.

No state may use or encourage the use of economic, political or any other type of measures to coerce another state in order to obtain from it the subordination of the exercise of its sovereign rights and to secure from it advantages of any kind. Also, no state shall organize, assist, foment, finance, incite or tolerate subversive, terrorist or armed activities directed towards the violent overthrow of the regime of another state, or interfere in civil strife in another state.

The use of force to deprive peoples of their national identity constitues a violation of their inalienable rights and of the principle of nonintervention.

Every state has an inalienable right to choose its political, economic, social and cultural systems, without interference in any form by another state.

Nothing in the foregoing paragraphs shall be construed as affecting the relevant provisions of the Charter relating to the maintenance of international peace and security.

The duty of states to cooperate with one another in accordance with the Charter

States have the duty to cooperate with one another, irrespective of the differences in their political, economic and social systems, in the various spheres of international relations, in order to maintain international peace and security and to promote international economic stability and progress, the general welfare of nations and international cooperation free from discrimination based on such differences.

To this end:

(a) States shall cooperate with other states in the maintenance of international peace and security;

(b) States shall cooperate in the promotion of universal respect for, and observance of, human rights and fundamental freedoms for all, and in the elimination of all forms of racial discrimination and all forms of religious intolerance;

(c) States shall conduct their international relations in the economic, social, cultural, technical and trade fields in accordance with the principles of sovereign equality and nonintervention;

(d) States Members of the United Nations have the duty to take joint and separate action in cooperation with the United Nations in accordance with the relevant provisions of the Charter.

States should cooperate in the economic, social, and cultural fields as well as in the field of science and technology and for the promotion of international cultural and educational progress. States should cooperate in the promotion of economic growth throughout the world, especially that of the developing countries

The principle of equal rights and self-determination of peoples

By virtue of the principle of equal rights and self-determination of peoples enshrined in the Charter of the United Nations, all peoples have the right freely to determine, without external interference, their political status and to pursue their economic, social and cultural development, and every state has the duty to respect this right in accordance with the provisions of the Charter.

Every state has the duty to promote, through joint and separate action, realization of the principle of equal rights and self-determination of peoples, in accordance with the provisions of the Charter, and to render assistance to the United Nations in carrying out the responsibilities entrusted to it by the Charter regarding the implementation of the principle, in order:

(a) To promote friendly relations and cooperation among states; and
(b) To bring a speedy end to colonialism, having due regard to the freely expressed will of the peoples concerned;

and bearing in mind that subjection of peoples to alien subjugation, domination and exploitation constitutes a violation of the principle, as well as a denial of fundamental human rights, and is contrary to the Charter.

Every state has the duty to promote through joint and separate action universal respect for and observance of human rights and fundamental freedoms in accordance with the Charter.

The establishment of a sovereign and independent state, the free association or integration with an independent state or the emergence into any other political status freely determined by a people constitute modes of implementing the right of self-determination by that people.

Every state has the duty to refrain from any forcible action which deprives peoples referred to above in the elaboration of the present principle of their right to self-determination and freedom and independence. In their actions against, and resistance to, such forcible action in pursuit of the exercise of their right to self-determination, such peoples are entitled to seek and to receive support in accordance with the purposes and principles of the Charter.

The territory of a colony or other non-self-governing territory has, under the Charter, a status separate and distinct from the territory of the state administering it; and such separate and distinct status under the Charter shall exist until the people of the colony or non-self-governing territory have exercised their right of self-determination in accordance with the Charter, and particularly its purposes and principles.

Nothing in the foregoing paragraphs shall be construed as authorizing or encouraging any action which would dismember or impair, totally or in part, the territorial integrity or political unity of sovereign and independent states conducting themselves in compliance with the principle of equal rights and self-determination of peoples as described above and thus possessed of a government representing the whole people belonging to the territory without distinction as to race, creed, or colour.

Every state shall refrain from any action aimed at the partial or total disruption of the national unity and territorial integrity of any other state or country.

The principle of sovereign equality of states

All states enjoy sovereign equality. They have equal rights and duties and are equal members of the international community, notwithstanding differences of an economic, social, political, or other nature.

In particular, sovereign equality includes the following elements:

(a) States are juridically equal;
(b) Each state enjoys the rights inherent in full sovereignty;
(c) Each state has the duty to respect the personality of other states;
(d) The territorial integrity and political independence of the state are inviolable;
(e) Each state has the right freely to choose and develop its political, social, economic, and cultural systems;
(f) Each state has the duty to comply fully and in good faith with its international obligations and to live in peace with other states.

The principle that states shall fulfil in good faith the obligations assumed by them in accordance with the Charter

Every state has the duty to fulfil in good faith the obligations assumed by it in accordance with the Charter of the United Nations.

Every state has the duty to fulfil in good faith its obligations under the generally recognized principles and rules of international law.

Every state has the duty to fulfil in good faith its obligations under international agreements valid under the generally recognized principles and rules of international law.

Where obligations arising under international agreements are in conflict with the obligations of Members of the United Nations under the Charter of the United Nations, the obligations under the Charter shall prevail.

GENERAL PART

2. *Declares* that:

In their interpretation and application the above principles are inter-related and each principle should be construed in the context of the other principles,

Nothing in this Declaration shall be construed as prejudicing in any manner the provisions of the Charter or the rights and duties of Member States under the Charter or the rights of peoples under the Charter, taking into account the elaboration of these rights in this Declaration,

3. *Declares further* that:

The principles of the Charter which are embodied in this Declaration constitute basic principles of international law, and consequently appeals to all states to be guided by these principles in their international conduct and to develop their mutual relations on the basis of the strict observance of these principles.

8. Treaty on the Nonproliferation of Nuclear Weapons

Signed at Washington, London, and Moscow simultaneously on July 1, 1968, the Treaty came into force after its ratification by the United States, the United Kingdom and the Soviet Union plus forty more Signatory States. UN Doc.A/7016/Add.1.

The States concluding this Treaty, hereinafter referred to as the "Parties to the Treaty,"

Considering the devastation that would be visited upon all mankind by a nuclear war and the consequent need to make every effort to avert the danger of such a war and to take measures to safeguard the security of peoples,

Believing that the proliferation of nuclear weapons would seriously enhance the danger of nuclear war,

In conformity with resolutions of the United Nations General Assembly calling for the conclusion of an agreement on the prevention of wider dissemination of nuclear weapons,

Undertaking to cooperate in facilitating the application of International Atomic Energy Agency safeguards on peaceful nuclear activities,

Expressing their support for research, development and other efforts to further the application, within the framework of the International Atomic Energy Agency safeguards system, of the principle of safeguarding effectively the flow of source and special fissionable materials by use of instruments and other techniques at certain strategic points,

Affirming the principle that the benefits of peaceful applications of nuclear technology, including any technological by-products which may be derived by nuclear-weapon States from the development of nuclear explosive devices, should be available for peaceful purposes to all Parties to the Treaty, whether nuclear-weapon or non-nuclear-weapon States,

Convinced that, in furtherance of this principle, all Parties to the Treaty are entitled to participate in the fullest possible exchange of scientific information for, and to contribute alone or in cooperation with other States to, the further development of the applications of atomic energy for peaceful purposes,

Declaring their intention to achieve at the earliest possible date the cessation of the nuclear arms race and to undertake effective measures in the direction of nuclear disarmament,

Urging the cooperation of all States in the attainment of this objective,

Recalling the determination expressed by the Parties to the 1963 Treaty banning nuclear weapon tests in the atmosphere in outer space and under water in its Preamble to seek to achieve the discontinuance of all test explosions of nuclear weapons for all time and to continue negotiations to this end,

Desiring to further the easing of international tension and the strengthening of trust between States in order to facilitate the cessation of the manufacture of nuclear weapons, the liquidation of all their existing stockpiles, and the elimination from national arsenals of nuclear weapons and the means of their delivery pursuant to a treaty on general and complete disarmament under strict and effective international control,

Recalling that, in accordance with the Charter of the United Nations, States must refrain in their international relations from the threat or use of force against the territorial integrity or political independence of any State, or in any other manner inconsistent with the Purposes of the United Nations, and that the establishment and maintenance of international peace and security are to be promoted with the least diversion for armaments of the world's human and economic resources,

Have agreed as follows:

ARTICLE I

Each nuclear-weapon State Party to the Treaty undertakes not to transfer to any recipient whatsoever nuclear weapons or other nuclear explosive devices or control over such weapons or explosive devices directly, or indirectly; and not in any way to assist, encourage, or induce any non-nuclear-weapon State to manufacture or otherwise acquire nuclear weapons or other nuclear explosive devices, or control over such weapons or explosive devices.

ARTICLE II

Each non-nuclear-weapon State Party to the Treaty undertakes not to receive the transfer from any transferor whatsoever of nuclear weapons or other nuclesr explosive devices or of control over such weapons or explosive devices directly, or indirectly; not to manufacture or otherwise acquire nuclear weapons or other nuclear explosive devices; and not to seek or receive any assistance in the manufacture of nuclear weapons or other nuclear explosive devices.

ARTICLE III

1. Each non-nuclear-weapon State Party to the Treaty undertakes to accept safeguards, as set forth in an agreement to be negotiated and concluded with the International Atomic Energy Agency in accordance with the Statute of the International Atomic Energy Agency and the Agency's safeguards system, for the exclusive purpose of verification of the fulfillment of its obligations assumed under this Treaty with a view to preventing diversion of nuclear energy from peaceful uses to nuclear weapons or other nuclear explosive devices. Procedures for the safeguards required by this article shall be followed with respect to source or special fissionable material whether it is being produced, processed, or used in any principal nuclear facility or is outside any such facility. The safeguards required by this article shall be applied on all source or special fissionable material in all peaceful nuclear activities within the territory of such State, under its jurisdiction, or carried out under its control anywhere.

2. Each State Party to the Treaty undertakes not to provide: (a) source or special fissionable material, or (b) equipment or material especially designed or prepared for the processing, use or production of special fissionable material, to any non-nuclear-weapon State for peaceful purposes, unless the source or special fissionable material shall be subject to the safeguards required by this article.

3. The safeguards required by this article shall be implemented in a manner designed to comply with article IV of this Treaty, and to avoid hampering the economic or technological development of the Parties or international cooperation in the field of peaceful nuclear activities, including the international exchange of nuclear material and equipment for the processing, use or production of nuclear material for peaceful purposes in accordance with the provisions of this article and the principle of safeguarding set forth in the Preamble of the Treaty.

4. Non-nuclear-weapon States Party to the Treaty shall conclude agreements with the International Atomic Energy Agency to meet the requirements of this article either individually or together with other States in accordance with the Statute of the International Atomic Energy Agency. Negotiation of such agreements shall commence within 180 days from the original entry into force of this Treaty. For States depositing their instruments of ratification or accession after the 180-day period, negotiation of such agreements shall commence not later than the date of such deposit. Such agreements shall enter into force not later than eighteen months after the date of initiation of negotiations.

ARTICLE IV

1. Nothing in this Treaty shall be interpreted as affecting the inalienable right of all the Parties to the Treaty to develop research, produc-

tion, and use of nuclear energy for peaceful purposes without discrimination and in conformity with articles I and II of this Treaty.

2. All the Parties to the Treaty undertake to facilitate, and have the right to participate in, the fullest possible exchange of equipment, materials, and scientific and technological information for the peaceful uses of nuclear energy. Parties to the Treaty in a position to do so shall also cooperate in contributing alone or together with other States or international organizations to the further development of the applications of nuclear energy for peaceful purposes, especially in the territories of non-nuclear-weapon States Party to the Treaty, with due consideration for the needs of the developing areas of the world.

ARTICLE V

Each Party to the Treaty undertakes to take appropriate measures to ensure that, in accordance with this Treaty, under appropriate international observation and through appropriate international procedures, potential benefits from any peaceful applications of nuclear explosions will be made available to non-nuclear-weapon States Party to the Treaty on a non-discriminatory basis and that the charge to such Parties for the explosive devices used will be as low as possible and exclude any charge for research and development. Non-nuclear-weapon States Party to the Treaty shall be able to obtain such benefits, pursuant to a special international agreement or agreements, through an appropriate international body with adequate representation of non-nuclear-weapon States. Negotiations on this subject shall commence as soon as possible after the Treaty enters into force. Non-nuclear-weapon States Party to the Treaty so desiring may also obtain such benefits pursuant to bilateral agreements.

ARTICLE VI

Each of the Parties to the Treaty undertakes to pursue negotiations in good faith on effective measures relating to cessation of the nuclear arms race at an early date and to nuclear disarmament, and on a treaty on general and complete disarmament under strict and effective international control.

ARTICLE VII

Nothing in this Treaty affects the right of any group of States to conclude regional treaties in order to assure the total absence of nuclear weapons in their respective territories.

ARTICLE VIII

1. Any Party to the Treaty may propose amendments to this Treaty. The text of any proposed amendment shall be submitted to the Depositary Governments which shall circulate it to all Parties to the Treaty.

Thereupon, if requested to do so by one-third or more of the Parties to the Treaty, the Depositary Governments shall convene a conference, to which they shall invite all the Parties to the Treaty, to consider such an amendment.

2. Any amendment to this Treaty must be approved by a majority of the votes of all the Parties to the Treaty, including the votes of all nuclear-weapon States Party to the Treaty and all other Parties which, on the date the amendment is circulated, are members of the Board of Governors of the International Atomic Energy Agency. The amendment shall enter into force for each Party that deposits its instrument of ratification of the amendment upon the deposit of such instruments of ratification by a majority of all the Parties, including the instruments of ratification of all nuclear-weapon States Party to the Treaty and all other Parties which, on the date the amendment is circulated, are members of the Board of Governors of the International Atomic Energy Agency. Thereafter, it shall enter into force for any other Party upon the deposit of its instrument of ratification of the amendment.

3. Five years after the entry into force of this Treaty, a conference of Parties to the Treaty shall be held in Geneva, Switzerland, in order to review the operation of this Treaty with a view to assuring that the purposes of the Preamble and the provisions of the Treaty are being realized. At intervals of five years thereafter, a majority of the Parties to the Treaty may obtain, by submitting a proposal to this effect to the Depositary Governments, the convening of further conferences with the same objective of reviewing the operation of the Treaty.

ARTICLE IX

1. This Treaty shall be open to all States for signature. Any State which does not sign the Treaty before its entry into force in accordance with paragraph 3 of this article may accede to it at any time.

2. This Treaty shall be subject to ratification by signatory States. Instruments of ratification and instruments of accession shall be deposited with the Governments of the United States of America, the United Kingdom of Great Britain and Northern Ireland and the Union of Soviet Socialist Republics, which are hereby designated the Depositary Governments.

3. This Treaty shall enter into force after its ratification by the States, the Governments of which are designated Depositaries of the Treaty, and forty other States signatory to this Treaty and the deposit of their instruments of ratification. For the purposes of this Treaty, a nuclear-weapon State is one which has manufactured and exploded a nuclear weapon or other nuclear explosive device prior to January 1, 1967.

4. For States whose instruments of ratification or accession are deposited subsequent to the entry into force of this Treaty, it shall enter into force on the date of the deposit of their instruments of ratification or accession.

5. The Depositary Governments shall promptly inform all signatory and acceding States of the date of each signature, the date of deposit of each instrument of ratification or of accession, the date of the entry into force of this Treaty, and the date of receipt of any requests for convening a conference or other notices.

6. This Treaty shall be registered by the Depositary Governments pursuant to article 102 of the Charter of the United Nations.

ARTICLE X

1. Each Party shall in exercising its national sovereignty have the right to withdraw from the Treaty if it decides that extraordinary events, related to the subject matter of this Treaty, have jeopardized the supreme interests of its country. It shall give notice of such withdrawal to all other Parties to the Treaty and to the United Nations Security Council three months in advance. Such notice shall include a statement of the extraordinary events it regards as having jeopardized its supreme interests.

2. Twenty-five years after the entry into force of the Treaty, a conference shall be convened to decide whether the Treaty shall continue in force indefinitely, or shall be extended for an additional fixed period or periods. This decision shall be taken by a majority of the Parties to the Treaty.

ARTICLE XI

This Treaty, the English, Russian, French, Spanish and Chinese texts of which are equally authentic, shall be deposited in the archives of the Depositary Governments. Duty certified copies of this Treaty shall be transmitted by the Depositary Governments to the Governments of the signatory and acceding States.

In witness whereof the undersigned, duty authorized, have signed this Treaty.

Done in triplicate, at the cities of Washington, London, and Moscow, this first day of July one thousand nine hundred sixty-eight.

9. Final Document on Disarmament

Adopted by the Tenth Special Session of the General Assembly on 1 July 1978. U.N. Document A/RES/S-10/2.

The General Assembly,

Alarmed by the threat to the very survival of mankind posed by the existence of nuclear weapons and the continuing arms race, and recalling the devastation inflicted by all wars,

Convinced that disarmament and arms limitation, particularly in the nuclear field, are essential for the prevention of the danger of nuclear war and the strengthening of international peace and security and for the economic and social advancement of all peoples, thus facilitating the achievement of the new international economic order,

Having resolved to lay the foundations of an international disarmament strategy which, through coordinated and persevering efforts in which the United Nations should play a more effective role, aims at general and complete disarmament under effective international control,

Adopts the following Final Document of this special session of the General Assembly devoted to disarmament:

I. INTRODUCTION

1. Attainment of the objective of security, which is an inseparable element of peace, has always been one of the most profound aspirations of humanity. States have for a long time sought to maintain their security through the possession of arms. Admittedly, their survival has, in certain cases, effectively depended on whether they could count on appropriate means of defense. Yet the accumulation of weapons, particularly nuclear weapons, today constitutes much more a threat than a protection for the future of mankind. The time has therefore come to put an end to this situation, to abandon the use of force in international relations and to seek security in disarmament, that is to say, through a gradual but effective process beginning with a reduction in the present level of armaments. The ending of the arms race and the achievement of real disarmament are tasks of primary importance and urgency. To meet this historic challenge is in the political and economic interests of all the nations and peoples of the world

as well as in the interests of ensuring their genuine security and peaceful future.

2. Unless its avenues are closed, the continued arms race means a growing threat to international peace and security and even to the very survival of mankind. The nuclear and conventional arms build-up threatens to stall the efforts aimed at reaching the goals of development, to become an obstacle on the road of achieving the new international economic order and to hinder the solution of other vital problems facing mankind.

3. Dynamic development of détente, encompassing all spheres of international relations in all regions of the world, with the participation of all countries, would create conditions conducive to the efforts of States to end the arms race, which has engulfed the world, thus reducing the danger of war. Progress on détente and progress on disarmament mutually complement and strengthen each other.

4 The Disarmament Decade solemnly declared in 1969 by the United Nations is coming to an end. Unfortunately, the objectives established on that occasion by the General Assembly appear to be as far away today as they were then, or even further because the arms race is not diminishing but increasing and outstrips by far the efforts to curb it. While it is true that some limited agreements have been reached, "effective measures relating to the cessation of the nuclear arms race at an early date and to nuclear disarmament" continue to elude man's grasp. Yet the implementation of such measures is urgently required. There has not been any real progress either that might lead to the conclusion of a treaty on general and complete disarmament under effective international control. Furthermore, it has not been possible to free any amount, however modest, of the enormous resources, both material and human, which are wasted on the unproductive and spiralling arms race and which should be made available for the purpose of economic and social development, especially since such a race "places a great burden on both the developing and the developed countries."

5. The Members of the United Nations are fully aware of the conviction of their peoples that the question of general and complete disarmament is of utmost importance and that peace, security and economic and social development are indivisible, and they have therefore recognized that the corresponding obligations are responsibilities are universal.

6. Thus a powerful current of opinion has gradually formed, leading to the convening of what will go down in the annals of the United Nations as the first special session of the General Assembly devoted entirely to disarmament.

7. The outcome of this special session, whose deliberations have to a large extent been facilitated by the five sessions of the Preparatory Committee which preceded it, is the present Final Document. This introduction

serves as a preface to the document which comprises also the following three sections: a Declaration, a Programme of Action and recommendations concerning the international machinery for disarmament negotiations.

8. While the final objective of the efforts of all States should continue to be general and complete disarmament under effective international control, the immediate goal is that of the elimination of the danger of a nuclear war and the implementation of measures to halt and reverse the arms race and clear the path towards lasting peace. Negotiations on the entire range of those issues should be based on the strict observance of the purposes and principles enshrined in the Charter of the United Nations, with full recognition of the role of the United Nations in the field of disarmament and reflecting the vital interest of all the peoples of the world in this sphere. The aim of the Declaration is to review and assess the existing situation, outline the objectives and the priority tasks and set forth fundamental principles for disarmament negotiations.

9. For disarmament—the aims and purposes of which the Declaration proclaims—to become a reality, it was essential to agree on a series of specific disarmament measures, selected by common accord as those on which there is a consensus to the effect that their subsequent realization in the short term appears to be feasible. There is also a need to prepare through agreed procedures a comprehensive disarmament programme. That programme, passing through all the necessary stages, should lead to general and complete disarmament under effective international control. Procedures for watching over the fulfilment of the obligations thus assumed had also to be agreed upon. That is the purpose of the Programme of Action.

10. Although the decisive factor for achieving real measures of disarmament is the "political will" of States, and especially of those possessing nuclear weapons, a significant role can also be played by the effective functioning of an appropriate international machinery designed to deal with the problems of disarmament in its various aspects. Consequently, it would be necessary that the two kinds of organs required to that end, the deliberative and the negotiating organs, have the appropriate organization and procedures that would be most conducive to obtaining constructive results. The last section of the Final Document, section IV, has been prepared with that end in view.

II. DECLARATION

11. Mankind today is confronted with an unprecedented threat of self-extinction arising from the massive and competitive accumulation of the most destructive weapons ever produced. Existing arsenals of nuclear weapons alone are more than sufficient to destroy all life on earth. Failure

of efforts to halt and reverse the arms race, in particular the nuclear arms race, increases the danger of the proliferation of nuclear weapons. Yet the arms race continues. Military budgets are constantly growing, with enormous consumption of human and material resources. The increase in weapons, especially nuclear weapons, far from helping to strengthen international security, on the contrary weakens it. The vast stockpiles and tremendous build-up of arms and armed forces and the competition for qualitative refinement of weapons of all kinds to which scientific resources and technological advances are diverted, pose incalculable threats to peace. This situation both reflects and aggravates international tensions, sharpens conflicts in various regions of the world, hinders the process of détente, exacerbates the differences between opposing military alliances, jeopardizes the security of all States, heightens the sense of insecurity among all States, including the non-nuclear-weapon States, and increases the threat of nuclear war.

12. The arms race, particularly in its nuclear aspect, runs counter to efforts to achieve further relaxation of international tension, to establish international relations based on peaceful coexistence and trust between all States, and to develop broad international cooperation and understanding. The arms race impedes the realization of the purposes, and is incompatible with the principles, of the Charter of the United Nations, especially respect for sovereignty, refraining from the threat or use of force against the territorial integrity or political independence of any State, peaceful settlement of disputes and nonintervention and noninterference in the internal affairs of States. It also adversely effects the rights of peoples freely to determine their systems of social and economic development, and hinders the struggle for self-determination and the elimination of colonial rule, racial or foreign domination or occupation. Indeed, the massive accumulation of armaments and the acquisition of armaments technology by racist regimes, as well as their possible acquisition of nuclear weapons, present a challenging and increasingly dangerous obstacle to a world community faced with the urgent need to disarm. It is, therefore, essential for purposes of disarmament to prevent any further acquisition of arms or arms technology by such regimes, especially through strict adherence by all States to relevant decisions of the Security Council.

13. Enduring international peace and security cannot be built on the accumulation of weaponry by military alliances nor be sustained by a precarious balance of deterrence or doctrines of strategic superiority. Genuine and lasting peace can only be created through the effective implementation of the security system provided for in the Charter of the United Nations and the speedy and substantial reduction of arms and armed forces, by international agreement and mutual example, leading ultimately to general and complete disarmament under effective international control. At the

same time, the causes of the arms race and threats to peace must be reduced and to this end effective action should be taken to eliminate tensions and settle disputes by peaceful means.

14. Since the process of disarmament affects the vital security interests of all States, they must all be actively concerned with and contribute to the measures of disarmament and arms limitation, which have an essential part to play in maintaining and strengthening international security. Therefore the role and responsibility of the United Nations in the sphere of disarmament, in accordance with its Charter, must be strengthened.

15. It is essential that not only Governments but also the peoples of the world recognize and understand the dangers in the present situation. In order that an international conscience may develop and that world public opinion may exercise a positive influence, the United Nations should increase the dissemination of information on the armaments race and disarmament with the full cooperation of Member States.

16. In a world of finite resources there is a close relationship between expenditure on armaments and economic and social development. Military expenditures are reaching ever higher levels, the highest percentage of which can be attributed to the nuclear-weapon States and most of their allies, with prospects of further expansion and the danger of further increases in the expenditures of other countries. The hundreds of billions of dollars spent annually on the manufacture of improvement of weapons are in sombre and dramatic contrast to the want and poverty in which two-thirds of the world's population live. This colossal waste of resources is even more serious in that it diverts to military purposes not only material but also technical and human resources which are urgently needed for development in all countries, particularly in the developing countries. Thus, the economic and social consequences of the arms race are so detrimental that its continuation is obviously incompatible with the implementation of the new international economic order based on justice, equity, and cooperation. Consequently, resources released as a result of the implementation of disarmament measures should be used in a manner which will help to promote the well-being of all peoples and to improve the economic conditions of the developing countries.

17. Disarmament has thus become an imperative and most urgent task facing the international community. No real progress has been made so far in the crucial field of reduction of armaments. However, certain positive changes in international relations in some areas of the world provide some encouragement. Agreements have been reached that have been important in limiting certain weapons or eliminating them altogether, as in the case of the Convention on the Prohibition of the Development, Production, and Stockpiling of Bacteriological (Biological) and Toxin Weapons and on Their Destruction[1] and excluding particular areas from the arms race. The

fact remains that these agreements relate only to measures of limited restraint while the arms race continues. These partial measures have done little to bring the world closer to the goal of general and complete disarmament. For more than a decade there have been no negotiations leading to a treaty on general and complete disarmament. The pressing need now is to translate into practical terms the provisions of this Final Document and to proceed along the road of binding and effective international agreements in the field of disarmament.

18. Removing the threat of a world war—a nuclear war—is the most acute and urgent task of the present day. Mankind is confronted with a choice: we must halt the arms race and proceed to disarmament or face annihilation.

19. The ultimate objective of the efforts of States in the disarmament process is general and complete disarmament under effective international control. The principal goals of disarmament are to ensure the survival of mankind and to eliminate the danger of war, in particular nuclear war, to ensure that war is no longer an instrument for settling international disputes and that the use and the threat of force are eliminated from international life, as provided for in the Charter of the United Nations. Progress towards this objective requires the conclusion and implementation of agreements on the cessation of the arms race and on genuine measures of disarmament, taking into account the need of States to protect their security.

20. Among such measures, effective measures of nuclear disarmament and the prevention of nuclear war have the highest priority. To this end, it is imperative to remove the threat of nuclear weapons, to halt and reverse the nuclear arms race until the total elimination of nuclear weapons and their delivery systems has been achieved, and to prevent the proliferation of nuclear weapons. At the same time, other measures designed to prevent the outbreak of nuclear war and to lessen the danger of the threat or use of nuclear weapons should be taken.

21. Along with these measures, agreements or other effective measures should be adopted to prohibit or prevent the development, production, or use of other weapons of mass destruction. In this context, an agreement on elimination of all chemical weapons should be concluded as a matter of high priority.

22. Together with negotiations on nuclear disarmament measures, negotiations should be carried out on the balanced reduction of armed forces and of conventional armaments, based on the principle of undiminished security of the parties with a view to promoting or enhancing stability at a lower military level, taking into account the need of all States to protect their security. These negotiations should be conducted with particular emphasis on armed forces and conventional weapons of nuclear-weapon States and other militarily significant countries. There should also

be negotiations on the limitation of international transfer of conventional weapons, based in particular on the same principle, and taking into account the inalienable right to self-determination and independence of peoples under colonial or foreign domination and the obligations of States to respect that right, in accordance with the Charter of the United Nations and the Declaration on Principles of International Law concerning Friendly Relations and Cooperation among States,[2] as well as the need of recipient States to protect their security.

23. Further international action should be taken to prohibit or restrict for humanitarian reasons the use of specific conventional weapons, including those which may be excessively injurious, cause unnecessary suffering or have indiscriminate effects.

24. Collateral measures in both the nuclear and conventional fields, together with other measures specifically designed to build confidence, should be undertaken in order to contribute to the creation of favourable conditions for the adoption of additional disarmament measures and to further the relaxation of international tension.

25. Negotiations and measures in the field of disarmament shall be guided by the fundamental principles set forth below.

26. All States Members of the United Nations reaffirm their full commitment to the purposes of the Charter of the United Nations and their obligation strictly to observe its principles as well as other relevant and generally accepted principles of international law relating to the maintenance of international peace and security. They stress the special importance of refraining from the threat or use of force against the sovereignty, territorial integrity or political independence of any State, or against peoples under colonial or foreign domination seeking to exercise their right to self-determination and to achieve independence; nonintervention and noninterference in the internal affairs of other States; the inviolability of international frontiers; and the peaceful settlement of disputes, having regard to the inherent right of States to individual and collective self-defence in accordance with the Charter.

27. In accordance with the Charter, the United Nations has a central role and primary responsibility in the sphere of disarmament. In order effectively to discharge this role and facilitate and encourage all measures in this field, the United Nations should be kept appropriately informed of all steps in this field, whether unilateral, bilateral, regional, or multilateral, without prejudice to the progress of negotiations.

28. All the peoples of the world have a vital interest in the success of disarmament negotiations. Consequently, all States have the duty to contribute to efforts in the field of disarmament. All States have the right to participate in disarmament negotiations. They have the right to participate on an equal footing in those multilateral disarmament negotiations which

have a direct bearing on their national security. While disarmament is the responsibility of all States, the nuclear-weapon States have the primary responsibility for nuclear disarmament and, together with other militarily significant States, for halting and reversing the arms race. It is therefore important to secure their active participation.

29. The adoption of disarmament measures should take place in such an equitable and balanced manner as to ensure the right of each State to security and to ensure that no individual State or group of States may obtain advantages over others at any stage. At each stage the objective should be undiminished security at the lowest possible level of armaments and military forces.

30. An acceptable balance of mutual responsibilities and obligations for nuclear and non-nuclear-weapon States should be strictly observed.

31. Disarmament and arms limitation agreements should provide for adequate measures of verification satisfactory to all parties concerned in order to create the necessary confidence and ensure that they are being observed by all parties. The form and modalities of the verification to be provided for in any specific agreement depend upon and should be determined by the purposes, scope and nature of the agreement. Agreements should provide for the participation of parties directly or through the United Nations system in the verification process. Where appropriate, a combination of several methods of verification as well as other compliance procedures should be employed.

32. All States, and in particular nuclear-weapon States, should consider various proposals designed to secure the avoidance of the use of nuclear weapons, and the prevention of nuclear war. In this context, while noting the declarations made by nuclear-weapon States, effective arrangements, as appropriate, to assure non-nuclear-weapon States against the use or the threat of use of nuclear weapons could strengthen the security of those States and international peace and security.

33. The establishment of nuclear-weapon-free zones on the basis of agreements or arrangements freely arrived at among the States of the zone concerned, and the full compliance with those agreements or arrangements, thus ensuring that the zones are genuinely free from nuclear weapons, and respect for such zones by nuclear-weapon States, constitute an important disarmament measure.

34. Disarmament, relaxation of international tension, respect for the right to self-determination and national independence, the peaceful settlement of disputes in accordance with the Charter of the United Nations and the strengthening of international peace and security are directly related to each other. Progress in any of these spheres has a beneficial effect on all of them; in turn, failure in one sphere has negative effects on others.

35. There is also a close relationship between disarmament and development. Progress in the former would help greatly in the realization of the latter. Therefore resources released as a result of the implementation of disarmament measures should be devoted to the economic and social development of all nations and contribute to the bridging of the economic gap between developed and developing countries.

36. Nonproliferation of nuclear weapons is a matter of universal concern. Measures of disarmament must be consistent with the inalienable right of all States, without discrimination, to develop, acquire and use nuclear technology, equipment and materials for the peaceful use of nuclear energy and to determine their peaceful nuclear programmes in accordance with their national priorities, needs and interests, bearing in mind the need to prevent the proliferation of nuclear weapons. International cooperation in the peaceful uses of nuclear energy should be conducted under agreed and appropriate international safeguards applied on a nondiscriminatory basis.

37. Significant progress in disarmament, including nuclear disarmament, would be facilitated by parallel measures to strengthen the security of States and to improve the international situation in general.

38. Negotiations on partial measures of disarmament should be conducted concurrently with negotiations on more comprehensive measures and should be followed by negotiations leading to a treaty on general and complete disarmament under effective international control.

39. Qualitative and quantitative disarmament measures are both important for halting the arms race. Efforts to that end must include negotiations on the limitation and cessation of the qualitative improvement of armaments, especially weapons of mass destruction and the development of new means of warfare so that ultimately scientific and technological achievements may be used solely for peaceful purposes.

40. Universality of disarmament agreements helps create confidence among States. When multilateral agreements in the field of disarmament are negotiated, every effort should be made to ensure that they are universally acceptable. The full compliance of all parties with the provisions contained in such agreements would also contribute to the attainment of that goal.

41. In order to create favourable conditions for success in the disarmament process, all States should strictly abide by the provisions of the Charter of the United Nations, refrain from actions which might adversely affect efforts in the field of disarmament, and display a constructive approach to negotiations and the political will to reach agreements. There are certain negotiations on disarmament under way at different levels, the early and successful completion of which could contribute to limiting the arms race. Unilateral measures of arms limitation or reduction could also contribute to the attainment of that goal.

42. Since prompt measures should be taken in order to halt and reverse the arms race, Member States hereby declare that they will respect the objectives and principles stated above and make every effort faithfully to carry out the Programme of Action set forth in section III below.

III. PROGRAMME OF ACTION

43. Progress towards the goal of general and complete disarmament can be achieved through the implementation of a programme of action on disarmament, in accordance with the goals and principles established in the Declaration on disarmament. The present Programme of Action contains priorities and measures in the field of disarmament that States should undertake as a matter of urgency with a view to halting and reversing the arms race and to giving the necessary impetus to efforts designed to achieve genuine disarmament leading to general and complete disarmament under effective international control.

44. The present Programme of Action enumerates the specific measures of disarmament which should be implemented over the next few years, as well as other measures and studies to prepare the way for future negotiations and for progress towards general and complete disarmament.

45. Priorities in disarmament negotiations shall be: nuclear weapons; other weapons of mass destruction, including chemical weapons; conventional weapons, including any which may be deemed to be excessively injurious or to have indiscriminate effects; and reduction of armed forces.

46. Nothing should preclude States from conducting negotiations on all priority items concurrently.

47. Nuclear weapons pose the greatest danger to mankind and to the survival of civilization. It is essential to halt and reverse the nuclear arms race in all its aspects in order to avert the danger of war involving nuclear weapons. The ultimate goal in this context is the complete elimination of nuclear weapons.

48. In the task of achieving the goals of nuclear disarmament, all the nuclear-weapon States, in particular those among them which possess the most important nuclear arsenals, bear a special responsibility.

49. The process of nuclear disarmament should be carried out in such a way, and requires measures to ensure, that the security of all States is guaranteed at progressively lower levels of nuclear armaments, taking into account the relative qualitative and quantitative importance of the existing arsenals of the nuclear-weapon States and other States concerned.

50. The achievement of nuclear disarmament will require urgent negotiation of agreements at appropriate stages and with adequate measures of verification satisfactory to the States concerned for:

(*a*) Cessation of the qualitative improvement and development of nuclear-weapon systems;

(*b*) Cessation of the production of all types of nuclear weapons and their means of delivery, and of the production of fissionable material for weapons purposes;

(*c*) A comprehensive, phased programme with agreed time-frames, whenever feasible, for progressive and balanced reduction of stockpiles of nuclear weapons and their means of delivery, leading to their ultimate and complete elimination at the earliest possible time.

Consideration can be given in the course of the negotiations to mutual and agreed limitation or prohibition, without prejudice to the security of any State, of any types of nuclear armaments.

51. The cessation of nuclear-weapon testing by all States within the framework of an effective nuclear disarmament process would be in the interest of mankind. It would make a significant contribution to the above aim of ending the qualitative improvement of nuclear weapons and the development of new types of such weapons and of preventing the proliferation of nuclear weapons. In this context the negotiations now in progress on "a treaty prohibiting nuclear-weapon tests, and a protocol covering nuclear explosions for peaceful purposes, which would be an integral part of the treaty," should be concluded urgently and the result submitted for full consideration by the multilateral negotiating body with a view to the submission of a draft treaty to the General Assembly at the earliest possible date. All efforts should be made by the negotiating parties to achieve an agreement which, following endorsement by the General Assembly, could attract the widest possible adherence. In this context, various views were expressed by non-nuclear-weapon States that, pending the conclusion of this treaty, the world community would be encouraged if all the nuclear-weapon States refrained from testing nuclear weapons. In this connection, some nuclear-weapon States expressed different views.

52. The Union of Soviet Socialist Republics and the United States of America should conclude at the earliest possible date the agreement they have been pursuing for several years in the second series of the strategic arms limitation talks (SALT II). They are invited to transmit in good time the text of the agreement to the General Assembly. It should be followed promptly by further strategic arms limitation negotiations between the two parties, leading to agreed significant reductions of, and qualitative limitations on strategic arms. It should constitute an important step in the direction of nuclear disarmament and, ultimately, of establishment of a world free of such weapons.

53. The process of nuclear disarmament described in the paragraph on this subject should be expedited by the urgent and vigorous pursuit to a suc-

cessful conclusion of ongoing negotiations and the urgent initiation of further negotiations among the nuclear-weapon States.

54. Significant progress in nuclear disarmament would be facilitated both by parallel political or international legal measures to strengthen the security of States and by progress in the limitation and reduction of armed forces and conventional armaments of the nuclear-weapon States and other States in the regions concerned.

55. Real progress in the field of nuclear disarmament could create an atmosphere conducive to progress in conventional disarmament on a world-wide basis.

56. The most effective guarantee against the danger of nuclear war and the use of nuclear weapons is nuclear disarmament and the complete elimination of nuclear weapons.

57. Pending the achievement of this goal, for which negotiations should be vigorously pursued, and bearing in mind the devastating results which nuclear war would have on belligerents and nonbelligerents alike, the nuclear-weapon States have special responsibilities to undertake measures aimed at preventing the outbreak of nuclear war, and of the use of force in international relations, subject to the provisions of the Charter of the United Nations, including the use of nuclear weapons.

58. In this context all States, and in particular nuclear-weapon States, should consider as soon as possible various proposals designed to secure the avoidance of the use of nuclear weapons, the prevention of nuclear war and related objectives, where possible through international agreement and thereby ensure that the survival of mankind is not endangered. All States should actively participate in efforts to bring about conditions in international relations among States in which a code of peaceful conduct of nations in international affairs could be agreed and which would preclude the use or threat of use of nuclear weapons.

59. In the same context, the nuclear-weapon States are called upon to take steps to assure the non-nuclear-weapon States against the use or threat of use of nuclear weapons. The General Assembly notes the declarations made by the nuclear-weapon States and urges them to pursue efforts to conclude, as appropriate, effective arrangements to assure non-nuclear-weapon States against the use or threat of use of nuclear weapons.

60. The establishment of nuclear-weapon-free zones on the basis of arrangements freely arrived at among the States of the region concerned constitutes an important disarmament measure.

61. The process of establishing such zones in different parts of the world should be encouraged with the ultimate objective of achieving a world entirely free of nuclear weapons. In the process of establishing such zones, the characteristics of each region should be taken into account. The

States participating in such zones should undertake to comply fully with all the objectives, purposes and principles of the agreements or arrangements establishing the zones, thus ensuring that they are genuinely free from nuclear weapons.

62. With respect to such zones, the nuclear-weapon States in turn are called upon to give undertakings, the modalities of which are to be negotiated with the competent authority of each zone, in particular:

(*a*) To respect strictly the status of the nuclear-weapon-free zone;

(*b*) To refrain from the use or threat of use of nuclear weapons against the States of the zone.

63. In the light of existing conditions, and without prejudice to other measures which may be considered in other regions, the following measures are especially desirable:

(*a*) Adoption by the States concerned of all relevant measures to ensure the full application of the Treaty for the Prohibition of Nuclear Weapons in Latin America (Treaty of Tlatelolco),[3] taking into account the views expressed at the tenth special session on the adherence to it;

(*b*) Signature and ratification of the Additional Protocols of the Treaty for the Prohibition of Nuclear Weapons in Latin America (Treaty of Tlatelolco) by the States entitled to become parties to those instruments which have not yet done so;

(*c*) In Africa, where the Organization of African Unity has affirmed a decision for the denuclearization of the region, the Security Council of the United Nations shall take appropriate effective steps whenever necessary to prevent the frustration of this objective;

(*d*) The serious consideration of the practical and urgent steps, as described in the paragraphs above, required for the implementation of the proposal to establish a nuclear-weapon-free zone in the Middle East, in accordance with the relevant General Assembly resolutions, where all parties directly concerned have expressed their support for the concept and where the danger of nuclear-weapon proliferation exists. The establishment of a nuclear-weapon-free zone in the Middle East would greatly enhance international peace and security. Pending the establishment of such a zone in the region, States of the region should solemnly declare that they will refrain on a reciprocal basis from producing, acquiring or in any other way possessing nuclear weapons and nuclear explosive devices, and from permitting the stationing of nuclear weapons on their territory by any third party and agree to place all their nuclear activities under International Atomic Energy Agency safeguards. Consideration should be given to a Security Council role in advancing the establishment of a nuclear-weapon-free zone in the Middle East;

(*e*) All States in the region of South Asia have expressed their determination to keep their countries free of nuclear weapons. No action should be taken by them which might deviate from that objective. In this context, the question of establishing a nuclear weapon-free zone in South Asia has been dealt with in several resolutions of the General Assembly, which is keeping the subject under consideration.

64. The establishment of zones of peace in various regions of the world under appropriate conditions, to be clearly defined and determined freely by the States concerned in the zone, taking into account the characteristics of the zone and the principles of the Charter of the United Nations, and in conformity with international law, can contribute to strengthening the security of States within such zones and to international peace and security as a whole. In this regard, the General Assembly notes the proposals for the establishment of zones of peace, *inter alia,* in:

(a) South-East Asia where States in the region have expressed interest in the establishment of such a zone, in conformity with their views;

(b) The Indian Ocean, taking into account the deliberations of the General Assembly and its relevant resolutions and the need to ensure the maintenance of peace and security in the region.

65. It is imperative, as an integral part of the effort to halt and reverse the arms race, to prevent the proliferation of nuclear weapons. The goal of nuclear nonproliferation is on the one hand to prevent the emergence of any additional nuclear-weapon Stages besides the existing five nuclear-weapon States, and on the other progressively to reduce and eventually eliminate nuclear weapons altogether. This involves obligations and responsibilities on the part of both nuclear-weapon States and non-nuclear-weapon States, the former undertaking to stop the nuclear arms race and to achieve nuclear disarmament by urgent application of the measures outlined in the relevant paragraphs of this Final Document, and all States undertaking to prevent the spread of nuclear weapons.

66. Effective measures can and should be taken at the national level and through international agreements to minimize the danger of the proliferation of nuclear weapons without jeopardizing energy supplies or the development of nuclear energy for peaceful purposes. Therefore, the nuclear-weapon States and the non-nuclear-weapon States should jointly take further steps to develop an international consensus of ways and means, on a universal and nondiscriminatory basis, to prevent the proliferation of nuclear weapons.

67. Full implementation of all the provisions of existing instruments on nonproliferation, such as the Treaty on the Non-Proliferation of Nuclear Weapons[4] and/or the Treaty for the Prohibition of Nuclear Weapons in Latin America (Treaty of Tlatelolco) by States parties to those instruments will be an important contribution to this end. Adherence to such instruments has increased in recent years and the hope has been expressed by the parties that this trend might continue.

68. Nonproliferation measures should not jeopardize the full exercise of the inalienable rights of all States to apply and develop their programmes for the peaceful uses of nuclear energy for economic and social development in conformity with their priorities, interests and needs. All States should also have access to and be free to acquire technology, equipment, and materials for peaceful uses of nuclear energy, taking into account the particular needs of the developing countries. International cooperation in this field should be under agreed and appropriate international safeguards applied through the International Atomic Energy Agency on a non-discriminatory basis in order to prevent effectively the proliferation of nuclear weapons.

69. Each country's choices and decisions in the field of the peaceful uses of nuclear energy should be respected without jeopardizing their respective fuel cycle policies or international cooperation, agreements and contracts for the peaceful use of nuclear energy, provided that the agreed safeguard measures mentioned above are applied.

70. In accordance with the principles and provisions of General Assembly resolution 32/50 of 8 December 1977, international cooperation for the promotion of the transfer and utilization of nuclear technology for economic and social development, especially in the developing countries, should be strengthened.

71. Efforts should be made to conclude the work of the International Nuclear Fuel Cycle Evaluation strictly in accordance with the objectives set out in the final communiqué of its Organizing Conference.[5]

72. All States should adhere to the Protocol for the Prohibition of the Use in War of Asphyxiating, Poisonous or Other Gases, and of Bacteriological Methods of Warfare, signed at Geneva on 17 June 1925.[6]

73. All States which have not yet done so should consider adhering to the Convention on the Prohibition of the Development, Production, and Stockpiling of Bacteriological (Biological) and Toxin Weapons and on Their Destruction.

74. States should also consider the possibility of adhering to multilateral agreements concluded so far in the disarmament field which are mentioned below in this section.

75. The complete and effective prohibition of the development, production, and stockpiling of all chemical weapons and their destruction represent one of the most urgent measures of disarmament. Consequently, conclusion of a convention to this end, on which negotiations have been going on for several years, is one of the most urgent tasks of multilateral negotiations. After its conclusion, all States should contribute to ensuring the broadest possible application of the convention through its early signature and ratification.

76. A convention should be concluded prohibiting the development, production, stockpiling, and use of radiological weapons.

77. In order to help prevent a qualitative arms race and so that scientific and technological achievements may ultimately be used solely for peaceful purposes, effective measures should be taken to avoid the danger and prevent the emergence of new types of weapons of mass destruction based on new scientific principles and achievements. Efforts should be appropriately pursued aiming at the prohibition of such new types and new systems of weapons of mass destruction. Specific agreements could be concluded on particular types of new weapons of mass destruction which may be identified. This question should be kept under continuing review.

78. The Committee on Disarmament should keep under review the need for a further prohibition of military or any other hostile use of environmental modification techniques in order to eliminate the dangers to mankind from such use.

79. In order to promote the peaceful use of and to avoid an arms race on the sea-bed and the ocean floor and in the subsoil thereof, the Committee on Disarmament is requested—in consultation with the States parties to the Treaty on the Prohibition of the Emplacement of Nuclear Weapons and Other Weapons of Mass Destruction on the Sea-Bed and the Ocean Floor and in the Subsoil Thereof,[7] and taking into account the proposals made during the 1977 Review Conference of the parties to that Treaty and any relevant technological developments—to proceed promptly with the consideration of further measures in the field of disarmament for the prevention of an arms race in that environment.

80. In order to prevent an arms race in outer space, further measures should be taken and appropriate international negotiations held in accordance with the spirit of the Treaty on Principles Governing the Activities of States in the Exploration and Use of Outer Space, including the Moon and Other Celestial Bodies.[8]

81. Together with negotiations on nuclear disarmament measures, the limitation and gradual reduction of armed forces and conventional weapons should be resolutely pursued within the framework of progress towards general and complete disarmament. States with the largest military arsenals have a special responsibility in pursuing the process of conventional armaments reductions.

82. In particular the achievement of a more stable situation in Europe at a lower level of military potential on the basis of approximate equality and parity, as well as on the basis of undiminished security of all States with a full respect for security interests and independence of States outside military alliances, by agreement on appropriate mutual reductions and limitations would contribute to the strengthening of security in Europe and

constitute a significant step towards enhancing international peace and security. Current efforts to this end should be continuted most energetically.

83. Agreements or other measures should be resolutely pursued on a bilateral, regional and multilateral basis with the aim of strengthening peace and security at a lower level of forces, by the limitation and reduction of armed forces and of conventional weapons, taking into account the need of States to protect their security, bearing in mind the inherent right of self-defence embodied in the Charter of the United Nations and without prejudice to the principle of equal rights and self-determination of peoples in accordance with the Charter, and the need to ensure balance at each stage and undiminished security of all States. Such measures might include those in the following two paragraphs.

84. Bilateral, regional and multilateral consultations and conferences where appropriate conditions exist with the participation of all the countries concerned for the consideration of different aspects of conventional disarmament, such as the initiative envisaged in the Declaration of Ayacucho subscribed to by eight Latin American countries on 9 December 1974.[9]

85. Consultations should be carried out among major arms supplier and recipient countries on the limitation of all types of international transfer of conventional weapons, based in particular on the principle of undiminished security of the parties with a view to promoting or enhancing stability at a lower military level, taking into account the need of all States to protect their security as well as the inalienable right to self-determination and independence of peoples under colonial or foreign domination and the obligations of States to respect that right, in accordance with the Charter of the United Nations and the Declaration on Principles of International Law concerning Friendly Relations and Cooperation among States.

86. The United Nations Conference on Prohibitions or Restrictions of Use of Certain Conventional Weapons Which May be Deemed to Be Excessively Injurious or to Have Indiscriminate Effects, to be held in 1979, should seek agreement, in the light of humanitarian and military considerations, on the prohibition or restriction of use of certain conventional weapons including those which may cause unnecessary suffering or have indiscriminate effects. The Conference should consider specific categories of such weapons, including those which were the subject-matter of previously conducted discussions.

87. All States are called upon to contribute towards carrying out this task.

88. The result of the Conferences should be considered by all States, and especially producer States, in regard to the question of the transfer of such weapons to other States.

89. Gradual reduction of military budgets on a mutually agreed basis, for example, in absolute figures or in terms of percentage points, particularly by nuclear-weapon States and other militarily significant States, would be a measure that would contribute to the curbing of the arms race and would increase the possibilities of reallocation of resources now being used for military purposes to economic and social development, particularly for the benefit of the developing countries. The basis for implementing this measure will have to be agreed by all participating States and will require ways and means of its implementation acceptable to all of them, taking account of the problems involved in assessing the relative significance of reductions as among different States and with due regard to the proposals of States on all the aspects of reduction of military budgets.

90. The General Assembly should continue to consider what concrete steps should be taken to facilitate the reduction of military budgets, bearing in mind the relevant proposals and documents of the United Nations on this question.

91. In order to facilitate the conclusion and effective implementation of disarmament agreements and to create confidence, States should accept appropriate provisions for verification in such agreements.

92. In the context of international disarmament negotiations, the problem of verification should be further examined and adequate methods and procedures in this field be considered. Every effort should be made to develop appropriate methods and procedures which are nondiscriminatory and which do not unduly interfere with the internal affairs of other States or jeopardize their economic and social development.

93. In order to facilitate the process of disarmament, it is necessary to take measures and pursue policies to strengthen international peace and security and to build confidence among States. Commitment to confidence-building measures could significantly contribute to preparing for further progress in disarmament. For this purpose, measures such as the following, and other measures yet to be agreed upon, should be undertaken:

(a) The prevention of attacks which take place by accident, miscalculation, or communications failure by taking steps to improve communications between Governments, particularly in areas of tension, by the establishment of "hot lines" and other methods of reducing the risk of conflict;

(b) States should assess the possible implications of their military research and development for existing agreements as well as for further efforts in the field of disarmament;

(c) The Secretary-General shall periodically submit reports to the General Assembly on the economic and social consequences of the arms race and its extremely harmful effects on world peace and security.

94. In view of the relationship between expenditure on armaments and economic and social development and the necessity to release real resources now being used for military purposes to economic and social development in the world, particularly for the benefit of the developing countries, the Secretary-General should, with the assistance of a group of qualified governmental experts appointed by him, initiate an expert study on the relationship between disarmament and development. The Secretary-General should submit an interim report on the subject to the General Assembly at its thirty-fourth session and submit the final results to the Assembly at its thirty-sixth session for subsequent action.

95. The expert study should have the terms of reference contained in the report of the *Ad Hoc* Group on the Relationship between Disarmament and Development[10] appointed by the Secretary-General in accordance with General Assembly resolution 32/88 A of 12 December 1977. It should investigate the three main areas listed in the report, bearing in mind the United Nations studies previously carried out. The study should be made in the context of how disarmament can contribute to the establishment of the new international economic order. The study should be forward-looking and policy-oriented and place special emphasis on both the desirability of a reallocation, following disarmament measures, of resources now being used for military purposes to economic and social development, particularly for the benefit of the developing countries and the substantive feasibility of such a reallocation. A principal aim should be to produce results that could effectively guide the formulation of practical measures to reallocate those resources at the local, national, regional, and international levels.

96. Taking further steps in the field of disarmament and other measures aimed at promoting international peace and security would be facilitated by carrying out studies by the Secretary-General in this field with appropriate assistance from governmental or consultant experts.

97. The Secretary-General shall, with the assistance of consultant experts appointed by him, continue the study of the interrelationship between disarmament and international security requested in Assembly resolution 32/87 C of 12 December 1977 and submit it to the thirty-fourth session of the General Assembly.

98. The thirty-third and subsequent sessions of the General Assembly should determine the specified guidelines for carrying out studies, taking into account the proposals already submitted including those made by individual countries at the special session, as well as other proposals which can be introduced later in this field. In doing so, the Assembly would take into consideration a report on these matters prepared by the Secretary-General.

99. In order to mobilize world public opinion on behalf of disarmament, the specific measures set forth below, designed to increase the

dissemination of information about the armaments race and the efforts to halt and reverse it, should be adopted.

100. Governmental and nongovernmental information organs and those of the United Nations and its specialized agencies should give priority to the preparation and distribution of printed and audio-visual material relating to the danger represented by the armaments race as well as to the disarmament efforts and negotiations on specific disarmament measures.

101. In particular, publicity should be given to the Final Document of the tenth special session.

102. The General Assembly proclaims the week starting 24 October, the day of the foundation of the United Nations, as a week devoted to fostering the objectives of disarmament.

103. To encourage study and research on disarmament, the United Nations Centre for Disarmament should intensify its activities in the presentation of information concerning the armaments race and disarmament. Also, the United Nations Educational, Scientific, and Cultural Organization is urged to intensify its activities aimed at facilitating research and publications on disarmament, related to its fields of competence, especially in developing countries, and should disseminate the results of such research.

104. Throughout this process of disseminating information about developments in the disarmament field of all countries, there should be increased participation by nongovernmental organizations concerned with the matter, through closer liaison between them and the United Nations.

105. Member States should be encouraged to ensure a better flow of information with regard to the various aspects of disarmament to avoid dissemination of false and tendentious information concerning armaments, and to concentrate on the danger of escalation of the armaments race and on the need for general and complete disarmament under effective international control.

106. With a view to contributing to a greater understanding and awareness of the problems created by the armaments race and of the need for disarmament, Governments and governmental and nongovernmental international organizations are urged to take steps to develop programmes of education for disarmament and peace studies at all levels.

107. The General Assembly welcomes the initiative of the United Nations Educational, Scientific, and Cultural Organization in planning to hold a world congress on disarmament education and, in this connexion, urges that Organization to step up its programme aimed at the development of disarmament education as a distinct field of study through the preparation, *inter alia,* of teachers' guides, textbooks, readers, and audio-visual materials. Member States should take all possible measures to encourage the incorporation of such materials in the curricula of their educational institutes.

108. In order to promote expertise in disarmament in more Member States, particularly in the developing countries, the General Assembly decides to establish a programme of fellowships on disarmament. The Secretary-General, taking into account the proposal submitted to the special session, should prepare guidelines for the programme. He should also submit the financial requirements of 20 fellowships to the General Assembly at its thirty-third session for inclusion in the regular budget of the United Nations, bearing in mind the savings that can be made within the existing budgetary appropriations.

109. Implementation of these priorities should lead to general and complete disarmament under effective international control, which remains the ultimate goal of all efforts exerted in the field of disarmament. Negotiations on general and complete disarmament shall be conducted concurrently with negotiations on partial measures of disarmament. With this purpose in mind, the Committee on Disarmament will undertake the elaboration of a comprehensive programme of disarmament encompassing all measures thought to be adivisable in order to ensure that the goal of general and complete disarmament under effective international control becomes a reality in a world in which international peace and security prevail and in which the new international economic order is strengthened and consolidated. The comprehensive programme should contain appropriate procedures for ensuring that the General Assembly is kept fully informed of the progress of the negotiations including an appraisal of the situation when appropriate and, in particular, a continuing review of the implementation of the programme.

110. Progress in disarmament should be accompanied by measures to strengthen institutions for maintaining peace and the settlement of international disputes by peaceful means. During and after the implementation of the programme of general and complete disarmament, there should be taken, in accordance with the principles of the Charter of the United Nations, the necessary measures to maintain international peace and security, including the obligation of States to place at the disposal of the United Nations agreed manpower necessary for an international peace force to be equipped with agreed types of armaments. Arrangements for the use of this force should ensure that the United Nations can effectively deter or suppress any threat or use of arms in violation of the purposes and principles of the United Nations.

111. General and complete disarmament under strict and effective international control shall permit States to have at their disposal only those non-nuclear forces, armaments, facilities, and establishments as are agreed to be necessary to maintain internal order and protect the personal security of citizens and in order that States shall support and provide agreed manpower for a United Nations peace force.

112. In addition to the several questions dealt with in this Programme of Action, there are a few others of fundamental importance, on which, because of the complexity of the issues involved and the short time at the disposal of the special session, it has proved impossible to reach satisfactory agreed conclusions. For those reasons they are treated only in very general terms and, in a few instances, not even treated at all in the Programme. It should be stressed, however, that a number of concrete approaches to deal with such questions emerged from the exchange of views carried out in the General Assembly which will undoubtedly facilitate the continuation of the study and negotiation of the problems involved in the competent disarmament organs.

IV. MACHINERY

113. While disarmament, particularly in the nuclear field, has become a necessity for the survival of mankind and for the elimination of the danger of nuclear war, little progress has been made since the end of the Second World War. In addition to the need to exercise political will, the international machinery should be utilized more effectively and also improved to enable implementation of the Programme of Action and help the United Nations to fulfil its role in the field of disarmament. In spite of the best efforts of the international community, adequate results have not been produced with the existing machinery. There is, therefore, an urgent need that existing disarmament machinery be revitalized and forums appropriately constituted for disarmament deliberations and negotiations with a better representative character. For maximum effectiveness, two kinds of bodies are required in the field of disarmament—deliberative and negotiating. All Member States should be represented on the former, whereas the latter, for the sake of convenience, should have a relatively small membership.

114. The United Nations, in accordance with the Charter, has a central role and primary responsibility in the sphere of disarmament. Accordingly, it should play a more active role in this field and, in order to discharge its functions effectively, the United Nations should facilitate and encourage all disarmament measures—unilateral, bilateral, regional, or multilateral—and be kept duly informed through the General Assembly, or any other appropriate United Nations channel reaching all Members of the Organization, of all disarmament efforts outside its aegis without prejudice to the progress of negotiations.

115. The General Assembly has been and should remain the main deliberative organ of the United Nations in the field of disarmament and should make every effort to facilitate the implementation of disarmament measures. An item entitled "Review of the implementation of the recommendations and decisions adopted by the General Assembly at its tenth

special session" shall be included in the Provisional agenda of the thirty-third and subsequent sessions of the General Assembly.

116. Draft multilateral disarmament conventions should be subjected to the normal procedures applicable in the law of treaties. Those submitted to the General Assembly for its commendation should be subject to full review by the Assembly.

117. The First Committee of the General Assembly should deal in the future only with questions of disarmament and related international security questions.

118. The General Assembly establishes, as successor to the Commission originally established by resolution 502 (VI) of 11 January 1952 a Disarmament Commission, composed of all States Members of the United Nations, and decides that:

(*a*) The Disarmament Commission shall be a deliberative body, a subsidiary organ of the General Assembly, the function of which shall be to consider and make recommendations on various problems in the field of disarmament and to follow up the relevant decisions and recommendations of the special session devoted to disarmament. The Disarmament Commission should, *inter alia,* consider the elements of a comprehensive programme for disarmament to be submitted as recommendations to the General Assembly and, through it, to the negotiating body, the Committee on Disarmament:

(*b*) The Disarmament Commission shall function under the rules of procedure relating to the committees of the General Assembly with such modifications as the Commission may deem necessary and shall make every effort to ensure that, in so far as possible, decisions on substantive issues be adopted by consensus;

(*c*) The Disarmament Commission shall report annually to the General Assembly and will submit for consideration by the Assembly at its thirty-third session a report on organizational matters; in 1979, the Disarmament Commission will meet for a period not exceeding four weeks, the dates to be decided at the thirty-third session of the Assembly;

(*d*) The Secretary-General shall furnish such experts, staff, and services as are necessary for the effective accomplishment of the Commission's functions.

119. A second special session of the General Assembly devoted to disarmament should be held on a date to be decided by the Assembly at its thirty-third session.

120. The General Assembly is conscious of the work that has been done by the international negotiating body that has been meeting since 14 March 1962 as well as the considerable and urgent work that remains to be accomplished in the field of disarmament. The Assembly is deeply aware of the continuing requirement for a single multilateral disarmament

negotiating forum of limited size taking decisions on the basis of consensus. It attaches great importance to the participation of all the nuclear-weapon States in an appropriately constituted negotiating body, the Committee on Disarmament. The Assembly welcomes the agreement reached following appropriate consultations among the Member States during the special session of the General Assembly devoted to disarmament that the Committee on Disarmament will be open to the nuclear-weapon States, the thirty-two to thirty-five other States to be chosen in consultation with the President of the thirty-second session of the Assembly; that the membership of the Committee on Disarmament will be reviewed at regular intervals; that the Committee on Disarmament will be convened in Geneva not later than January 1979 by the Country whose name appears first in the alphabetical list of membership; and that the Committee on Disarmament will:

(*a*) Conduct its work by consensus;

(*b*) Adopt its own rules of procedure;

(*c*) Request the Secretary-General of the United Nations, following consultations with the Committee on Disarmament, to appoint the Secretary of the Committee, who shall also act as his personal representative, to assist the Committee and its Chairman in organizing the business and time-tables of the Committee;

(*d*) Rotate the chairmanship of the Committee among all its members on a monthly basis;

(*e*) Adopt its own agenda taking into account the recommendations made to it by the members of the Committee;

(*f*) Submit a report to the General Assembly annually, or more frequently as appropriate, and provide its formal and other relevant documents to the States Members of the United Nations on a regular basis;

(*g*) Make arrangements for interested States, not members of the Committee, to submit to the Committee written proposals or working documents on measures of disarmament that are the subject of negotiation in the Committee and to participate in the discussion of the subject-matter of such proposals or working documents;

(*h*) Invite States not members of the Committee, upon their request, to express views in the Committee when the particular concerns of those States are under discussion;

(*i*) Open its plenary meetings to the public unless otherwise decided.

121. Bilateral and regional disarmament negotiations may also play an important role and could facilitate negotiations of multilateral agreements in the field of disarmament.

122. At the earliest appropriate time, a world disarmament conference should be convened with universal participation and with adequate preparation.

123. In order to enable the United Nations to continue to fulfil its role in the field of disarmament and to carry out the additional tasks assigned to it by this special session, the United Nations Centre for Disarmament should be adequately strengthened and its research and information functions accordingly extended. The Centre should also take account fully of the possibilities offered by specialized agencies and other institutions and programmes within the United Nations system with regard to studies and information on disarmament. The Centre should also increase contacts with nongovernmental organizations and research institutions in view of the valuable role they play in the field of disarmament. This role could be encouraged also in other ways that may be considered as appropriate.

124. The Secretary-General is requested to set up an advisory board of eminent persons, selected on the basis of their personal expertise and taking into account the principle of equitable geographical representation, to adivse him on various aspects of studies and to be made under the auspices of the United Nations in the field of disarmament and arms limitation, including a programme of such studies.

***

125. The General Assembly notes with satisfaction that the active participation of the Member States in the consideration of the agenda items of the special session and the proposals and suggestions submitted by them and reflected to a considerable extent in the Final Document have made a valuable contribution to the work of the special session and to its positive conclusion. Since a number of those proposals and suggestions,[11] which have become an integral part of the work of the special session of the General Assembly, deserve to be studied further and more thoroughly, taking into consideration the many relevant comments and observations made in both the general debate of the plenary and the deliberations of the *Ad Hoc* Committee of the Tenth Special Session, the Secretary-General is requested to transmit, together with this Final Document, to the appropriate deliberative and negotiating organs dealing with the questions of disarmament all the official records of the special session devoted to disarmament, in accordance with the recommendations which the Assembly may adopt at its thirty-third session. Some of the proposals put forth for the consideration of the special session are listed below:

(*a*) Text of the decision of the Central Committee of the Romanian Communist Party concerning Romania's position on disarmament and, in particular, on nuclear disarmament, adopted on 9 May 1978;[12]

(*b*) Views on the Swiss Government on problems to be discussed at the tenth special session of the General Assembly;[13]

(*c*) Proposals of the Union of Soviet Socialist Republics on practical measures for ending the arms race;[14]

(*d*) Memorandum from France concerning the establishment of an International Satellite Monitoring Agency.[15]

(*e*) Memorandum from France concerning the establishment of an International Institute for Research on Disarmament;[16]

(*f*) Proposal by Sri Lanka for the establishment of a World Disarmament Authority;[17]

(*g*) Working paper submitted by the Federal Republic of Germany entitled "Contribution to the seismological verification of a comprehensive test ban";[18]

(*h*) Working paper submitted by the Federal Republic of Germany entitled "Invitation to attend an international chemical-weapon verification workshop in the Federal Republic of Germany";[19]

(*i*) Working paper submitted by China on disarmament;[20]

(*j*) Working paper submitted by the Federal Republic of Germany concerning zones of confidence-building measures as a first step towards the preparation of a world-wide convention on confidence-building measures;[21]

(*k*) Proposal by Ireland for a study of the possibility of establishing a system of incentives to promote arms control and disarmament;[22]

(*l*) Working paper submitted by Romania concerning a synthesis of the proposals in the field of disarmament;[23]

(*m*) Proposal by the United States of America on the establishment of a United Nations Peace-keeping Reserve and on confidence-building measures and stabilizing measures in various regions, including notification of manoeuvres, invitation of observers to manoeuvres, and United Nations machinery to study and promote such measures;[24]

(*n*) Proposal by Uruguay on the possibility of establishing a polemological agency;[25]

(*o*) Proposal by Belgium, Canada, Denmark, Germany, Federal Republic of, Ireland, Italy, Japan, Luxembourg, the Netherlands, New Zealand, Norway, Sweden, the United Kingdom of Great Britain and Northern Ireland and the United States of America on the strengthening of the security role of the United Nations in the peaceful settlement of disputes and peace-keeping;[26]

(*p*) Memorandum from France concerning the establishment of an International Disarmament Fund for Development;[27]

(*q*) Proposal by Norway entitled "Evaluation of the impact of new weapons on arms control and disarmament efforts";[28]

(*r*) Note verbale transmitting the text, signed in Washington on 22 June 1978 by the Ministers for Foreign Affairs of Argentina, Bolivia, Chile, Colombia, Ecuador, Panama, Peru, and Venezuela, reaffirming the principles of the Declaration of Ayacucho with respect to the limitation of conventional weapons;[29]

(*s*) Memorandum from Liberia entitled "Declaration of a new philosophy on disarmament";[30]

(*t*) Statements made by the representatives of China, on 22 June 1978, on the draft Final Document of the tenth special session;[31]

(*u*) Proposal by the President of Cyprus for the total demilitarization and disarmament of the Republic of Cyprus and the implementation of the resolutions of the United Nations;[32]

(*v*) Proposal by Costa Rica on economic and social incentives to halt the arms race;[33]

(*w*) Amendments submitted by China to the draft Final Document of the tenth special session;[34]

(*x*) Proposals by Canada for the implementation of a strategy of suffocation of the nuclear arms race;[35]

(*y*) Draft resolution submitted by Cyprus, Ethiopia and India on the urgent need for cessation of further testing of nuclear weapons;[36]

(*z*) Draft resolution submitted by Ethiopia and India on the nonuse of nuclear weapons and prevention of nuclear war;[37]

(*aa*) Proposal by the nonaligned countries on the establishment of a zone of peace in the Mediterranean;[38]

(*bb*) Proposal by the Government of Senegal for a tax on military budgets;[39]

(*cc*) Proposal by Austria for the transmission to Member States of working paper A/AC.187/109 and the ascertainment of their views on the subject of verification;[40]

(*dd*) Proposal by the nonaligned countries for the dismantling of foreign military bases in foreign territories and withdrawal of foreign troops from foreign territories;[41]

(*ee*) Proposal by Mexico for the opening, on a provisional basis, of an *ad hoc* account in the United Nations Development Programme to use for development the funds which may be released as a result of disarmament measures;[42]

(*ff*) Proposal by Italy on the role of the Security Council in the field of disarmament in accordance with Article 26 of the Charter of the United Nations;[43]

(*gg*) Proposal by the Netherlands for a study on the establishment of an international disarmament organization.[44]

126. In adopting this Final Document, the States Members of the United Nations solemnly reaffirm their determination to work for general and complete disarmament and to make further collective efforts aimed at strengthening peace and international security; eliminating the threat of war, particularly nuclear war; implementing practical measures aimed at halting and reversing the arms race; strengthening the procedures for the peaceful settlement of disputes; and reducing military expenditures and

utilizing the resources thus released in a manner which will help to promote the well-being of all peoples and to improve the economic conditions of the developing countries.

127. The General Assembly expresses its satisfaction that the proposals submitted to its special session devoted to disarmament and the deliberations thereon have made it possible to reaffirm and define in this Final Document fundamental principles, goals, priorities, and procedures for the implementation of the above purposes, either in the Declaration or the Programme of Action or in both. The Assembly also welcomes the important decisions agreed upon regarding the deliberative and negotiating machinery and is confident that these organs will discharge their functions in an effective manner.

128. Finally, it should be borne in mind that the number of States that participated in the general debate, as well as the high level of representation and the depth and scope of that debate, are unprecedented in the history of disarmament efforts. Several Heads of State or Government addressed the General Assembly. In addition, other Heads of State or Government sent messages and expressed their good wishes for the success of the special session of the Assembly. Several high officials of specialized agencies and other institutions and programmes within the United Nations system and spokesmen of twenty-five nongovernmental ogranizations and six research institutes also made valuable contributions to the proceedings of the session. It must be emphasized, moreover, that the special session marks not the end but rather the beginning of a new phase of the efforts of the United Nations in the field of disarmament.

129. The General Assembly is convinced that the discussions of the disarmament problems at the special session and its Final Document will attract the attention of all peoples, further mobilize world public opinion and provide a powerful impetus for the cause of disarmament.

NOTES

1. General Assembly resolution 2826 (XXVI), annex.
2. General Assembly resolution 2625 (XXV), annex.
3. United Nations, *Treaty Series,* vol. 634, No. 9068.
4. General Assembly resolution 2373 (XXII), annex.
5. See A/C.1/32/7.
6. League of Nations, *Treaty Series,* vol. XCIV (1929), No. 2138.
7. General Assembly resolution 2660 (XXV), annex.
8. General Assembly resolution 2222 (XXI), annex.
9. See A/10044, annex.
10. A/S-10/9.
11. See A/S-10/PV.1-25, A/S-10/1-14 and 17, A/S-10/AC.1/PV.1-16, A/S-10/AC.1/1-40, A/S-10/AC.1/L.1-17.
12. A/S-10/14.

13. A/S-10/AC1/2.
14. A/S-10/AC.1/4.
15. A/S-10/AC.1/7.
16. A/S-10/AC.1/8.
17. A/S-10/AC.1/9 and Add.1.
18. A/S-10/AC.1/12.
19. A/S-10/AC.1/13.
20. A/S-10/AC.1/17.
21. A/S-10/AC.1/20.
22. A/S-10/AC.1/21.
23. A/S-10/AC.1/23.
24. A/S-10/AC.1/24.
25. A/S-10/AC.1/25.
26. A/S-10/AC.1/26 and Corr.1 and 2.
27. A/S-10/AC.1/28.
28. A/S-10/AC.1/31.
29. A/S-10/AC.1/34.
30. A/S-10/AC.1/35.
31. A/S-10/AC.1/36.
32. A/S-10/AC.1/39.
33. A/S-10/AC.1/40.
34. A/S-10/AC.1/L.2–4, A/S-10/AC.1/L.7 and 8.
35. A/S-10/AC.1/L.6.
36. A/S-10/AC.1/L.10.
37. A/S-10/AC.1/L.11.
38. A/S-10/AC.1/37, para. 72.
39. A/S-10/AC.1/37, para. 101.
40. A/S-10/AC.1/37, para. 113.
41. A/S-10/AC.1/37, para. 126.
42. A/S-10/AC.1/37, para. 141.
43. A/S-10/AC.1/37, para. 179.
44. A/S-10/AC.1/37, para. 186.

10. Declaration on the Granting of Independence to Colonial Countries and Peoples

Adopted by Resolution 1514(XV) of the General Assembly on December 14, 1960. General Assembly, Official Records, XV, Supp. 16 (A/4684), pp. 66–67.

The General Assembly

Mindful of the determination proclaimed by the peoples of the world in the Charter of the United Nations to reaffirm faith in fundamental human rights, in the dignity and worth of the human person, in the equal rights of men and women and of nations large and small and to promote social progress and better standards of life in larger freedom,

Conscious of the need for the creation of conditions of stability and well-being and peaceful and friendly relations based on respect for the principles of equal rights and self-determination of all peoples, and of universal respect for, and observance of, human rights and fundamental freedoms for all without distinction as to race, sex, language or religion,

Recognizing the passionate yearning for freedom in all dependent peoples and the decisive role of such peoples in the attainment of their independence,

Aware of the increasing conflicts resulting from the denial of or impediments in the way of the freedom of such peoples, which constitute a serious threat to world peace.

Considering the important role of the United Nations in assisting the movement for independence in trust and nonself-governing territories,

Recognizing that the peoples of the world ardently desire the end of colonialism in all its manifestations,

Convinced that the continued existence of colonialism prevents the development of international economic cooperation, impedes the social, cultural and economic development of dependent peoples and militates against the United Nations ideal of universal peace,

Affirming that peoples may, for their own ends, freely dispose of their natural wealth and resources without prejudice to any obligations arising out of international economic cooperation, based upon the principle of mutual benefit, and international law,

Believing that the process of liberation is irresistible and irreversible and that, in order to avoid serious crises, an end must be put to colonialism and all practices of segregation and discrimination associated therewith,

Welcoming the emergence in recent years of a large number of dependent territories into freedom and independence, and recognizing the increasingly powerful trends towards freedom in such territories which have not yet attained independence,

Convinced that all peoples have an inalienable right to complete freedom, the exercise of their sovereignty and the integrity of their national territory,

Solemnly proclaims the neccessity of bringing to a speedy and unconditional end colonialism in all its forms and manifestations;

And to this end

Declares that:

1. The subjection of peoples to alien subjugation, domination and exploitation constitutes a denial of fundamental human rights, is contrary to the Charter of the United Nations and is an impediment to the promotion of world peace and cooperation.

2. All peoples have the right to self-determination, by virtue of that right they freely determine their political status and freely pursue their economic, social and cultural development.

3. Inadequacy of political, economic, social or educational preparedness should never serve as a pretext for delaying independence.

4. All armed action or repressive measures of all kinds directed against dependent peoples shall cease in order to enable them to exercise peacefully and freely their right to complete independence, and the integrity of their national territory shall be respected.

5. Immediate steps shall be taken, in trust and nonself-governing territories or all other territories which have not yet attained independence, to transfer all powers to the peoples of those territories, without any conditions or reservations, in accordance with their freely expressed will and desire, without any distinction as to race, creed or color, in order to enable them to enjoy complete independence and freedom.

6. Any attempt aimed at the partial or total disruption of the national unity and the territorial integrity of a country is incompatible with the purposes and principles of the Charter of the United Nations.

7. All states shall observe faithfully and strictly the provisions of the Charter of the United Nations, the Universal Declaration of Human Rights and the present Declaration on the basis of equality, noninterference in the internal affairs of all states and respect for the sovereign rights of all peoples and their territorial integrity.

11. Universal Declaration of Human Rights

Adopted by Resolution 217A(III) of the General Assembly, December 10, 1948. General Assembly, Official Records, 3rd Session, Part I, Resolutions (A/810) pp. 71-7.

Whereas recognition of the inherent dignity and of the equal and inalienable rights of all members of the human family is the foundation of freedom, justice and peace in the world,

Whereas disregard and contempt for human rights have resulted in barbarous acts which have outraged the conscience of mankind, and the advent of a world in which human beings shall enjoy freedom of speech and belief and freedom from fear and want has been proclaimed as the highest aspiration of the common people,

Whereas it is essential, if man is not to be compelled to have recourse, as a last resort, to rebellion against tyranny and oppression, that human rights should be protected by the rule of law,

Whereas it is essential to promote the development of friendly relations between nations,

Whereas the peoples of the United Nations have in the Charter reaffirmed their faith in fundamental human rights, in the dignity and worth of the human person and in the equal rights of men and women and have determined to promote social progress and better standards of life in larger freedom,

Whereas Member States have pledged themselves to achieve, in cooperation with the United Nations, the promotion of universal respect for and observance of human rights and fundamental freedoms,

Whereas a common understanding of these rights and freedoms is of the greatest importance for the full realization of this pledge,

Now, therefore,

The General Assembly

Proclaims this Universal Declaration of Human Rights as a common standard of achievement for all peoples and all nations, to the end that every individual and every organ of society, keeping this Declaration constantly in mind, shall strive by teaching and education to promote respect for these rights and freedoms and by progressive measures, national and international, to secure their universal and effective recognition and observance, both among the peoples of Member States themselves and among the peoples of territories under their jurisdiction.

ARTICLE 1
All human beings are born free and equal in dignity and rights. They are endowed with reason and conscience and should act towards one another in a spirit of brotherhood.

ARTICLE 2
Everyone is entitled to all the rights and freedoms set forth in this Declaration, without distinction of any kind, such as race, colour, sex, language, religion, political or other opinion, national or social origin, property, birth or other status.

Furthermore, no distinction shall be made on the basis of the political, jurisdictional or international status of the country or territory to which a person belongs, whether it be independent, trust, nonself-governing or under any other limitation of sovereingnty.

ARTICLE 3
Everyone has the right to life, liberty and the security of person.

ARTICLE 4
No one shall be held in slavery or servitude; slavery and the slave trade shall be prohibited in all their forms.

ARTICLE 5
No one shall be subjected to torture or to cruel, inhuman or degrading treatment or punishment.

ARTICLE 6
Everyone has the right to recognition everywhere as a person before the law.

ARTICLE 7
All are equal before the law and are entitled without any discrimination to equal protection of the law. All are entitled to equal protection against any discrimination in violation of this Declaration and against any incitement to such discrimination.

ARTICLE 8
Everyone has the right to an effective remedy by the competent national tribunals for acts violating the fundamental rights granted him by the constitution or by law.

ARTICLE 9

No one shall be subjected to arbitrary arrest, detention or exile.

ARTICLE 10

Everyone is entitled in full equality to a fair and public hearing by an independent and impartial tribunal, in the determination of his rights and obligations and of any criminal charge against him.

ARTICLE 11

1. Everyone charged with a penal offence has the right to be presumed innocent until proved guilty according to law in a public trial at which he has had all the guarantees necessary for his defence.

2. No one shall be held guilty of any penal offence on account of any act or omission which did not constitute a penal offence, under national or international law, at the time when it was committed. Nor shall a heavier penalty be imposed than the one that was applicable at the time the penal offence was committed.

ARTICLE 12

No one shall be subjected to arbitrary interference with his privacy, family, home, or correspondence, nor to attacks upon his honour and reputation. Everyone has the right to the protection of the law against such interference or attacks.

ARTICLE 13

1. Everyone has the right to freedom of movement and residence within the borders of each state.

2. Everyone has the right to leave any country, including his own, and to return to his country.

ARTICLE 14

1. Everyone has the right to seek and to enjoy in other countries asylum from persecution.

2. This right may not be invoked in the case of prosecutions genuinely arising from nonpolitical crimes or from acts contrary to the purposes and principles of the United Nations.

ARTICLE 15

1. Everyone has the right to a nationality.

2. No one shall be arbitrarily deprived of his nationality nor denied the right to change his nationality.

ARTICLE 16

1. Men and women of full age, without any limitation due to race, nationally or religion, have the right to marry and to found a family. They are entitled to equal rights as to marriage, during marriage and at its dissolution.

2. Marriage shall be entered into only with the free and full consent of the intending spouses.

3. The family is the natural and fundamental group unit of society and is entitled to protection by society and the State.

ARTICLE 17

1. Everyone has the right to own property alone as well as in association with others.

2. No one shall be arbitrarily deprived of his property.

ARTICLE 18

Every one has the right to freedom of thought, conscience and religion; this right includes freedom to change his religion or belief, and freedom, either alone or in community with others and in public or private, to manifest his religion or belief in teaching, practice, worship, and observance.

ARTICLE 19

Everyone has the right to freedom of opinion and expression; this right includes freedom to hold opinions without interference and to seek, receive and impart information and ideas through any media and regardless of frontiers.

ARTICLE 20

1. Everyone has the right to freedom of peaceful assembly and association.

2. No one may be compelled to belong to an association.

ARTICLE 21

1. Everyone has the right to take part in the Government of his country, directly or through freely chosen representatives.

2. Everyone has the right of equal access to public service in his country.

3. The will of the people shall be the basis of the authority of government; this will shall be expressed in periodic and genuine elections which shall be by universal and equal suffrage and shall be held by secret vote or by equivalent free voting procedures.

ARTICLE 22

Everyone, as a member of society, has the right to social security and is entitled to realization, through national effort and international cooperation and in accordance with the organization and resources of each State, of the economic, social and cultural rights indispensable for his dignity and the free development of his personality.

ARTICLE 23

1. Everyone has the right to work, to free choice of employment, to just and favourable conditions of work and to protection against unemployment.

2. Everyone, without any discrimination, has the right to equal pay for equal work.

3. Everyone who works has the right to just and favourable remuneration insuring for himself and his family an existence worthy of human dignity, and supplemented, if necessary, by other means of social protection.

4. Everyone has the right to form and to join trade unions for the protection of his interests.

ARTICLE 24

Everyone has the right to rest and leisure, including reasonable limitation of working hours and periodic holidays with pay.

ARTICLE 25

1. Everyone has the right to a standard of living adequate for the health and well-being of himself and of his family, including food, clothing, housing, and medical care and necessary social services, and the right to security in the event of unemployment, sickness, disability, widowhood, old age, or other lack of livelihood in circumstances beyond his control.

2. Motherhood and childhood are entitled to special care and assistance. All children, whether born in or out of wedlock, shall enjoy the same social protection.

ARTICLE 26

1. Everyone has the right to education. Education shall be free, at least in the elementary and fundamental stages. Elementary education shall be compulsory. Technical and professional education shall be made generally available and higher education shall be equally accessible to all on the basis of merit.

2. Education shall be directed to the full development of the human personality and to the strengthening of respect for human rights and fundamental freedoms. It shall promote understanding, tolerance and friend-

ship among all nations, racial or religious groups, and shall further the activities of the United Nations for the maintenance of peace.

3. Parents have a prior right to choose the kind of education that shall be given to their children.

ARTICLE 27

1. Everyone has the right freely to participate in the cultural life of the community, to enjoy the arts and to share in scientific advancement and its benefits.

2. Everyone has the right to the protection of the moral and material interests resulting from any scientific, literary or artistic production of which he is the author.

ARTICLE 28

Everyone is entitled to a social and international order in which the rights and freedoms set forth in this Declaration can be fully realized.

ARTICLE 29

1. Everyone has duties to the community in which alone the free and full development of his personality is possible.

2. In the exercise of his rights and freedoms, everyone shall be subject only to such limitations as are determined by law solely for the purpose of securing due recognition and respect for the rights and freedoms of others and of meeting the just requirements of morality, public order and the general welfare in a democratic society.

3. These rights and freedoms may in no case be exercised contrary to the purposes and principles of the United Nations.

ARTICLE 30

Nothing in this Declaration may be interpreted as implying for any State, group or person any right to engage in any activity or to perform any act aimed at the destruction of any of the rights and freedoms set forth herein.

12. International Covenant on Economic, Social and Cultural Rights

Adopted by Resolution 2200(XXI) of the General Assembly, December 16, 1966. General Assembly, Official Records, 21st Session, Supp. 16 (A/6316). pp. 49–52.

PREAMBLE

The States Parties to the present Covenant,

Considering that, in accordance with the principles proclaimed in the Charter of the United Nations, recognition of the inherent dignity and of the equal and inalienable rights of all members of the human family is the foundation of freedom, justice and peace in the world,

Recognizing that these rights derive from the inherent dignity of the human persons,

Recognizing that, in accordance with the Universal Declaration of Human Rights, the ideal of free human beings enjoying freedom from fear and want can only be achieved if conditions are created whereby everyone may enjoy his economic, social and cultural rights, as well as his civil and political rights,

Considering the obligation of States under the Charter of the United Nations to promote universal respect for, and observance of, human rights and freedoms,

Realizing that the individual, having duties to other individuals and to the community to which he belongs, is under a responsibility to strive for the promotion and observance of the rights recognized in the present Covenant,

Agree upon the following articles:

PART I

ARTICLE 1

1. All peoples have the right of self-determination. By virtue of the right they freely determine their political status and freely pursue their economic, social and cultural development.

2. All peoples may, for their own ends, freely dispose of their natural wealth and resources without prejudice to any obligations arising out of international economic cooperation, based upon the principle of mutual benefit, and international law. In no case may a people be deprived of its own means of subsistence.

3. The States Parties to the present Covenant, including those having responsibility for the administration of Non-Self-Governing and Trust Territories, shall promote the realization of the right of self-determination, and shall respect that right, in conformity with the provisions of the United Nations Charter.

PART II

ARTICLE 2

1. Each State Party to the present Covenant undertakes to take steps, individually and through international assistance and cooperation especially economic and technical, to the maximum of its available resources, with a view to achieving progressively the full realization of the rights recognized in the present Covenant by all appropriate means, including particularly the adoption of legislative measures.

2. The States Parties to the present Covenant undertake to guarantee that the rights enunciated in the present Covenant will be exercised without discrimination of any kind as to race, colour, sex, language, religion, political or other opinion, national or social origin, property, birth or other status.

3. Developing countries, with due regard to human rights and their national economy, may determine to what extent they would guarantee the economic rights recognized in the present Covenant to nonnationals.

ARTICLE 3

The States Parties to the present Covenant undertake to ensure the equal right of men and women to the enjoyment of all economic, social and cultural rights set forth in this Covenant.

ARTICLE 4

The States Parties to the present Covenant recognize that in the enjoyment of those rights provided by the State in conformity with the present Covenant, the State may subject such rights only to such limitations as are determined by law only in so far as this may be compatible with the nature of these rights and solely for the purpose of promoting the general welfare in a democratic society.

ARTICLE 5

1. Nothing in the present Covenant may be interpreted as implying for any State, group or person, any right to engage in any activity or to perform any act aimed at the destruction of any of the rights or freedoms recognized herein, or at their limitation to a greater extent than is provided for in the present Covenant.

2. No restriction upon or derogation from any of the fundamental human rights recognized or existing in any country in virtue of law, conventions, regulations or custom shall be admitted on the pretext that the present Covenant does not recognize such rights or that it recognizes them to a lesser extent.

PART III

ARTICLE 6

1. The States Parties to the present Covenant recognize the right to work, which includes the right of everyone to the opportunity to gain his living by work which he freely chooses or accepts, and will take appropriate steps to safeguard this right.

2. The steps to be taken by a State Party to the present Covenant to achieve the full realization of this right shall include technical and vocational guidance and training programmes, policies and techniques to achieve steady economic, social and cultural development and full and productive employment under conditions safeguarding fundamental political and economic freedoms to the individual.

ARTICLE 7

The States Parties to the present Covenant recognize the right of everyone to the enjoyment of just and favourable conditions of work, which ensure, in particular:

(a) Remuneration which provides all workers as a minimum with:

(i) Fair wages and equal remuneration for work of equal value without distinction of any kind, in particular women being guaranteed conditions of work not inferior to those enjoyed by men, with equal pay for equal work; and

(ii) A decent living for themselves and their families in accordance with the provisions of the present Covenant;

(b) Safe and healthy working conditions;

(c) Equal opportunity for everyone to be promoted in his employment to an appropriate higher level, subject to no considerations other than those of seniority and competence;

(d) Rest, leisure and reasonable limitation of working hours and periodic holidays with pay, as well as remuneration for public holidays.

ARTICLE 8

1. The States Parties to the present Covenant undertake to ensure:

(a) The right of everyone to form trade unions and join the trade union of his choice subject only to the rules of the organization concerned, for the promotion and protection of his economic and social interests. No restrictions may be placed on the exercise of this right other than those prescribed by law and which are necessary in a democratic society in the interests of national security or public order or for the protection of the rights and freedom of others;

(b) The right of trade unions to establish national federations or confederations and the right of the latter to form or join international trade-union organizations;

(c) The right of trade unions to function freely subject to no limitations other than those prescribed by law and which are necessary in a democratic society in the interests of national security or public order or for the protection of the rights and freedoms of others;

(d) The right to strike, provided that it is exercised in conformity with the laws of the particular country.

2. This article shall not prevent the imposition of lawful restrictions on the exercise of these rights by members of the armed forces, or of the police, or of the administration of the State.

3. Nothing in this article shall authorize States Parties to the International Labour Convention of 1948 on Freedom of Association and Protection of the Right to Organize to take legislative measures which would prejudice, or apply the law in such a manner as would prejudice, the guarantees provided for in that Convention.

ARTICLE 9

The States Parties to the present Covenant recognize the right of everyone to social security including social insurance.

ARTICLE 10

The States Parties to the present Covenant recognize that:

1. The widest possible protection and assistance should be accorded to the family, which is the natural and fundamental group unit of society, particularly for its establishment and while it is responsible for the care and education of dependent children. Marriage must be entered into with the free consent of the intending spouses;

2. Special protection should be accorded to mothers during a reasonable period before and after childbirth. During such period working mothers should be accorded paid leave or leave with adequate social security benefits;

3. Special measures of protection and assistance should be taken on behalf of all children and young persons without any discrimination for reasons of parentage or other conditions. Children and young persons should be protected from economic and social exploitation. Their employment in work harmful to their morals or health or dangerous to life or likely to hamper their normal development should be punishable by law. States should also set age limits below which the paid employment of child labour should be prohibited and punishable by law.

ARTICLE 11

1. The States Parties to the present Covenant recognize the right of everyone to an adequate standard of living for himself and his family, including adequate food, clothing and housing, and to the continuous improvement of living conditions. The States Parties will take appropriate steps to ensure the realization of this right, recognizing to this effect the essential importance of international cooperation based on free consent.

2. The States Parties to the present Covenant, recognizing the fundamental right of everyone to be free from hunger, shall take, individually and through international cooperation, the measures, including specific programmes, which are needed:

(a) To improve methods of production, conservation and distribution of food by making full use of technical and scientific knowledge, by disseminating knowledge of the principles of nutrition and by developing or reforming agrarian systems in such a way as to achieve the most efficient development and utilization of natural resources; and

(b) Take into account the problems of both food-importing and food-exporting countries, to ensure an equitable distribution of world food supplies in relation to need.

ARTICLE 12

1. The States Parties to the present Covenant recognize the right of everyone to the enjoyment of the highest attainable standard of physical and mental health.

2. The steps to be taken by the States Parties to the present Covenant to achieve the full realization of this right shall include those necessary for:

(a) The provision for the reduction of the still-birth-rate and of infant mortality and for the healthy development of the child;

(b) The improvement of all aspects of environmental and industrial hygiene;

(c) The prevention, treatment and control of epidemic, endemic, occupational and other diseases;

(d) The creation of conditions which would assure to all medical service and medical attention in the event of sickness.

ARTICLE 13

1. The States Parties to the present Covenant recognize the right of everyone to education. They agree that education shall be directed to the full development of the human personality and the sense of its dignity, and shall strengthen the respect for human rights and fundamental freedoms. They further agree that education shall enable all persons to participate effectively in a free society, promote understanding, tolerance and friendship among all nations and all racial, ethnic or religious groups, and further the activities of the United Nations for the maintenance of peace.

2. The States Parties to the present Covenant recognize that, with a view to achieving the full realization of this right:

(a) Primary education shall be compulsory and available free to all;

(b) Secondary education in its different forms, including technical and vocational secondary education, shall be made generally available and accessible to all by every appropriate means, and in particular by the progressive introduction of free education;

(c) Higher education shall be made equally accessible to all, on the basis of capacity, by every appropriate means, and in particular by the progressive introduction of free education;

(d) Fundamental education shall be encouraged or intensified as far as possible for those persons who have not received or completed the whole period of their primary education;

(e) The development of a system of schools at all levels shall be actively pursued, an adequate fellowship system shall be established, and the material conditions of teaching staff shall be continuously improved.

3. The States Parties to the present Covenant undertake to have respect for the liberty of parents and, when applicable, legal guardians, to choose for their children schools other than those established by the public authorities which conform to such minimum educational standards as may be laid down or approved by the State and to ensure the religious and moral education of their children in conformity with their own convictions.

4. No part of this article shall be construed so as to interfere with the liberty of individuals and bodies to establish and direct educational institutions, subject always to the observance of the principles set forth in paragraph 1 and to the requirement that the education given in such institutions shall conform to such minimum standards as may be laid down by the State.

ARTICLE 14

Each State Party to the present Covenant which, at the time of becoming a Party, has not been able to secure in its metropolitan territory or other territories under its jurisdiction compulsory primary education, free of charge, undertakes, within two years, to work out and adopt a detailed plan of action for the progressive implementation, within a reasonable number of years, to be fixed in the plan, of the principle of compulsory education free of charge for all.

ARTICLE 15

1. The States Parties to the present Covenant recognize the right of everyone:

(a) To take part in cultural life;

(b) To enjoy the benefits of scientific progress and its applications;

(c) To benefit from the protection of the moral and material interests resulting from any scientific, literary or artistic production of which he is the author.

2. The steps to be taken by the States Parties to the present Covenant to achieve the full realization of this right shall include those necessary for the conservation, the development and the diffusion of science and culture.

3. The States Parties to the present Covenant undertake to respect the freedom indispensable for scientific research and creative activity.

4. The States Parties to the present Covenant recognize the benefits to be derived from the encouragement and development of international contacts and cooperation in the scientific and cultural fields.

PART IV

ARTICLE 16

1. The States Parties to the present Covenant undertake to submit in conformity with this part of the Covenant reports on the measures which they have adopted and the progress made in achieving the observance of the rights recognized herein.

2. (a) All reports shall be submitted to the Secretary-General of the United Nations who shall transmit copies to the Economic and Social Council for consideration in accordance with the provisions of the present Covenant.

(b) The Secretary-General of the United Nations shall also transmit to the specialized agencies copies of the reports, or any relevant parts therefrom, from States Parties to the present Covenant which are also members of these specialized agencies in so far as these reports, or parts therefrom, relate to any matters which fall within the responsibilities of the said agencies in accordance with their constitutional instruments.

ARTICLE 17

1. The States Parties to the present Covenant shall furnish their reports in stages, in accordance with a programme to be established by the

Economic and Social Council within one year of the entry into force of the present Covenant after consultation with the States Parties and the specialized agencies concerned.

2. Reports may indicate factors and difficulties affecting the degree of fulfilment of obligations under the present Covenant.

3. Where relevant information has previously been furnished to the United Nations or to any specialized agency by any State Party to the present Covenant it will not be necessary to reproduce that information but a precise reference to the information so furnished will suffice.

ARTICLE 18

Pursuant to its responsibilities under the Charter in the field of human rights and fundamental freedoms, the Economic and Social Council may make arrangements with the specialized agencies in respect of their reporting to it on the progress made in achieving the observance of the provisions of the present Covenant falling within the scope of their activities. These reports may include particulars of decisions and recommendations on such implementation adopted by their competent organs.

ARTICLE 19

The Economic and Social Council may transmit to the Commission on Human Rights for study and general recommendation or as appropriate for information the reports concerning human rights submitted by States in accordance with articles 16 and 17, and those concerning human rights submitted by the specialized agencies in accordance with article 18.

ARTICLE 20

The States Parties to the present Covenant and the specialized agencies concerned may submit comments to the Economic and Social Council on any general recommendation under article 19 or reference to such general recommendation in any report of the Commission or any documentation referred to therein.

ARTICLE 21

The Economic and Social Council may submit from time to time to the General Assembly reports with recommendations of a general nature and a summary of the information received from the States Parties to the present Covenant and the specialized agencies on the measures taken and the progress made in achieving general observance of the rights recognized in the present Covenant.

ARTICLE 22

The Economic and Social Council may bring to the attention of other organs of the United Nations, their subsidiary organs and specialized agencies concerned with furnishing technical assistance, any matters arising out of the reports referred to in this part of the present Covenant which may assist such bodies in deciding each within its field of competence, on the advisability of international measures likely to contribute to the effective progressive implementation of the present Covenant.

ARTICLE 23

The States Parties to the present Covenant agree that international action for the achievement of the rights recognized in the present Covenant includes such methods as the conclusion of conventions, the adoption of recommendations, the furnishing of technical assistance and the holding of regional meetings and technical meetings for the purpose of consultation and study organized in conjunction with the Governments concerned.

ARTICLE 24

Nothing in the present Covenant shall be interpreted as impairing the provisions of the Charter of the United Nations and of the constitutions of the specialized agencies which define the respective responsibilities of the various organs of the United Nations and of the specialized agencies in regard to the matters dealt with in the present Covenant.

ARTICLE 25

Nothing in the present Covenant shall be interpreted as impairing the inherent right of all peoples to enjoy and utilize fully and freely their natural wealth and resources.

PART V

ARTICLE 26

1. The present Covenant is open for signature by any State Member of the United Nations or member of any of its specialized agencies, by any State Party to the Statute of the International Court of Justice, and by any other State which has been invited by the General Assembly of the United Nations to become a party to the present Covenant.

2. The present Covenant is subject to ratification. Instruments of ratification shall be deposited with the Secretary-General of the United Nations.

3. The present Covenant shall be open to accession by any State referred to in paragraph 1 of this article.

4. Accession shall be effected by the deposit of an instrument of accession with the Secretary-General of the United Nations.

5. The Secretary-General of the United Nations shall inform all States which have signed the present Covenant or acceded to it of the deposit of each instrument of ratification or accession.

ARTICLE 27

1. The Present Covenant shall enter into force three months after the date of the deposit with the Secretary-General of the United Nations of the thirty-fifth instrument of ratification or instrument of accession.

2. For each State ratifying the present Covenant or acceding to it after the deposit of the thirty-fifth instrument of ratification or instrument of accession, the present Covenant shall enter into force three months after the date of the deposit of its own instrument of ratification or instrument of accession.

ARTICLE 28

The provisions of the present Covenant shall extend to all parts of federal States without any limitations or exceptions.

ARTICLE 29

1. Any State Party to the present Covenant may propose an amendment and file it with the Secretary-General of the United Nations. The Secretary-General of the United Nations shall thereupon communicate any proposed amendments to the States Parties to the present Covenant with a request that they notify him whether they favour a conference of States Parties for the purpose of considering and voting upon the proposal. In the event that at least one-third of the States Parties favours such a conference the Secretary-General of the United Nations shall convene the conference under the auspices of the United Nations. Any amendment adopted by a majority of the States Parties present and voting at the conference shall be submitted to the General Assembly of the United Nations for approval.

2. Amendments shall come into force when they have been approved by the General Assembly and accepted by a two-thirds majority of the States Parties to processes.

3. When amendments come into force they shall be bindin on those States Parties which have accepted them, other State Parties being still bound by the provisions of the present Covenant and any earlier amendment which they have accepted.

ARTICLE 30

Irrespective of the notifications made under article 26, paragraph 5, the Secretary-General of the United Nations shall inform all States referred to in paragraph 1 of the same article of the following particulars:

(a) Signatures, ratifications and accessions under article 26;

(b) The date of the entry into force of the present Covenant under article 27 and the date of the entry into force of any amendments under article 29.

ARTICLE 31

1   The present Covenant, of which the Chinese, English, French, Russian and Spanish texts are equally authentic, shall be deposited in the archives of the United Nations.

2. The Secretary-General of the United Nations shall transmit certified copies of the present Covenant to all States referred to in article 26.

13. International Covenant on Civil and Political Rights

Adopted by Resolution 2200(XXI) of the General Assembly, December 16, 1966. General Assembly, Official Records, 21st Session, Supp. 16 (A/6316), pp. 52–58.

PREAMBLE

The State Parties to the present Covenant,

Considering that, in accordance with the principles proclaimed in the Charter of the United Nations, recognition of the inherent dignity and of the equal and inalienable rights of all members of the human family is the foundation of freedom, justice and peace in the world,

Recognizing that these rights derive from the inherent dignity of the human person,

Recognizing that, in accordance with the Universal Declaration of Human Rights, the ideal of free human beings enjoying civil and political freedom and freedom from fear and want can only be achieved if conditions are created whereby everyone may enjoy his civil and political rights, as well as his economic, social and cultural rights,

Considering the obligation of States under the Charter of the United Nations to promote universal respect for, and observance of, human rights and freedoms,

Realizing that the individual, having duties to other individuals and to the community to which he belongs, is under a responsibility to strive for the promotion and observance of the rights recognized in the present Covenant,

Agree upon the following articles:

PART I

ARTICLE 1

1. All peoples have the right of self-determination. By virtue of the right they freely determine their political status and freely pursue their economic, social and cultural development.

2. All peoples may, for their own ends, freely dispose of their natural wealth and resources without prejudice to any obligations arising out of international economic cooperation, based upon the principle of mutual benefit, and international law. In no case may a people be deprived of its own means of subsistence.

3. The States Parties to the present Covenant, including those having responsibility for the administration of Non-Self-Governing and Trust Territories, shall promote the realization of the right of self-determination, and shall respect that right, in conformity with the provisions of the United Nations Charter.

PART II

ARTICLE 2

1. Each State Party to the present Covenant undertakes to respect and to ensure to all individuals within its territory and subject to its jurisdiction the rights recognized in the present Covenant, without distinction of any kind, such as race, colour, sex, language, religion, political or other opinion, national or social origin, property, birth or other status.

2. Where not already provided for by existing legislative or other measures, each State Party to the present Covenant undertakes to take the necessary steps, in accordance with its constitutional processes and with the provisions of the present Covenant, to adopt such legislative or other measures as may be necessary to give effect to the rights recognized in the present Covenant.

3. Each State Party to the present Covenant undertakes:

(a) To ensure that any person whose rights or freedoms as herein recognized are violated shall have an effective remedy notwithstanding that the violation has been committed by persons acting in an official capacity;

(b) To ensure that any person claiming such a remedy shall have his right thereto determined by competent judicial, administrative or legislative authorities, or by any other competent authority provided for by the legal system of the State, and to develop the possibilities of judicial remedy;

(c) To ensure that the competent authorities shall enforce such remedies when granted.

ARTICLE 3

The States Parties to the present Covenant under-take to ensure the equal right of men and women to the enjoyment of all civil and political rights set forth in the present Covenant.

ARTICLE 4

1. In time of public emergency which threatens the life of the nation and the existence of which is officially proclaimed, the States Parties to the present Covenant may take measures derogating from their obligations under the present Covenant to the extent strictly required by the exigencies of the situation, provided that such measures are not inconsistent with their other obligations under international law and do not involve discrimination solely on the ground of race, colour, sex, language, religion or social origin.

2. No derogation from articles 6, 7, 8 (paragraphs 1 and 2), 11, 15, 16 and 18 may be made under this provision.

3. Any State Party to the present Covenant availing itself of the right of derogation shall inform immediately the other States Parties to the present Covenant, through the intermediary of the Secretary-General of the United Nations of the provisions from which it has derogated and of the reasons by which it was actuated. A further communication shall be made, through the same intermediary on the date on which it terminates such derogation.

ARTICLE 5

1. Nothing in the present Covenant may be interpreted as implying for any State, group or person any right to engage in any activity or perform any act aimed at the destruction of any of the rights and freedoms recognized herein or at their limitation to a greater extent than is provided for in the present Covenant.

2. There shall be no restriction upon or derogation from any of the fundamental human rights recognized or existing in any State Party to the present Covenant pursuant to law; conventions, regulations or custom on the pretext that the present Covenant does not recognize such rights or that it recognizes them to a lesser extent.

PART III

ARTICLE 6

1. Every human being has the inherent right to life. This right shall be protected by law. No one shall be arbitrarily deprived of his life.

2. In countries which have not abolished the death penalty, sentence of death may be imposed only for the most serious crimes in accordance with law in force at the time of the commission of the crime and not contrary to the provisions of the present Covenant and to the Convention on the Prevention and Punishment of the Crime of Genocide. This penalty can only be carried out pursuant to a final judgment rendered by a competent court.

3. When deprivation of life constitutes the crime of genocide, it is understood that nothing in this article shall authorize any State Party to the present Covenant to derogate in any way from any obligation assumed under the provisions of the Convention on the Prevention and Punishment of the Crime of Genocide.

4. Anyone sentenced to death shall have the right to seek pardon or commutation of the sentence. Amnesty, pardon or commutation of the sentence of death may be granted in all cases.

5. Sentence of death shall not be imposed for crimes committed by persons below eighteen years of age and shall not be carried out on pregnant women.

6. Nothing in this article shall be invoked to delay or to prevent the abolition of capital punishment by any State Party to the present Covenant.

ARTICLE 7
No one shall be subjected to torture or to cruel, inhuman or degrading treatment or punishment. In particular, no one shall be subjected without his free consent to medical or scientific experimentation.

ARTICLE 8
1. No one shall be held in slavery; slavery and the slave-trade in all their forms shall be prohibited.

2. No one shall be held in servitude.

3. (a) No one shall be required to perform forced or compulsory labour;

(b) The preceding subparagraph shall not be held to preclude in countries where imprisonment with hard labour may be imposed as a punishment for a crime, the performance of hard labour in pursuance of a sentence to such punishment by a competent court;

(c) For the purpose of this paragraph the term "forced or compulsory labour" shall not include:

(i) Any work or service, not referred to in subparagraph (b), normally required of a person who is under detention in consequence of a lawful order of a court, or of a person during conditional release from such detention;

(ii) Any service of a military character and, in countries where conscientious objection is recognized, any national service required by law of conscientious objectors;

(iii) Any service exacted in cases of emergency or calamity threatening the life or well-being of the community;

(iv) Any work or service which forms part of normal civil obligations.

ARTICLE 9

1. Everyone has the right to liberty and security of person. No one shall be subjected to arbitrary arrest or detention. No one shall be deprived of his liberty except on such grounds and in accordance with such procedures as are established by law.

2. Anyone who is arrested shall be informed, at the time of arrest, of the reasons for his arrest and shall be promptly informed of any charges against him.

3. Anyone arrested or detained on a criminal charge shall be brought promptly before a judge or other officer authorized by law to exercise judicial power and shall be entitled to trial within a reasonable time or to release. It shall not be the general rule that persons awaiting trial shall be detained in custody, but release may be subject to guarantees to appear for trial, at any other stage of the judicial proceedings, and, should occasion arise, for execution of the judgment.

4. Anyone who is deprived of his liberty by arrest or detention shall be entitled to take proceedings before a court, in order that such court may decide without delay on the lawfulness of his detention and order his release if the detention is not lawful.

5. Anyone who has been the victim of unlawful arrest or detention shall have an enforceable right to compensation.

ARTICLE 10

1. All persons deprived of their liberty shall be treated with humanity and with respect for the inherent dignity of the human person.

2. (a) Accused persons shall, save in exceptional circumstances, be segregated from convicted persons, and shall be subject to separate treatment appropriate to their status as unconvicted persons;

(b) Accused juvenile persons shall be separated from adults and brought as speedily as possible for adjudication.

3. The penitentiary system shall comprise treatment of prisoners the essential aim of which shall be their reformation and social rehabilitation. Juvenile offenders shall be segregated from adults and be accorded treatment appropriate to their age and legal status.

ARTICLE 11

No one shall be imprisoned merely on the ground of inability to fulfil a contractual obligation.

ARTICLE 12

1. Everyone lawfully within the territory of a State shall, within that territory, have the right to liberty of movement and freedom to choose his residence.

2. Everyone shall be free to leave any country, including his own.

3. The above-mentioned rights shall not be subject to any restrictions except those which are provided by law, are necessary to protect national security, public order ("*ordre public*"), public health or morals or the rights and freedoms of others, and are consistent with the other rights recognized in the present Covenant.

4. No one shall be arbitrarily deprived of the right to enter his own country.

ARTICLE 13

An alien lawfully in the territory of a State Party to the present Covenant may be expelled therefrom only in pursuance of a decision reached in accordance with law and shall, except where compelling reasons of national security otherwise require, be allowed to submit the reasons against his expulsion and to have his case reviewed by, and be represented for the purpose before, the competent authority or a person or persons especially designated by the competent authority.

ARTICLE 14

1. All persons shall be equal before the courts and tribunals. In the determination of any criminal charge against him, or of his rights and obligations in a suit at law, everyone shall be entitled to a fair and public hearing by a competent, independent and impartial tribunal established by law. The Press and the public may be excluded from all or part of a trial for reasons of morals, public order ("*ordre public*") or national security in a democratic society, or when the interest of the private lives of the parties so requires, or to the extent strictly necessary in the opinion of the court in special circumstances where publicity would prejudice the interests of justice; but any judgment rendered in a criminal case or in a suit at law shall be made public except where the interest of juveniles otherwise requires or the proceedings concern matrimonial disputes or the guardianship of children.

2. Everyone charged with a criminal offence shall have the right to be presumed innocent until proved guilty according to law.

3. In the determination of any criminal charge against him, everyone shall be entitled to the following minimum guarantees, in full equality:

(a) To be informed promptly and in detail in a language which he understands of the nature and cause of the charge against him;

(b) To have adequate time and facilities for the preparation of his defence and to communicate with counsel of his own choosing;

(c) To be tried without undue delay;

(d) To be tried in his presence, and to defend himself in person or through legal assistance of his own choosing; to be informed, if he does not have legal assistance, of this right; and to have legal assistance assigned to him, in any case where the interests of justice so require, and without payment by him in any such case if he does not have sufficient means to pay for it;

(e) To examine, or have examined, the witnesses against him and to obtain the attendance and examination of witnesses on his behalf under the same conditions as witnesses against him;

(f) To have the free assistance of an interpreter if he cannot understand or speak the language used in court;

(g) Not to be conpelled to testify against himself, or to confess guilt.

4. In the case of juveniles, the procedure shall be such as will take account of their age and the desirability of promoting their rehabilitation.

5. Everyone convicted of a crime shall have the right to his conviction and sentence being reviewed by a higher tribunal according to law.

6. When a person has by a final decision been convicted of a criminal offence and when subsequently his conviction has been reversed or he has been pardoned on the ground that a new or newly discovered fact shows conclusively that there has been a miscarriage of justice, the person who has suffered punishment as a result of such conviction shall be compensated according to law, unless it is proved that the nondisclosure of the unknown fact in time is wholly or partly attributable to him.

7. No one shall be liable to be tried or punished again for an offence for which he has already been finally convicted or acquitted in accordance with the law and penal procedure of each country.

ARTICLE 15

1. No one shall be held guilty of any criminal offence on account of any act or omission which did not constitute a criminal offence, under national or international law, at the time when it was committed. Nor shall a heavier penalty be imposed than the one that was applicable at the time when the criminal offence was committed. If, subsequently to the commission of the offence, provision is made by law for the imposition of a lighter penalty, the offender shall benefit thereby.

2. Nothing in this article shall prejudice the trial and punishment of any person for any act or omission which, at the time when it was committed, was criminal according to the general principles of law recognized by the community of nations.

ARTICLE 16

Everyone shall have the right to recognition everywhere as a person before the law.

AERTICLE 17

1. No one shall be subjected to arbitrary or unlawful interference with his privacy, family, home or correspendence, nor to unlawful attacks on his honour and reputation.

2. Everyone has the right to the protection of the law against such interference or attacks.

ARTICLE 18

1. Everyone shall have the right to freedom of thought, conscience and religion. This right shall include freedom to have or to adopt a religion or belief of his choice, and freedom either individually or in community with others and in public or private, to manifest his religion or belief in worship, observance, practice and teaching.

2. No one shall be subject to coercion which would impair his freedom to have or to adopt a religion or belief of his choice.

3. Freedom to manifest one's religion or beliefs may be subject only to such limitations as are prescribed by law and are necessary to protect public safety, order, health, or morals or the fundamental rights and freedoms of others.

4. The States Parties to the present Covenant undertake to have respect for the liberty of parents and, when applicable, legal guardians, to ensure the religious and moral education of their children in conformity with their own convictions.

ARTICLE 19

1. Everyone shall have the right to hold opinions without interference.

2. Everyone shall have the right to freedom of expression; this right shall include freedom to seek, receive and impart information and ideas of all kinds, regardless of frontiers, either orally, in writing or in print, in the form of art, or through any other media of his choice.

3. The exercise of the rights provided for in the foregoing paragraph carries with it special duties and responsibilities. It may therefore be subject to certain restrictions, but these shall be such only as are provided by law and are necessary, (1) for respect of the rights or reputations of others, (2) for the protection of national security or of public order (*"ordre public"*), or of public health or morals.

ARTICLE 20

1. Any propaganda for war shall be prohibited by law.

2. Any advocacy of national, racial, or religious hatred that constitutes incitement to discrimination, hostility or violence shall be prohibited by law.

ARTICLE 21

The right of peaceful assembly shall be recognized. No restrictions may be placed on the exercise of this right other than those imposed in conformity with the law and which are necessary in a democratic society in the interests of national security or public safety, public order (*"ordre public"*), the protection of public health or morals or the protection of the rights and freedoms of others.

ARTICLE 22

1. Everyone shall have the right to freedom of association with others, including the right to form and join trade unions for the protection of his interests.

2. No restrictions may be placed on the exercise of this right other than those prescribed by law and which are necessary in a democratic society in the interests of national security or public safety, public order (*"ordre public"*), the protection of public health or morals or the protection of the rights and freedoms of others. This article shall not prevent the imposition of lawful restrictions on members of the armed forces and of the police in their exercise of this right.

3. Nothing in this article shall authorize States Parties to the International Labour Convention of 1948 on Freedom of Association and Protection of the Right to Organise to take legislative measures which would prejudice, or to apply the law in such a manner as to prejudice, the guarantees provided for in the Convention.

ARTICLE 23

1. The family is the natural and fundamental group unit of society and is entitled to protection by society and the State.

2. The right of men and women of marriageable age to marry and to found a family shall be recognized.

3. No marriage shall be entered into without the free and full consent of the intending spouses.

4. States Parties to the present Covenant shall take appropriate steps to ensure equality of rights and responsibilities of spouses as to marriage, during marriage and at its dissolution. In the case of dissolution, provision shall be made for the necessary protection of any children.

ARTICLE 24

1. Every child shall have, without any discrimination as to race, colour, sex, language, religion, national or social origin, property or birth, the right to such measures of protection as required by his status as a minor, on the part of his family, the society and the State.

2. Every child shall be registered immediately after birth and shall have a name.

3. Every child has the right to acquire a nationality.

ARTICLE 25

Every citizen shall have the right and the opportunity, without any of the distinctions mentioned in article 2 and without unreasonable restrictions:

(a) To take part in the conduct of public affairs, directly or through freely chosen representatives;

(b) To vote and to be elected at genuine periodic elections which shall be by universal and equal suffrage and shall be held by secret ballot, guaranteeing the free expression of the will of the electors;

(c) To have access, on general terms of equality, to public service in his country.

ARTICLE 26

All persons are equal before the law and are entitled without any discrimination to equal protection of the law. In this respect the law shall prohibit any discrimination and guarantee to all persons equal and effective protection against discrimination on any ground such as race, colour, sex, language, religion, political or other opinion, national or social origin, property, birth or other status.

ARTICLE 27

In those States in which ethnic, religious or linguistic minorities exist, persons belonging to such minorities shall not be denied the right, in the community with the other members of their group, to enjoy their own culture, to profess and practise their own religion, or to use their own language.

PART IV

ARTICLE 28

1. There shall be established a Human Rights Committee (hereafter referred to in the present Covenant as "the Committee"). It shall consist of eighteen members and shall carry out the functions hereinafter provided.

2. The Committee shall be composed of nationals of the State Parties to the present Covenant who shall be persons of high moral character and recognized competence in the field of human rights, consideration being given to the usefulness of the participation of some persons having legal experience.

3. The members of the Committee shall be elected and shall serve in their personal capacity.

ARTICLE 29

1. The members of the Committee shall be elcted by secret ballot from a list of persons possessing the qualifications prescribed in article 28 and nominated for the purpose by the States Parties to the present Covenant.

2. Each State Party to the present Covenant may nominate not more than two persons. These persons shall be nationals of the nominating State.

3. A person shall be eligible for renomination.

ARTICLE 30

1. The initial election shall be held no later than six months after the date of the entry into force of the present Covenant.

2. At least four months before the date of each election of the Committee, other than an election to fill a vacancy declared in accordance with article 34, the Secretary-General of the United Nations shall address a written invitation to the States Parties to the present Covenant to submit their nominations for membership of the Committee within three months.

3. The Secretary-General of the United Nations shall prepare a list in alphabetical order of all the persons thus nominated, with an indication of the States Parties which have nominated them, and shall submit it to the States Parties to the present Covenant no later than one month before the date of each election.

4. Elections of the members of the Committee shall be held at a meeting of the States Parties to the present Covenant convened by the Secretary-General of the United Nations at the Headquarters of the United Nations. At that meeting, for which two-thirds of the States Parties to the present Covenant shall constitute a quorum, the persons elected to the Committee shall be those nominees who obtain the largest number of votes and an absolute majority of the votes of the representatives of States Parties present and voting.

ARTICLE 31

1. The Committee may not include more than one national of the same State.

2. In the election of the Committee consideration shall be given to equitable geographical distribution of membership and to the representation of the different forms of civilization as well as of the principal legal systems.

ARTICLE 32

1. The members of the Committee shall be elected for a term of four years. They shall be eligible for reelection if renominated. However, the

terms of nine of the members elected at the first election shall expire at the end of two years; immediately after the first election the names of these nine members shall be chosen by lot by the Chairman of the meeting referred to in paragraph 4 of article 30.

2. Elections at the expiry of office shall be held in accordance with the preceding articles of this part of the present Covenant.

ARTICLE 33

1. If, in the unanimous opinion of the other members, a member of the Committee has ceased to carry out his functions for any cause other than absence of a temporary character, the Chairman of the Committee shall notify the Secretary-General of the United Nations who shall then declare the seat of that member to be vacant.

2. In the event of the death or the resignation of a member of the Committee, the Chairman shall immediately notify the Secretary-General of the United Nations who shall declare the seat vacant from the date of death or the date on which the resignation takes effect.

ARTICLE 34

1. When a vacancy is declared in accordance with article 33 and if the term of office of the member to be replaced does not expire within six months of the declaration of the vacancy, the Secretary-General of the United Nations shall notify each of the States Parties to the present Covenant which may within two months submit nominations in accordance with article 29 for the purpose of filling the vacancy.

2. The Secretary-General of the United Nations shall prepare a list in alphabetical order of the persons thus nominated and shall submit it to the States Parties to the present Covenant. The election to fill the vacancy shall then take place in accordance with the relevant provisions of this part of the present Covenant.

3. A member of the Committee elected to fill a vacancy declared in accordance with article 33 shall hold office for the remainder of the term of the member who vacated the seat on the Committee under the provisions of that article.

ARTICLE 35

The members of the Committee shall, with the approval of the General Assembly of the United Nations, receive emoluments from United Nations resources on such terms and conditions as the General Assembly may decide having regard to the importance of the Committee's responsibilities.

ARTICLE 36

The Secretary-General of the United Nations shall provide the necessary staff and facilities for the effective performance of the functions of the Committee under this Covenant.

ARTICLE 37

1. The Secretary-General of the United Nations shall convene the initial meeting of the Committee at the Headquarters of the United Nations.

2. After its initial meeting, the Committee shall meet at such times as shall be provided in its rules of procedure.

3. The Committee shall normally meet at the Headquarters of the United Nations or at the United Nations office at Geneva.

ARTICLE 38

Every member of the Committee shall, before taking up his duties, make a solemn declaration in open committee that he will perform his functions impartially and conscientiously.

ARTICLE 39

1. The Committee shall elect its officers for a term of two years. They may be reelected.

2. The Committee shall establish its own rules of procedure, but these rules shall provide, *inter alia,* that:

(a) Twelve members shall constitute a quorum;

(b) Decisions of the Committee shall be made by a majority vote of the members present.

ARTICLE 40

1. The States Parties to the present Covenant undertake to submit reports on the measures they have adopted which give effect to the rights recognized herein and on the progress made in the enjoyment of those rights; (a) within one year of the entry into force of the present Covenant for the States Parties concerned and (b) thereafter whenever the Committee so requests.

2. All reports shall be submitted to the Secretary-General of the United Nations who shall transmit them to the Committee for consideration. Reports shall indicate the factors and difficulties, if any, affecting the implementation of the present Covenant.

3. The Secretary-General of the United Nations may after consultation with the Committee transmit to the specialized agencies concerned copies of such parts of the reports as may fall within their field of competence.

4. The Committee shall study the reports submitted by the States Parties to the present Covenant. It shall transmit its reports and such general

comments as it may consider appropriate to the States Parties. The Committee may also transmit to the Economic and Social Council these comments along with the copies of the reports it has received from States Parties to the present Covenant.

5. The States Parties to the present Covenant may submit to the Committee observations on any comments that may be made in accordance with paragraph 4 of this article.

ARTICLE 41

1. A State Party to the present Covenant may at any time declare under this article that it recognizes the competence of the Committee to receive and consider communications to the effect that a State Party claims that another State Party is not fulfilling its obligations under the present Covenant. Communications under this article may be received and considered only if submitted by a State Party which has made a declaration recognizing in regard to itself the competence of the Committee. No communication shall be received by the Committee if it concerns a State Party which has not made such a declaration. Communications received under this article shall be dealt with in accordance with the following procedure:

(a) If a State Party to the present Covenant considers that another State Party is not giving effect to the provisions of the present Covenant, it may, by written communication, bring the matter to the attention of that State Party. Within three months after the receipt of the communication, the receiving State shall afford the State which sent the communication an explanation or any other statement in writing clarifying the matter, which should include, to the extent possible and pertinent, reference to domestic procedures and remedies taken, pending, or available in the matter.

(b) If the matter is not adjusted to the satisfaction of both States Parties concerned within six months after the receipt by the receiving State of the initial communication, either State shall have the right to refer the matter to the Committee, by notice given to the Committee and to the other State.

(c) The Committee shall deal with a matter referred to it only after it has ascertained that all available domestic remedies have been invoked and exhausted in the matter, in conformity with the generally recognized principles of international law. This shall not be the rule where the application of the remedies is unreasonably prolonged.

(d) The Committee shall hold closed meetings when examining communications under this article.

(e) Subject to the provisions of subparagraph (c), the Committee shall make available its good offices to the States Parties concerned with a view to a friendly solution of the matter on the basis of respect for human rights and fundamental freedoms as recognized in this Covenant.

(f) In any matter referred to it, the Committee may call upon the States Parties concerned, referred to in subparagraph (b), to supply any relevant information.

(g) The States Parties concerned, referred to in subparagraph (b), shall have the right to be represented when the matter is being considered in the Committee and to make submissions orally and/or in writing.

(h) The Committee shall, within twelve months after the date of receipt of notice under subparagraph (b), submit a report:

(i) If a solution within the terms of subparagraph (c) is reached, the Committee shall confine its report to a brief statement of the facts and of the solution reached;

(ii) If a solution is not reached, within the terms of subparagraph (e), the Committee shall confine its report to a brief statement of the facts; the written submissions and record of the oral submissions made by the States Parties concerned shall be attached to the report.

In every matter the report shall be communicated to the States Parties concerned.

2. The provisions of this article shall come into force when ten States Parties to the present Covenant have made declarations under paragraph 1 of this article. Such declarations shall be deposited by the States Parties with the Secretary-General of the United Nations who shall transmit copies thereof to the other States Parties. A declaration may be withdrawn at any time by notification to the Secretary-General. Such a withdrawal shall not prejudice the consideration of any matter which is the subject of a communication already transmitted under this article; no further communication by any State Party shall be received after the notification of withdrawal of the declaration has been received by the Secretary-General of the United Nations unless the State Party concerned had made a new declaration.

ARTICLE 42

1. (a) If a matter referred to the Committee in accordance with article 41 is not resolved to the satisfaction of the States Parties concerned, the Committee may, with the prior consent of the States Parties concerned, appoint an *ad hoc* Conciliation Commission (hereinafter referred to as "the Commission"). The good offices of the Commission shall be made available to the States Parties concerned with a view to an amicable solution of the matter on the basis of respect for the present Covenant;

(b) The Commission shall consist of five persons acceptable to the States Parties concerned. If the States Parties concerned fail to reach agreement within three months on all or part of the composition of the Commission the members of the Commission concerning whom no agreement was reached shall be elected by secret ballot by a two-thirds majority vote of the Committee from among its members.

2. The members of the Commission shall serve in their personal capacity. They shall not be nationals of the States Parties concerned, or of a State not party to the present Covenant, or of a State Party which has not made a declaration under article 41.

3. The Commission shall elect its own Chairman and adopt its own rules of procedure.

4. The meetings of the Commission shall normally be held at the Headquarters of the United Nations or at the United Nations Office at Geneva. However, they may be held at such other convenient places as the Commission may determine in consultation with the Secretary-General of the United Nations and the States Parties concerned.

5. The secretariat provided in accordance with article 36 shall also service the Commissions appointed under this article.

6. The information received and collated by the Committee shall be made available to the Commission and the Commission may call upon the States Parties concerned to supply any other relevant information.

7. When the Commission has fully considered the matter, but in any event not later than twelve months after having been seized of the matter, it shall submit to the Chairman of the Committee a report for communication to the States Parties concerned.

(a) If the Commission is unable to complete its consideration of the matter within twelve months, it shall confine its report to a brief statement of the status of its consideration of the matter.

(b) If an amicable solution to the matter on the basis of respect for human rights as recognized in the present Covenant is reached, the Commission shall confine its report to a brief statement of the facts and of the solution reached.

(c) If a solution within the terms of subparagraph (b) is not reached, the Commission's report shall embody its findings on all questions of fact relevant to the issues between the States Parties concerned, as well as its views on the possibilities of amicable solution of the matter. This report shall also contain the written submissions and a record of the oral submissions made by the States Parties concerned.

(d) If the Commission's report is submitted under subparagraph (c), the States Parties concerned shall, within three months of the receipt of the report, inform the Chairman of the Committee whether or not they accept the contents of the report of the Commission.

8. The provisions of this article are without prejudice to the responsibilities of the Committee under article 41.

9. The States Parties concerned shall share equally all the expenses of the members of the Commission in accordance with estimates to be provided by the Secretary-General of the United Nations.

10. The Secretary-General of the United Nations shall be empowered to pay the expenses of the members of the Commission, if necessary, before reimbursement by the States Parties concerned with paragraph 9 of this article.

ARTICLE 43

The members of the Committee and of the *ad hoc* conciliation commissions which may be appointed under article 41, shall be entitled to the facilities, privileges and immunities of experts on mission for the United Nations as laid down in the relevant sections of the Convention on the Privileges and Immunities of the United Nations.

ARTICLE 44

The provisions for the implementation of the present Covenant shall apply without prejudice to the procedures prescribed in the field of human rights by or under the constituent instruments and the conventions of the United Nations and of the specialized agencies and shall not prevent the States Parties to the present Covenant from having recourse to other procedures for settling a dispute in accordance with general or special international agreements in force between them.

ARTICLE 45

The Committee shall submit to the General Assembly, through the Economic and Social Council, an annual report on its activities.

PART V

ARTICLE 46

Nothing in the present Covenant shall be interpreted as impairing the provisions of the Charter of the United Nations and of the constitutions of the specialized agencies which define the respective responsibilities of the various organs of the United Nations and of the specialized agencies in regard to the matters dealt with in the present Covenant.

ARTICLE 47

Nothing in the Covenant shall be interpreted as impairing the inherent right of all peoples to enjoy and utilize fully and freely their natural wealth and resources.

PART VI

ARTICLE 48

1. The present Covenant is open for signature by any State Member of the United Nations or member of any of its specialized agencies, by any

State Party to the Statute of the International Court of Justice, and by any other State which has been invited by the General Assembly of the United Nations to become a party to the present Covenant.

2. The present Covenant is subject to ratification. Instruments of ratification shall be deposited with the Secretary-General of the United Nations.

3. The present Covenant shall be open to accession by any State referred to in paragraph 1 of this article.

4. Accession shall be effected by the deposit of an instrument of accession with the Secretary-General of the United Nations.

5. The Secretary-General of the United Nations shall inform all States which have signed this Covenant or acceded to it of the deposit of each instrument of ratification or accession.

ARTICLE 49

1. The present Covenant shall enter into force three months after the date of the deposit with the Secretary-General of the United Nations of the thirty-fifth instrument of ratification or instrument of accession.

2. For each State ratifying the present Covenant or acceding to it after the deposit of the thirty-fifth instrument of ratification or instrument of accession, the present Covenant shall enter into force three months after the date of the deposit of its own instrument of ratification or instrument of accession.

ARTICLE 50

The provisions of the present Covenant shall extend to all parts of federal States without any limitations or exceptions.

ARTICLE 51

1. Any State Party to the present Covenant may propose an amendment and file it with the Secretary-General of the United Nations. The Secretary-General of the United Nations shall thereupon communicate any proposed amendments to the States Parties to the present Covenant with a request that they notify him whether they favour a conference of States Parties for the purpose of considering and voting upon the proposal. In the event that at least one-third of the States Parties favours such a conference the Secretary-General of the United Nations shall convene the conference under the auspices of the United Nations. Any amendment adopted by a majority of the States Parties present and voting at the conference shall be submitted to the General Assembly of the United Nations for approval.

2. Amendments shall come into force when they have been approved by the General Assembly and accepted by a two-thirds majority of the

States Parties to the present Covenant in accordance with their respective constitutional processes.

3. When amendments come into force they shall be binding on those States Parties which have accepted them, other States Parties being still bound by the provisions of the present Covenant and any earlier amendment which they have accepted.

ARTICLE 52

Irrespective of the notifications made under article 48, paragraph 5, the Secretary-General of the United Nations shall inform all States referred to in paragraph 1 of the same article of the following particulars:

(a) Signatures, ratifications and accessions under article 48;

(b) The date of the entry into force of the present Covenant under article 49 and the date of the entry into force of any amendments under article 51.

ARTICLE 53

1. The present Covenant, of which the Chinese, English, French, Russian and Spanish texts are equally authentic, shall be deposited in the archives of the United Nations.

2. The Secretary-General of the United Nations shall transmit certified copies of the present Covenant to all States referred to in article 48.

14. Optional Protocol to the International Covenant on Civil and Political Rights

Adopted by Resolution 2200(XXI) of the General Assembly, December 16, 1966. General Assembly, Official Records, 21st Session, Supp. 16 (A/6316), pp. 59–60.

The States Parties to the present Protocol,

Considering that in order further to achieve the purposes of the Covenant on Civil and Political Rights (hereinafter referred to as "the Covenant") and the implementation of its provisions it would be appropriate to enable the Human Rights Committee set up in part IV of the Covenant (hereinafter referred to as "the Committee") to receive and consider, as provided in the present Protocol, communications from individuals claiming to be victims of violations of any of the rights set forth in the Covenant,

Have agreed as follows:

ARTICLE 1

A State Party to the Covenant that becomes a party to the present Protocol recognizes the competence of the Committee to receive and consider communications from individuals, subject to its jurisdiction, claiming to be victims of a violation by that State Party of any of the rights set forth in the Covenant. No communication shall be received by the Committee if it concerns a State Party to the Covenant which is not a Party to the present Protocol.

ARTICLE 2

Subject to the provision of article 1, individuals claiming that any of their rights enumerated in the Covenant have been violated and who have exhausted all available domestic remedies may submit a written communication to the Committee for consideration.

ARTICLE 3

The Committee shall consider inadmissible any communication under this Protocol which is anonymous, or which it considers to be an abuse of the right of submission of such communications or to be incompatible with the provisions of the Covenant.

ARTICLE 4

1. Subject to the provisions of article 3, the Committee shall bring any communications submitted to it under the present Protocol to the attention of the State Party to the present Protocol alleged to be violating any provision of the Covenant.

2. Within six months, the receiving State shall submit to the Committee written explanations or statements clarifying the matter and the remedy, if any, that may have been taken by that State.

ARTICLE 5

1. The Committee shall consider communications received under the present Protocol in the light of all written information made available to it by the individual and by the State Party concerned.

2. The Committee shall not consider any communication from an individual unless it has ascertained that:

(a) the same matter is not being examined under another procedure of international investigation or settlement;

(b) the individual has exhausted all available domestic remedies. This shall not be the rule where the application of the remedies is unreasonably prolonged.

3. The Committee shall hold closed meetings when examining communications under the present Protocol.

4. The Committee shall forward its views to the State Party concerned and to the individual.

ARTICLE 6

The Committee shall include in its annual report under article 45 of the Covenant a summary of its activities under the present Protocol.

ARTICLE 7

Pending the achievement of the objectives of General Assembly resolution 1514 (XV) of 14 December 1960 concerning the Declaration on the Granting of Independence to Colonial Countries and Peoples, the provisions of the present Protocol shall in no way limit the right of petition granted to these peoples by the Charter of the United Nations and other international conventions and instruments under the United Nations and its specialized agencies.

ARTICLE 8

1. The present Protocol is open for signature by any State which has signed the Covenant.

2. The present Protocol is subject to ratification by any State which has ratified or acceded to the Covenant. Instruments of ratification shall be deposited with the Secretary-General of the United Nations.

3. The present Protocol shall be open to accession by any State which has ratified or acceded to the Covenant.

4. Accession shall be effected by the deposit of an instrument of accession with the Secretary-General of the United Nations.

5. The Secretary-General of the United Nations shall inform all States which have signed the present Protocol or acceded to it of the deposit of each instrument of ratification or accession.

ARTICLE 9

1. Subject to the entry into force of the Covenant, the present Protocol shall enter into force three months after the date of the deposit with the Secretary-General of the United Nations of the tenth instrument of ratification or instrument of accession.

2. For each State ratifying the present Protocol or acceding to it after the deposit of the tenth instrument of ratification or instrument of accession, the present Protocol shall enter into force three months after the date of the deposit of its own instrument of ratification or instrument of accession.

ARTICLE 10

The provision of the present Protocol shall extend to all parts of federal States without any limitations or exceptions.

ARTICLE 11

1. Any State Party to the present Protocol may propose an amendment and file it with the Secretary-General of the United Nations. The Secretary-General of the United Nations shall thereupon communicate any proposed amendments to the States Parties to the present Protocol with a request that they notify him whether they favour a conference of States Parties for the purpose of considering and voting upon the proposal. In the event that at least one-third of the States Parties favours such a conference the Secretary-General of the United Nations shall convene the conference under the auspices of the United Nations. Any amendment adopted by a majority of the States Parties present and voting at the conference shall be submitted to the General Assembly of the United Nations for approval.

2. Amendments shall come into force when they have been approved by the General Assembly and accepted by a two-thirds majority of the States Parties to the present Protocol in accordance with their respective constitutional processes.

3. When amendments come into force they shall be binding on those States Parties which have accepted them, other States Parties being still bound by the provisions of the present Protocol and any earlier amendment which they have accepted.

ARTICLE 12

1. Any State Party may denounce the present Protocol at any time by written notification addressed to the Secretary-General of the United Nations. Denunciation shall take effect three months after the date of receipt of the notification by the Secretary-General of the United Nations.

2. Denunciation shall be without prejudice to the continued application of the provisions of the present Protocol to any communication submitted under article 2 before the effective date of denunciation.

ARTICLE 13

Irrespective of the notifications made under article 8, paragraph 5, of the present Protocol, the Secretary-General of the United Nations shall inform all States referred to in article 48, paragraph 1, of the Covenant of the following particulars:

(a) Signatures, ratifications and accessions under article 8;

(b) The date of the entry into force of the present Protocol under article 9 and the date of the entry into force of any amendments under article 11;

(c) Denunciations under article 12.

ARTICLE 14

1. The present Protocol, of which the Chinese, English, French, Russian, and Spanish texts are equally authentic, shall be deposited in the archives of the United Nations.

2. The Secretary-General of the United Nations shall transmit certified copies of the present Protocol to all States referred to in Article 48 of the Covenant.

15. Declaration on the Establishment of a New International Economic Order

Adopted by Resolution 3201(S-VI) of the General Assembly at its Sixth Special Session on 1 May 1974. General Assembly, Report A/9556 (Part II).

The General Assembly
Adopts the following Declaration:

DECLARATION ON THE ESTABLISHMENT OF A NEW INTERNATIONAL ECONOMIC ORDER

We, the Members of the United Nations,

Having convened a special session of the General Assembly to study for the first time the problems of raw materials and development, devoted to the consideration of the most important economic problems facing the world community,

Bearing in mind the spirit, purposes, and principles of the Charter of the United Nations to promote the economic advancement and social progress of all peoples,

Solemnly proclaim our united determination to work urgently for

THE ESTABLISHMENT OF A NEW INTERNATIONAL ECONOMIC ORDER

based on equity, sovereign equality, interdependence, common interest and cooperation among all States, irrespective of their economic and social systems, which shall correct inequalities and redress existing injustices, make it possible to eliminate the widening gap between the developed and the developing countries and ensure steadily accelerating economic and social development in peace and justice for present and future generations.

1. The greatest and most significant achievement during the last decades has been the independence from colonial and alien domination of a large number of peoples and nations which has enabled them to become members of the community of free peoples. Technological progress has also been made in all spheres of economic activities in the last three decades, thus providing a solid potential for improving the well-being of all peoples.

However, the remaining vestiges of alien and colonial domination, foreign occupation, racial discrimination, *apartheid* and neo-colonialism in all its forms continue to be among the greatest obstacles to the full emancipation and progress of the developing countries and all the peoples involved. The benefits of technological progress are not shared equitably by all members of the international community. The developing countries, which constitute 70 percent of the world population, account for only 30 percent of the world's income. It has proved impossible to achieve an even and balanced development of the international community under the existing international economic order. The gap between the developed and the developing countries continues to widen in a system which was established at a time when most of the developing countries did not even exist as independent States and which perpetuates inequality.

2. The present international economic order is in direct conflict with current developments in international political and economic relations. Since 1970, the world economy has experienced a series of grave crises which have had severe repercussions, especially on the developing countries because of their generally greater vulnerability to external economic impulses. The developing world has become a powerful factor that makes its influence felt in all fields of international activity. These irreversible changes in the relationship of forces in the world necessitate the active, full and equal participation of the developing countries in the formulation and application of all decisions that concern the international community.

3. All these changes have thrust into prominence the reality of interdependence of all the members of the world community. Current events have brought into sharp focus the realization that the interests of the developed countries and the interests of the developing countries can no longer be isolated from each other; that there is close interrelationship between the prosperity of the developed countries and the growth and development of the developing countries, and that the prosperity of the international community as a whole depends upon the prosperity of its constituent parts. International cooperation for development is the shared goal and common duty of all countries. Thus the political, economic, and social well-being of present and future generations depends more than ever on cooperation between all members of the international community on the basis of sovereign equality and the removal of the disequilibrium that exists between them.

4. The new international economic order should be founded on full respect for the following principles:

(a) Sovereign equality of States, self-determination of all peoples, inadmissibility of the acquisition of territories by force, territorial integrity and noninterference in the internal affairs of other States;

(b) Broadest cooperation of all the member States of the international community, based on equity, whereby the prevailing disparities in the world may be banished and prosperity secured for all;

(c) Full and effective participation on the basis of equality of all countries in the solving of world economic problems in the common interest of all countries, bearing in mind the necessity to ensure the accelerated development of all the developing countries, while devoting particular attention to the adoption of special measures in favour of the least developed, land-locked and island developing countries as well as those developing countries most seriously affected by economic crises and natural calamities, without losing sight of the interests of other developing countries;

(d) Every country has the right to adopt the economic and social system that it deems to be the most appropriate for its own development and not to be subjected to discrimination of any kind as a result;

(e) Full permanent sovereignty of every State over its natural resources and all economic activities. In order to safeguard these resources, each State is entitled to exercise effective control over them and their exploitation with means suitable to its own situation, including the right to nationalization or transfer of ownership to its nationals, this right being an expression of the full permanent sovereignty of the State. No State may be subjected to economic, political, or any other type of coercion to prevent the free and full exercise of this inalienable right;

(f) All States, territories and peoples under foreign occupation, alien and colonial domination or *apartheid* have the right to restitution and full compensation for the exploitation and depletion of, and damages to, the natural and all other resources of those States, territories and peoples;

(g) Regulation and supervision of the activities of transnational corporations by taking measures in the interest of the national economies of the countries where such transnational corporations operate on the basis of the full sovereignty of those countries;

(h) Right of the developing countries and the peoples of territories under colonial and racial domination and foreign occupation to achieve their liberation and to regain effective control over their natural resources and economic activities;

(i) Extending of assistance to developing countries, peoples, and territories under colonial and alien domination, foreign occupation, racial discrimination or *apartheid* or which are subjected to economic, political or any other type of measures to coerce them in order to obtain from them the subordination of the exercise of their sovereign rights and to secure from them advantages of any kind, and to neocolonialism in all its forms and which have established or are endeavouring to establish effective control over their natural resources and economic activities that have been or are still under foreign control;

(j) Just and equitable relationship between the prices of raw materials, primary products, manufactured and semimanufactured goods exported by developing countries and the prices of raw materials, primary commodities, manufactures, capital goods and equipment imported by them with the aim of bringing about sustained improvement in their unsatisfactory terms of trade and the expansion of the world economy;

(k) Extension of active assistance to developing countries by the whole international community, free of any political or military conditions;

(l) Ensuring that one of the main aims of the reformed international monetary system shall be the promotion of the development of the developing countries and the adequate flow of real resources to them;

(m) Improving the competitiveness of natural materials facing competition from synthetic substitutes;

(n) Preferential and nonreciprocal treatment for developing countries wherever feasible, in all fields of international economic cooperation, wherever feasible;

(o) Securing favourable conditions for the transfer of financial resources to developing countries;

(p) To give to the developing countries access to the achievements of modern science and technology, to promote the transfer of technology and the creation of indigenous technology for the benefit of the developing countries in forms and in accordance with procedures which are suited to their economies;

(q) Necessity for all States to put an end to the waste of natural resources, including food products;

(r) The need for developing countries to concentrate all their resources for the cause of development;

(s) Strengthening—through individual and collective actions—of mutual economic, trade, financial and technical cooperation among the developing countries mainly on a preferential basis;

(t) Facilitating the role which producers associations may play, within the framework of international cooperation, and in pursuance of their aims, *inter alia,* assisting in promotion of sustained growth of world economy and accelerating development of developing countries.

5. The unanimous adoption of the International Development Strategy for the Second Development Decade was an important step in the promotion of international economic cooperation on a just and equitable basis. The accelerated implementation of obligations and commitments assumed by the international community within the framework of the Strategy, particularly those concerning imperative development needs of developing countries, would contribute significantly to the fulfilment of the aims and objectives of the present Declaration.

6. The United Nations as a universal organization should be capable of dealing with problems of international economic cooperation in a comprehensive manner and ensuring equally the interests of all countries. It must have an even greater role in the establishment of a new international economic order. The Charter of Economic Rights and Duties of States, for the preparation of which this Declaration will provide an additional source of inspiration, will constitute a significant contribution in this respect. All the States Members of the United Nations are therefore called upon to exert maximum efforts with a view to securing the implementation of this Declaration, which is one of the principal guarantees for the creation of better conditions for all peoples to reach a life worthy of human dignity.

7. This Declaration on the Establishment of a New International Economic Order shall be one of the most important bases of economic relations between all peoples and all nations.

16. Programme of Action on the Establishment of a New International Economic Order

Adopted by Resolution 3202(S–VI) of the General Assembly at its Sixth Special Session on 1 May 1974. General Assembly, Report A/9556 (Part II).

The General Assembly
Adopts the following Programme of Action:

PROGRAMME OF ACTION ON THE ESTABLISHMENT OF A NEW INTERNATIONAL ECONOMIC ORDER

In view of the continuing severe economic imbalance in the relations between developed and developing countries, and in the context of the constant and continuing aggravation of the imbalance of the economies of the developing countries and the consequent need for the mitigation of their current economic difficulties, urgent and effective measures need to be taken by the international community to assist the developing countries while devoting particular attention to the least developed, land-locked and island developing countries and those developing countries most seriously affected by economic crises and natural calamities leading to serious retardation of development processes.

With a view to ensuring the application of the Declaration on the Establishment of a New International Economic Order it will be necessary to adopt and implement within a specified period a programme of action of unprecedented scope and to bring about maximum economic cooperation and understanding among all States, particularly between developed and developing countries based on the principles of dignity and sovereign equality.

PROGRAMME OF ACTION

I. *Fundamental problems of raw materials and primary commodities as related to trade and development*
1. *Raw materials*
   All efforts should be made:
   (a) To put an end to all forms of foreign occupation, racial discrimination, *apartheid,* colonial, neocolonial and alien

domination and exploitation through the exercise of permanent sovereignty over natural resources.

(b) To take measures for the recovery, exploitation, development, marketing and distribution of natural resources, particularly of developing countries, to serve their national interests, to promote collective self-reliance among them, and to strengthen mutually beneficial international economic cooperation with a view to bringing about the accelerated development of developing countries.

(c) To facilitate the functioning, and to further the aims, of producers associations, including their joint marketing arrangements, orderly commodity trading, improvement in export income of producing developing countries and in their terms of trade, and sustained growth of world economy for the benefit of all.

(d) To evolve a just and equitable relationship between prices of raw materials, primary commodities, semi-manufactured and manufactured goods exported by developing countries and the raw materials, primary commodities, food, manufactured and semi-manufactured goods and capital equipment imported by them and to work for a link between the prices of exports of developing countries and the prices of their imports from developed countries.

(e) To take measures to reverse the continued trend of stagnation or decline in the real price of several commodities exported by developing countries, despite a general rise in commodity prices, resulting in a decline in the export earnings of these developing countries.

(f) To take measures to expand the markets for natural products in relation to synthetics, taking into account the interests of the developing countries, and to utilize fully the ecological advantages of these products.

(g) To take measures to promote the processing of raw materials in the producer developing countries.

2. *Food*

All efforts should be made:

(a) To take full account of specific problems of developing countries, particularly in times of food shortages, in the international efforts connected with the food problem.

(b) To take into account that, owing to lack of means, some developing countries have vast potentialities of unexploited or underexploited land which, if reclaimed and put into practical use, would contribute considerably to the solution of the food crisis.

(c) By the international community to undertake concrete and speedy measures with a view to arresting desertification, salination, and damage by locusts or any other similar phenomenon involving several developing countries, particularly in Africa, and gravely affecting the capacity of agricultural production of these countries. Furthermore, the international community should assist the developing countries affected by this phenomenon to develop the affected zones with a view to contributing to the solution of their food problems.

(d) To refrain from damaging or deteriorating natural resources and food resources, especially those derived from the sea, by preventing pollution and taking appropriate steps to protect and reconstitute those resources.

(e) By developed countries in evolving their policies relating to production, stocks, imports and exports of food to take full account of the interests of:

    (i) Developing importing countries which cannot afford high prices for their imports, and

    (ii) Developing exporting countries which need increased market opportunities for their exports.

(f) To ensure that developing countries can import the necessary quantity of food without undue strain on their foreign exchange resources and without unpredictable deterioration in their balance of payments. In this context, special measures should be taken in respect of the least developed, the land-locked and island developing countries as well as those developing countries most seriously affected by economic crises and natural calamities.

(g) To ensure that concrete measures to increase food production and storage facilities in developing countries should be introduced, *inter alia,* by ensuring an increase in all available essential inputs, including fertilizers, from developed countries on favourable terms.

(h) To promote exports of food products of developing countries through just and equitable arrangements, *inter alia,* by the progressive elimination of such protective and other measures as constitute unfair competition.

3. *General trade*

   All efforts should be made:

   (a) To take the following measures for the amelioration of terms of trade of developing countries and concrete steps to eliminate chronic trade deficits of developing countries:

   (i) Fulfilment of relevant commitments already undertaken in the United Nations Conference on Trade and Development and in the International Development Strategy.

   (ii) Improved access to markets in developed countries through the progressive removal of tariff and non-tariff barriers and of restrictive business practices.

   (iii) Expeditious formulation of commodity agreements where appropriate, in order to regulate as necessary and to stabilize the world markets for raw materials and primary commodities.

   (iv) Preparation of an overall integrated programme, setting out guidelines and taking into account the current work in this field, for a comprehensive range of commodities of export interest to developing countries.

   (v) Where products of developing countries compete with the domestic production in developed countries, each developed country should facilitate the expansion of imports from developing countries and provide a fair and reasonable opportunity to the developing countries to share in the growth of the market.

   (vi) When the importing developed countries derive receipts from customs duties, taxes and other protective measures applied to imports of these products, consideration should be given to the claim of the developing countries that these receipts should be reimbursed in full to the exporting developing countries or devoted to providing additional resources to meet their development needs.

   (vii) Developed countries should make appropriate adjustments in their economies so as to facilitate the expansion and diversification of imports from developing countries and thereby permit a rational, just and equitable international division of labour.

   (viii) Setting up general principles for pricing policy for exports of commodities of developing countries, with a view to rectifying and achieving satisfactory terms of trade for them.

(ix) Until satisfactory terms of trade are achieved for all developing countries, consideration should be given to alternative means, including improved compensatory financing schemes for meeting the development needs of developing countries concerned.

(x) Implementation, improvement and enlargement of the Generalized System of Preferences for exports of agricultural primary commodities, manufactures and semi-manufactures from developing to developed countries and consideration of its extension to commodities, including those which are processed or semi-processed. Developing countries which are or will be sharing their existing tariff advantages in some developed countries as the result of the introduction and eventual enlargement of the Generalized System of Preferences should, as a matter of urgency, be granted new openings in the markets of other developed countries which should offer them export opportunities that at least compensate for the sharing of those advantages.

(xi) Setting up of buffer stocks within the framework of commodity arrangements and their financing by international financial institutions, wherever necessary, the developed countries and—when they are able to do so—by the developing countries, the aim being to favour the producing and consuming developing countries and to contribute to the expansion of world trade as a whole.

(xii) In cases where natural materials can satisfy the requirements of the market, new investment for the expansion of capacity of production of synthetic materials and substitutes should not be made.

(b) To be guided by the principles of nonreciprocity and preferential treatment of developing countries in multilateral trade negotiations between developed and developing countries, and to seek sustained and additional benefits for the international trade of developing countries, so as to achieve a substantial increase in their foreign exchange earnings, diversification of their exports and acceleration of the rate of their economic growth.

Transportation and insurance:

All efforts should be made:

(i) To promote an increasing and equitable participation of developing countries in the world shipping tonnage;

(ii) To arrest and reduce the ever-increasing freight rates in order to reduce the cost of imports to, and exports from, the developing countries;

(iii) To minimize cost of insurance and reinsurance for developing countries and to assist the growth of domestic insurance and reinsurance markets in developing countries and the establishment to this end, where appropriate, of institutions in these countries or at the regional level;

(iv) To ensure the early implementation of the code of conduct for liner conferences.

(v) To take urgent measures to increase the import and export capability of the least developed countries and to offset the disadvantages of the adverse geographic situation of land-locked countries, particularly with regard to their transportation and transit costs, as well as developing island countries in order to increase their trading ability.

(vi) By the developed countries to refrain from imposing measures or implementing policies designed to prevent the importation, at equitable prices, of commodities from the developing countries or from frustrating the implementation of legitimate measures and policies adopted by the developing countries in order to improve prices and encourage the export of such commodities.

II. *International monetary system and financing of development of developing countries*

All efforts should be made:

1. To reform the international monetary system with, *inter alia,* the following objectives:

(a) Measures to check the inflation already experienced by the developed countries, to prevent it from being transferred to developing countries and to study and devise possible arrangements within the International Monetary Fund to mitigate the effects of inflation in developed countries on the economies of developing countries;

(b) Measures to eliminate the instability of the international monetary system, in particular the uncertainty of the exchange rates especially as it affects adversely the trade in commodities;

(c) Maintenance of the real value of the currency reserves of the developing countries by preventing their erosion from inflation and exchange rate depreciation of reserve currencies;

(d) Full and effective participation of developing countries in all phases of decision-making for the formulation of an equitable and durable monetary system and adequate participation of developing countries in all bodies entrusted with this reform and, particularly, in the Board of Governors;

(e) Adequate and orderly creation of additional liquidity with particular regard to the needs of the developing countries through the additional allocation of Special Drawing Rights based on the concept of world liquidity needs to be appropriately revised in the light of the new international environment. Any creation of international liquidity should be made through international multilateral mechanisms;

(f) Early establishment of a link between Special Drawing Rights and additional development financing in the interest of developing countries, consistent with the monetary characteristics of Special Drawing Rights;

(g) The International Monetary Fund should review. the relevant provisions in order to ensure effective participation by developing countries in the decision-making process;

(h) Arrangements to promote an increasing net transfer of real resources from the developed to the developing countries;

(i) Review the methods of operation of the International Monetary Fund, in particular the terms for both credit repayments and "standby" arrangements, the system of compensatory financing, and the terms of the financing of commodity buffer stocks, so as to enable the developing countries to make more effective use of them.

2. To take the following urgent measures to finance the development of developing countries and to meet the balance-of-payment crises in the developing world:

(a) Implementation at an accelerated pace by the developed countries of the time-bound programme, as already laid down in the International Development Strategy for the

Second United Nations Development Decade, for the net amount of financial resource transfers to developing countries. Increase in the official component of the net amount of financial resource transfers to developing countries so as to meet and even to exceed the target of the International Development Strategy;

(b) International financing institutions to effectively play their role as development financing banks without discrimination on account of the political or economic system of any member country, assistance being united;

(c) More effective participation by developing countries, whether recipients or contributors, in the decision-making process in the competent organs of the International Bank for Reconstruction and Development and the International Development Association through the establishment of a more equitable pattern of voting rights;

(d) Exemption, wherever possible, of the developing countries from all import and capital outflow controls imposed by the developed countries;

(e) Promotion of foreign investment both public and private from developed to developing countries in accordance with the needs and requirements in sectors of their economies as determined by the recipient countries;

(f) Appropriate urgent measures, including international action, to be taken to mitigate adverse consequences for the current and future development of developing countries arising from the burden of external debt contracted on hard terms;

(g) Debt renegotiation on a case-by-case basis with a view to concluding agreements on debt cancellation, moratorium, rescheduling, or interest subsidization;

(h) International financial institutions to take into account the special situation of each developing country in reorienting their lending policies to suit these urgent needs. There is also need for improvement in practices of international financial institutions in regard to, *inter alia,* development financing and international monetary problems;

(i) Appropriate steps to be taken to give priority to the least developed, land-locked and island developing countries and to the countries most seriously affected by economic crises and natural calamities, in the availability of loans for development purposes which should include more favourable terms and conditions.

III. *Industrialization*

All efforts should be made by the international community to take measures to encourage the industrialization of the developing countries. To this end:

(a) The developed countries should respond favourably, within the framework of their official aid as well as international financial institutions, to the requests of developing countries for the financing of industrial projects;

(b) The developed countries should encourage investors to finance industrial production projects, particularly export-oriented production, in developing countries, in agreement with the latter and within the context of their laws and regulations;

(c) With a view to bringing about a new international economic structure which should increase the share of the developing countries in world industrial production, the developed countries and the agencies of the United Nations system, is cooperation with the developing countries, should contribute to setting up new industrial capacities including raw material and commodity transforming facilities as a matter of priority in the developing countries that produce those raw materials and commodities;

(d) Continue and expand, with the aid of the developed countries and the international institutions, the operational and instruction-oriented technical assistance programmes including vocational training and management development of national personnel of the developing countries in the light of their special development requirements.

IV. *Transfer of technology*

All efforts should be made:

(a) To formulate an international code of conduct for the transfer of technology corresponding to needs and conditions prevalent in developing countries;

(b) To give access on improved terms to modern technology and the adaptation of that technology, as appropriate, to specific economic, social and ecological conditions and varying stages of development in developing countries;

(c) To expand significantly in assistance from developed to developing countries in programmes of research and development and creation of suitable indigenous technology;

(d) To adapt commercial practices governing transfer of technology to the requirements of the developing countries, and to prevent abuse of the rights of sellers;

(e) To promote international cooperation in research and development, in exploration and exploitation, conservation and legitimate utilization of natural resources and all sources of energy;

In taking the above measures, the special needs of the least developed and land-locked countries should be borne in mind.

V. *Regulation and control over the activities of transnational corporations*

All efforts should be made to formulate adoption and implementation of an international code of conduct for transnational corporations in order to:

(a) Prevent interference in the internal affairs of the countries where they operate and their collaboration with racist régimes and colonial administrations;

(b) Regulate their activities in host countries, to eliminate restrictive business practices and to conform to the national development plans and objectives of developing countries, and in this context facilitate, as necessary, review and revision of previously concluded arrangements;

(c) Bring about assistance, transfer of technology and management skills to developing countries on equitable and favourable terms;

(d) Regulate the repatriation of the profits accruing from their operations, taking into account the legitimate interests of all parties concerned;

(e) Promote reinvestment of their profits in developing countries.

VI. *Charter of Economic Rights and Duties of States*

The Charter of Economics Rights and Duties of States, the draft of which is presently being prepared by a working group of the United Nations and which the General Assembly has already expressed the intention of adopting at its forthcoming twenty-ninth session, shall constitute an effective instrument towards the establishment of a new system of international economic relations based on equity, sovereign equality, and interdependence of the interests of developed and developing countries. It is therefore of vital importance that the charter be adopted by the General Assembly at its next regular session.

VII. *Promotion of cooperation among developing countries*

1. Collective self-reliance and growing cooperation among developing countries will further strengthen their role in the new international economic order. Developing countries, with a view

to expanding cooperation at the regional, subregional and inter-regional levels, should take further steps *inter alia:*

(a) To support the establishment and/or improvement of appropriate mechanism to defend the prices of their export-able commodities and to improve access to and to stabilize markets for them. In this context the increasingly effective mobilization by the whole group of oil exporting countries of their natural resources for the benefit of their economic development is to be welcomed. At the same time there is the paramount need for cooperation among the developing countries in evolving urgently and in a spirit of solidarity all possible means to assist developing countries to cope with the immediate problems resulting from this legitimate and perfectly justified action. The measures already taken in this regard are a positive indication of the evolving coop-eration between developing countries.

(b) To protect their inalienable right to permanent sovereignty over their natural resources.

(c) To promote, establish or strengthen economic integration at the regional and subregional levels.

(d) To increase considerably their imports from other develop-ing countries.

(e) No developing country should accord to imports from developed countries more favourable treatment than that accorded to imports from developing countries. Taking in-to account the existing international agreements, current limitations and possibilities and also their future evolution, preferential treatment should be given to the procurement of import requirements from other developing countries. Wherever possible, preferential treatment should be given to imports from developing countries and the exports of those countries.

(f) To promote close cooperation in the fields of finance, credit relations and monetary issues, including the develop-ment of credit relations on a preferential basis and on favourable terms.

(g) To strengthen efforts which are already being made by developing countries to utilize available financial resources for financing development in the developing countries through investment, financing of export-oriented and emergency projects and other long-term assistance.

(h) To promote and establish effective instruments of cooperation in the fields of industry, science and technology, transport, shipping and mass communication media.

2. Developed countries should support initiatives in the regional subregional and interregional cooperation of developing countries through the extension of financial and technical assistance through more effective and concrete actions, particularly in the field of commercial policy.

VIII. *Assistance in the exercise of permanent sovereignty of States over natural resources*

All efforts should be made:

(a) To defeat attempts to prevent the free and effective exercise of the rights of every State to full and permanent sovereignty over its natural resources.

(b) By competent agencies of the United Nations system to meet requests for assistance from developing countries in connexion with the operation of nationalized means of production.

IX. *Strengthening the role of the United Nations systems in the field of international economic cooperation*

1. In furtherance of the objectives of the International Development Strategy and in accordance with the aims and objectives of the Declaration on the Establishment of a New International Economic Order, all Member States pledge to make full use of the United Nations system in the implementation of this Programme of Action they have jointly adopted in working for the establishment of a new international economic order and therby strengthening the role of the United Nations in the field of world-wide cooperation for economic and social development.

2. The General Assembly of the United Nations shall conduct an overall review of the implementation of the Programme of Action as a priority item. All the activities of the United Nations system to be undertaken under the Programme of Action as well as those already planned, such as the World Population Conference, the World Food Conference, the Second General Conference of the United Nations Industrial Development Organization and the mid-term review and appraisal of the International Development Strategy, should be so directed as to enable the special session of the General Assembly on development, called for under General Assembly resolution 3172 (XXVIII), to make its full contribution to the establishment of the new international economic order. All Member States are

urged jointly and individually to direct their efforts and policies towards the success of that special session.

3. The Economic and Social Council shall define the policy framework and coordinate the activities of all organizations, institutions and subsidiary bodies within the United Nations system which shall be entrusted with the task of implementing this Programme. In order to enable the Economic and Social Council to carry out its tasks effectively:

   (a) All organizations, institutions and subsidiary bodies concerned within the United Nations system shall submit to the Economic and Social Council progress reports on the implementation of this Programme within their respective fields of competence as often as necessary, but not less than once a year.

   (b) The Economic and Social Council shall examine the progress reports as a matter of urgency, to which end it may be convened as necessary, in special sessions or, if need be, may function continuously. It shall draw the attention of the General Assembly to the problem and difficulties arising in connexion with the implementation of this Programme.

4. All organizations, institutions, subsidiary bodies and conferences of the United Nations system are entrusted with the implementation of this Programme of Action. The activities of the United Nations Conference on Trade and Development (established under General Assembly resolution 1995 (XIX)) should be strengthened for the purpose of following in collaboration with other competent organizations the development of international trade in raw materials throughout the world.

5. Urgent and effective measures should be taken to review the lending policies of international financial institutions, taking into account the special situation of each developing country, to suit urgent needs; to improve the practices of these institutions in regard to, *inter alia,* development financing and international monetary problems, and to ensure more effective participation by developing countries—whether recipients or contributors— in the decision-making process through appropriate revision of the pattern of voting rights.

6. The developed countries and others in a position to do so should contribute substantially to the various organizations, programmes and funds established within the United Nations system for the purpose of accelerating economic and social development in developing countries.

7. This Programme of Action complements and strengthens the goals and objectives embodied in the International Development Strategy as well as the new measures formulated by the General Assembly at its twenty-eighth session to offset the short-falls in achieving those goals and objectives.

8. The implementation of the Programme of Action should be taken into account at the time of medium-term review and appraisal of the International Development Strategy for the Second United Nations Development Decade. New commitments, changes, additions and adaptations in the International Development Strategy should be made, as appropriate, taking into account the Declaration on the Establishment of a New International Economic Order and this Programme of Action.

X. *Special Programme*

The General Assembly adopts the following Special Programme, including particularly emergency measures to mitigate the difficulties of the developing countries most seriously affected by economic crisis bearing in mind the particular problem of the least developed and land-locked countries:

The General Assembly,

Considering that:

(a) The sharp increase in the prices of their essential imports such as food, fertilizers, energy products, capital goods, equipment and services, including transportation and transit costs, have gravely exacerbated the increasingly adverse terms of trade of a number of developing countries, added to the burden of their foreign debt and, cumulatively, created a situation which, if left untended, will make it impossible for them to finance their essential imports and development and result in a further deterioration in the levels and conditions of life in these countries. The present crisis is the outcome of all the problems that have accumulated over the years: in the field of trade, in monetary reform, the world-wide inflationary situation, inadequacy and delay in provision of financial assistance and many other similar problems in the economic and developmental fields. In facing the crisis, this complex situation must be borne in mind so as to ensure that the special programme adopted by the international community provides emergency relief and timely assistance to the most seriously affected countries. Simultaneously, steps are taken to resolve these outstanding problems through a fundamental restructuring of the world economic system, in order to allow these countries while solving the present difficulties to reach an acceptable level of development.

(b) The special measures adopted to assist the most seriously affected countries must encompass not only the relief which they require on an emergency basis to maintain their import requirements but also, beyond that, steps to consciously promote the capacity of these countries to produce and earn more. Unless such a comprehensive approach is adopted there is every likelihood that the difficulties of the most seriously affected countries may be perpetuated. Nevertheless, the first and most pressing task of the international community is to enable these countries to meet the shortfall in their balance of payments positions. But this must be simultaneously supplemented by additional development assistance to maintain and thereafter accelerate their rate of economic development.

(c) The countries which have been most seriously affected are precisely those which are at the greatest disadvantage in the world economy: the least developed, the land-locked and other low-income developing countries as well as other developing countries whose economies have been seriously dislocated as a result of the present economic crisis, natural calamities, and foreign aggression and occupation. An indication of the countries thus affected, the level of the impact on their economies and the kind of relief and assistance they require can be assessed on the basis, *inter alia,* of the following criteria:

   (i)   Low *per capita* income as a reflection of relative poverty, low productivity, low level of technology and development.

   (ii) Sharp increase in their import cost of essentials relative to export earnings.

   (iii) High ratio of debt servicing to export earnings.

   (iv) Insufficiency in export earnings, comparative inelasticity of export incomes and unavailability of exportable surplus.

   (v)   Low level of foreign exchange reserves or their inadequacy for requirements.

   (vi) Adverse impact of higher transportation and transit costs.

   (vii) Relative importance of foreign trade in development process.

(d) The assessment of the extent and nature of the impact on the economies of the most seriously affected countries must be made flexible keeping in mind the present uncertainty in the world economy, the adjustment policies that may be adopted by the developed countries, the flow of capital and investment. Estimates of the payments situation and needs of these countries can be assessed and projected reliably only on the basis of their average performance over a number of years. Long-term projections, at this time, cannot but be uncertain.

(e) It is important that in the special measures to mitigate the difficulties of the most seriously affected countries all the developed countries as well as developing countries should contribute according to their level of development and the capacity and strength of their economies. It is notable that some developing countries, despite their own difficulties and development needs, have shown a willingness to play a concrete and helpful role in ameliorating the difficulties faced by the poorer developing countries. The various initiatives and measures taken recently by certain developing countries with adequate resources on a bilateral and multilateral basis to contribute to alleviating the difficulties of other developing countries are a reflection of their commitment to the principle of effective economic cooperation among developing countries.

(f) The response of the developed countries which have by far the greater capacity to assist the affected countries in overcoming their present difficulties must be commensurate with their responsibilities. Their assistance should be in addition to the presently available levels of aid. They should fulfill and if possible exceed the targets of the International Development Strategy on financial assistance to the developing countries, especially that relating to official development assistance. They should also give serious consideration to the cancellation of the external debts of the most seriously affected countries. This would provide the simplest and quickest relief to the affected countries. Favourable consideration should also be given to debt moratorium and rescheduling. The current situation should not lead the industrialized countries to adopt what will ultimately prove to be a self-defeating policy aggravating the present crisis.

Recalling the constructive proposals made by His Imperial Majesty the Shahanshah of Iran and His Excellency President Boumediène of Algeria,

1. *Decides* to launch a Special Programme to provide emergency relief and development assistance to the developing countries most seriously affected, as a matter of urgency, and for the period of time necessary, at least until the end of the Second

United Nations Development Decade, to help them overcome their present difficulties and to achieve self-sustaining economic development;

2. *Decides* as a first step in the Special Programme to request the Secretary-General to launch an emergency operation to provide timely relief to the most seriously affected developing countries as defined in paragraph 3 of the preamble with the aim of maintaining unimpaired essential imports for the duration of the coming 12 months and to invite the industrialized countries and other potential contributors to announce their contributions for emergency assistance or intimate their intention to do so by 15 June 1974 to be provided through bilateral or multilateral channels, taking into account commitments and measures of assistance announced or already taken by some countries and *further requests* the Secretary-General to report the progress of the emergency operation to the twenty-ninth session of the General Assembly through the Economic and Social Council at its fifty-seventh session;

3. *Calls upon* the industrialized countries and other potential contributors to extend immediate relief and assistance to the most seriously affected countries which must be of an order of magnitude that is commensurate with the needs of these countries. Such assistance should be in addition to the existing level of aid and provided at a very early date to the maximum possible extent on grant basis and where not possible on soft terms. The disbursement and relevant operational procedures and terms must reflect this exceptional situation. The assistance could be provided either through bilateral or multilateral channels, including such new institutions and facilities that have been or are to be set up. The special measures may include the following:

   (a) Special arrangements on particularly favourable terms and conditions including possible subsidies for and assured supplies of essential commodities and goods;

   (b) Deferred payments for all or part of imports of essential commodities and goods;

   (c) Commodity assistance, including food aid, on grant basis or deferred payments in local currencies, bearing in mind that this should not adversely affect the exports of developing countries;

   (d) Long-term suppliers' credits on easy terms;

   (e) Long-term financial assistance on concessionary terms;

    (f) Drawings from special International Monetary Fund facilities on concessional terms;

    (g) Establishment of a link between the creation of Special Drawing Rights and development assistance, taking into account the additional financial requirement of the most seriously affected countires;

    (h) Subsidies, provided bilaterally or multilaterally, for interest on funds available on commercial terms borrowed by most seriously affected countries;

    (i) Debt renegotiation on a case-by-case basis with a view to concluding agreements on debt cancellation, moratorium or rescheduling;

    (j) Provision on more favourable terms of capital goods and technical assistance to accelerate the industrialization of the affected countries;

    (k) Investment in industrial and development projects on favourable terms;

    (l) Subsidizing the additional transit and transport costs, especially of the land-locked countries;

4. *Appeals* to the developed countries to consider favourably the cancellation, moratorium or rescheduling of the debts of the most seriously affected developing countries on their request as an important contribution to mitigating the grave and urgent difficulties of these countries;

5. *Decides* to establish a Special Fund under the auspices of the United Nations, through voluntary contributions from industrialized countries and other potential contributors, as a part of the Special Programme, to provide emergency relief and development assistance, which will commence its operations at the latest by 1 January 1975;

6. *Establishes* an *Ad Hoc* Committee on the Special Programme, composed of thirty-six Member States appointed by the President of the General Assembly after appropriate consultations, bearing in mind the purposes of the Special Fund and its terms of references, to:

    (a) Make recommendations on the scope, machinery, modes of operation etc., of the Special Fund, taking into account the need for:

        (i) Equitable representation on its governing body;

        (ii) Equitable distribution of its resources;

        (iii) Full utilization of the services and facilities of existing international organizations;

(iv) The possibility of merging the United Nations Capital Development Fund with the operations of the Special Fund;

(v) A central monitoring body to oversee the various measures being taken both bilaterally and multilaterally;

and, to this end, bearing in mind the different ideas and proposals made at the sixth special session, including those contained in documents A/AC.166/L.15 and A/PV.2208 and comments thereon and the possibility of utilizing the Special Fund to provide an alternative channel for normal development assistance after the emergency period;

(b) Monitor, pending commencement of the operations of the Special Fund, the various measures being taken both bilaterally and multilaterally to assist the most seriously affected countries;

(c) Prepare, on the basis of information provided by the countries concerned and by appropriate agencies of the United Nations system, a broad assessment of:

(i) The magnitude of the difficulties facing the most seriously affected countries;

(ii) The kind and quantities of the commodities and goods essentially required by them;

(iii) Their need for financial assistance;

(iv) Their technical assistance requirements, including especially access to technology;

7. *Requests* the Secretary-General of the United Nations, the Secretary-General of the United Nations Conference on Trade and Development, the President of the International Bank for Reconstruction and Development, the Managing Director of the International Monetary Fund, the Administrator of the United Nations Development Programme and the heads of the other competent international organizations to assist the *Ad Hoc* Committee in performing the functions assigned to it under operative paragraph 6, and help, as appropriate, in the operations of the Special Fund;

8. *Requests* the International Monetary Fund to expedite decisions on:

(a) The establishment of an extended special facility with a view to enabling the most seriously affected developing countries to participate in it on favourable terms;

    (b) The creation of Special Drawing Rights and the early establishment of the link between the allocation of Special Drawing Rights and development financing; and

    (c) The establishment and operation of the proposed new special facility to extend credits and subsidize interest charges on commercial funds borrowed by Member States bearing in mind the interest of the developing countries and especially the addition financial requirements of the most seriously affected countries;

9. *Requests* the World Bank Group and the International Monetary Fund to place their managerial, financial and technical services at the disposal of Governments contributing to emergency financial relief so as to enable them to assist without delay in channelling funds to the recipients, making such institutional and procedural changes as may be required;

10. *Invites* the United Nations Development Programme to take the necessary steps, particularly at the country level, to respond on an emergency basis to requests for additional assistance which it may be called upon to render within the framework of the Special Programme;

11. *Requests* the *Ad Hoc* Committee to submit its report and recommendations to the Economic and Social Council at its fifty-seventh session and invites the Council, on the basis of its consideration of this report, to submit suitable recommendations to the General Assembly at its twenty-ninth session;

12. *Decides* to consider, within the framework of a new international economic order, as a matter of high priority at the twenty-ninth session of the General Assembly, the question of special measures for the most seriously affected countries.

17. Charter of Economic Rights and Duties of States

Adopted by Resolution 3281 (XXIX) of the General Assembly on 12 December 1974. G.A. Report A/9946.

PREAMBLE

The General Assembly,

Reaffirming the fundamental purposes of the United Nations, in particular, the maintenance of international peace and security, the development of friendly relations among nations and the achievement of international cooperation in solving international problems in the economic and social fields,

Affirming the need for strengthening international cooperation in these fields,

Reaffirming further the need for strengthening international cooperation for development,

Declaring that it is a fundamental purpose of this Charter to promote the establishment of the new international economic order, based on equity, sovereign equality, interdependence, common interest and cooperation among all States, irrespective of their economic and social systems,

Desirous of contributing to the creation of conditions for:

(a) The attainment of wider prosperity among all countries and of higher standards of living for all peoples,

(b) The promotion by the entire international community of economic and social progress of all countries, especially developing countries,

(c) The encouragement of cooperation, on the basis of mutual advantage and equitable benefits for all peace-loving States which are willing to carry out the provisions of this Charter, in the economic, trade, scientific, and technical fields, regardless of political, economic, or social systems,

(d) The overcoming of main obstacles in the way of the economic development of the developing countries,

(e) The acceleration of the economic growth of developing countries with a view to bridging the economic gap between developing and developed countries,

(f) The protection, preservation and enhancement of the environment,

Mindful of the need to establish and maintain a just and equitable economic and social order through:

(a) The achievement of more rational and equitable international economic relations and the encouragement of structural changes in the world economy,

(b) The creation of conditions which permit the further expansion of trade and intensification of economic cooperation among all nations,

(c) The strengthening of the economic independence of developing countries,

(d) The establishment and promotion of international economic relations, taking into account the agreed differences in development of the developing countries and their specific needs,

Determined to promote collective economic security for development, in particular of the developing countries, with strict respect for the sovereign equality of each State and through the cooperation of the entire international community,

Considering that genuine cooperation among States, based on joint consideration of and concerted action regarding international economic problems, is essential for fulfilling the international community's common desire to achieve a just and rational development of all parts of the world,

Stressing the importance of ensuring appropriate conditions for the conduct of normal economic relations among all States, irrespective of differences in social and economic systems, and for the full respect for the rights of all peoples, as well as the strengthening of instruments of international economic cooperation as means for the consolidation of peace for the benefit of all,

Convinced of the need to develop a system of international economic relations on the basis of sovereign equality, mutual and equitable benefit and the close interrelationship of the interests of all States,

Reiterating that the responsibility for the development of every country rests primarily upon itself but that concomitant and effective international cooperation is an essential factor for the full achievement of its own development goals,

Firmly convinced of the urgent need to evolve a substantially improved system of international economic relations,

Solemnly adopts the present Charter of Economic Rights and Duties of States.

I. FUNDAMENTALS OF INTERNATIONAL
ECONOMIC RELATIONS

Economic as well as political and other relations among States shall be governed, *inter alia,* by the following principles:

(a) Sovereignty, territorial integrity and political independence of States;
(b) Sovereign equality of all States;
(c) Nonaggression;
(d) Nonintervention;
(e) Mutual and equitable benefit;
(f) Peaceful coexistence;
(g) Equal rights and self-determination of peoples;
(h) Peaceful settlement of disputes;
(i) Remedying of injustices which have been brought about by force and which deprive a nation of the natural means necessary for its normal development;
(j) Fulfilment in good faith of international obligations;
(k) Respect for human rights and fundamental freedoms;
(l) No attempt to seek hegemony and spheres of influence;
(m) Promotion of international social justice;
(n) International cooperation for development;
(o) Free access to and from the sea by land-locked countries within the framework of the above principles.

II. ECONOMIC RIGHTS AND DUTIES OF STATES
ARTICLE 1

Every State has the sovereign and inalienable right to choose its economic system as well as its political, social, and cultural systems in accordance with the will of its people, without outside interference, coercion or threat in any form whatsoever.

ARTICLE 2

1. Every State has and shall freely exercise full permanent sovereignty, including possession, use, and disposal, over all its wealth, natural resources and economic activities.

2. Each State has the right:

(a) To regulate and exercise authority over foreign investment within its national jurisdiction in accordance with its laws and regulations and in conformity with its national objectives and priorities. No State shall be compelled to grant preferential treatment to foreign investment;

(b) To regulate and supervise the activities of transnational corporations within its national jurisdiction and take measures to ensure that such activities comply with its laws, rules and regulations and conform with its economic and social policies. Transnational corporations shall not intervene in the internal affairs of a host State. Every State should, with full regard for its sovereign rights, cooperate with other States in the exercise of the right set forth in this subparagraph;

(c) To nationalize, expropriate or transfer ownership of foreign property, in which case appropriate compensation should be paid by the State adopting such measures, taking into account its relevant laws and regulations and all circumstances that the State considers pertinent. In any case where the question of compensation gives rise to a controversy, it shall be settled under the domestic law of the nationalizing State and by its tribunals, unless it is freely and mutually agreed by all States concerned that other peaceful means be sought on the basis of the sovereign equality of States and in accordance with the principle of free choice of means.

ARTICLE 3
In the exploitation of natural resources shared by two or more countries, each State must cooperate on the basis of a system of information and prior consultations in order to achieve optimum use of such resources without causing damage to the legitimate interest of others.

ARTICLE 4
Every State has the right to engage in international trade and other forms of economic cooperation irrespective of any differences in political, economic, and social systems. No State shall be subjected to discrimination of any kind based solely on such differences. In the pursuit of international trade and other forms of economic cooperation, every State is free to choose the forms of organization of its foreign economic relations and to enter into bilateral and multilateral arrangements consistent with its international obligations and with the needs of international economic cooperation.

ARTICLE 5
All States have the right to associate in organizations of primary commodity producers in order to develop their national economies to achieve stable financing for their development, and in pursuance of their aims, to assist in the promotion of sustained growth of the world economy, in particular accelerating the development of developing countries. Correspondingly all States have the duty to respect that right by refraining from applying economic and political measures that would limit it.

ARTICLE 6

It is the duty of States to contribute to the development of international trade of goods, particularly by means of arrangements and by the conclusion of long-term multilateral commodity agreements, where appropriate, and taking into account the interests of producers and consumers. All States share the responsibility to promote the regular flow and access of all commercial goods traded at stable, remunerative and equitable prices, thus contributing to the equitable development of the world economy, taking into account, in particular, the interests of developing countries.

ARTICLE 7

Every State has the primary responsibility to promote the economic, social and cultural development of its people. To this end, each State has the right and the responsibility to choose its means and goals of development, fully to mobilize and use its resources, to implement progressive economic and social reforms and to ensure the full participation of its people in the process and benefits of development. All States have the duty, individually and collectively, to cooperate in order to eliminate obstacles that hinder such mobilization and use.

ARTICLE 8

States should cooperate in facilitating more rational and equitable international economic relations and in encouraging structural changes in the context of a balanced world economy in harmony with the needs and interests of all countries, expecially developing countries, and should take appropriate measures to this end.

ARTICLE 9

All States have the responsibility to cooperate in the economic, social, cultural, scientific, and technological fields for the promotion of economic and social progress throughout the world, especially that of the developing countries.

ARTICLE 10

All States are juridically equal and, as equal members of the international community, have the right to participate fully and effectively in the international decision-making process in the solution of world economic, financial, and monetary problems, *inter alia,* through the appropriate international organizations in accordance with their existing and evolving rules, and to share equitably in the benefits resulting therefrom.

ARTICLE 11

All States should cooperate to strengthen and continuously improve the efficiency of international organizations in implementing measures to stimulate the general economic progress of all countries, particularly of developing countries, and therefore should cooperate to adapt them, when appropriate, to the changing needs of international economic cooperation.

ARTICLE 12

1. States have the right, in agreement with the parties concerned, to participate in subregional, regional, and interregional cooperation in the pursuit of their economic and social development. All States engaged in such cooperation have the duty to ensure that the policies of those groupings to which they belong correspond to the provisions of the Charter and are outward-looking, consistent with their international obligations and with the needs of international economic cooperation and have full regard for the legitimate interests of third countries, especially developing countries.

2. In the case of groupings to which the States concerned have transferred or may transfer certain competences as regards matters that come within the scope of the present Charter, its provisions shall also apply to those groupings, in regard to such matters, consistent with the responsibilities of such States as members of such groupings. Those States shall cooperate in the observance by the groupings of the provisions of this Charter.

ARTICLE 13

1. Every State has the right to benefit from the advances and developments in science and technology for the acceleration of its economic and social development.

2. All States should promote international scientific and technological cooperation and the transfer of technology, with proper regard for all legitimate interests including, *inter alia,* the rights and duties of holders, suppliers, and recipients of technology. In particular, all States should facilitate the access of developing countries to the achievements of modern science and technology, the transfer of technology and the creation of indigenous technology for the benefit of the developing countries in forms and in accordance with procedures which are suited to their economies and their needs.

3. Accordingly, developed countries should cooperate with the developing countries in the establishment, strengthening and development of their scientific and technological infrastructures and their scientific research and technological activities so as to help to expand and transform the economies of developing countries.

4. All States should cooperate in exploring with a view to evolving further internationally accepted guidelines or regulations for the transfer of technology, taking fully into account the interests of developing countries.

ARTICLE 14

Every State has the duty to cooperate in promoting a steady and increasing expansion and liberalization of world trade and an improvement in the welfare and living standards of all peoples, in particular those of developing countries. Accordingly, all States should cooperate, *inter alia,* towards the progressive dismantling of obstacles to trade and the improvement of the international framework for the conduct of world trade and, to these ends, coordinated efforts shall be made to solve in an equitable way the trade problems of all countries, taking into account the specific trade problems of the developing countries. In this connexion, States shall take measures aimed at securing additional benefits for the international trade of developing countries so as to achieve a substantial increase in their foreign exchange earnings, the diversification of their exports, the acceleration of the rate of growth of their trade, taking into account their development needs, an improvement in the possibilities for these countries to participate in the expansion of world trade and a balance more favourable to developing countries in the sharing of the advantages resulting from this expansion, through, in the largest possible measure, a substantial improvement in the conditions of access for the products of interest to the developing countries and, wherever appropriate, measures designed to attain stable, equitable and remunerative prices for primary products.

ARTICLE 15

All States have the duty to promote the achievement of general and complete disarmament under effective international control and to utilize the resources freed by effective disarmanent measures for the economic and social development of countries, allocating a substantial portion of such resources as additional means for the development needs of developing countries.

ARTICLE 16

1. It is the right and duty of all States, individually and collectively, to eliminate colonialism, *apartheid,* racial discrimination, neocolonialism and all forms of foreign aggression, occupation and domination, and the economic and social consequences thereof, as a prerequisite for development. States which practise such coercive policies are economically responsible to the countries, territories, and peoples affected for the restitution and full compensation for the exploitation and depletion of, and damages to, the natural and all other resources of those countries, territories, and peoples. It is the duty of all States to extend assistance to them.

2. No State has the right to promote or encourage investments that may constitute an obstacle to the liberation of a territory occupied by force.

ARTICLE 17

International cooperation for development is the shared goal and common duty of all States. Every State should cooperate with the efforts of developing countries to accelerate their economic and social development by providing favourable external conditions and by extending active assistance to them, consistent with their development needs and objectives, with strict respect for the sovereign equality of States and free of any conditions derogating from their sovereignty.

ARTICLE 18

Developed countries should extend, improve, and enlarge the system of generalized nonreciprocal and nondiscriminatory tariff preferences to the developing countries consistent with the relevant agreed conclusions and relevant decisions as adopted on this subject, in the framework of the competent international organizations. Developed countries should also give serious consideration to the adoption of other differential measures, in areas where this is feasible and appropriate and in ways which will provide special and more favourable treatment, in order to meet the trade and development needs of the developing countries. In the conduct of international economic relations the developed countries should endeavour to avoid measures having a negative effect on the development of the national economies of the developing countries, as promoted by generalized tariff preferences and other generally agreed differential measures in their favour.

ARTICLE 19

With a view to accelerating the economic growth of developing countries and bridging the economic gap between developed and developing countries, developed countries should grant generalized preferential, nonreciprocal and nondiscriminatory treatment to developing countries in those fields of international economic cooperation where it may be feasible.

ARTICLE 20

Developing countries should, in their efforts to increase their over-all trade, give due attention to the possibility of expanding their trade with socialist countries, by granting to these countries conditions for trade not inferior to those granted normally to the developed market economy countries.

ARTICLE 21

Developing countries should endeavour to promote the expansion of their mutual trade and to this end may, in accordance with the existing and evolving provisions and procedures of international agreements where applicable, grant trade preferences to other developing countries without being obliged to extend such preferences to developed countries, provided these arrangements do not constitute an impediment to general trade liberalization and expansion.

ARTICLE 22

1. All States should respond to the generally recognized or mutually agreed development needs and objectives of developing countries by promoting increased net flows of real resources to the developing countries from all sources, taking into account any obligations and commitments undertaken by the States concerned, in order to reinforce the efforts of developing countries to accelerate their economic and social development.

2. In this context, consistent with the aims and objectives mentioned above and taking into account any obligations and commitments undertaken in this regard, it should be their endeavour to increase the net amount of financial flows from official sources to developing countries and to improve the terms and conditions thereof.

3. The flow of development assistance resources should include economic and technical assistance.

ARTICLE 23

To enhance the effective mobilization of their own resources, the developing countries should strengthen their economic cooperation and expand their mutual trade so as to accelerate their economic and social development. All countries, especially developed countries, individually as well as through the competent international organizations of which they are members, should provide appropriate and effective support and cooperation.

ARTICLE 24

All States have the duty to conduct their mutual economic relations in a manner which takes into account the interests of other countries. In particular, all States should avoid prejudicing the interests of developing countries.

ARTICLE 25

In furtherance of world economic development, the international community, especially its developed members, shall pay special attention to the particular needs and problems of the least developed among the developing countries, of land-locked developing countries and also island developing countries, with a view to helping them to overcome their particular difficulties and thus contribute to their economic and social development.

ARTICLE 26

All States have the duty to coexist in tolerance and live together in peace, irrespective of differences in political, economic, social, and cultural systems, and to facilitate trade between States having different economic and social systems. International trade should be conducted without prejudice to generalized nondiscriminatory and nonreciprocal preferences in favour of developing countries, on the basis of mutual advantage, equitable benefits and the exchange of most-favoured-nation treatment.

ARTICLE 27

1. Every State has the right to enjoy fully the benefits of world invisible trade and to engage in the expansion of such trade.

2. World invisible trade, based on efficiency and mutual and equitable benefit, furthering the expansion of the world economy, is the common goal of all States. The role of developing countries in world invisible trade should be enhanced and strengthened consistent with the above objectives, particular attention being paid to the special needs of developing countries.

3. All States should cooperate with developing countries in their endeavours to increase their capacity to earn foreign exchange from invisible transactions, in accordance with the potential and needs of each developing country and consistent with the objectives mentioned above.

ARTICLE 28

All States have the duty to cooperate in achieving adjustments in the prices of exports of developing countries in relation to prices of their imports so as to promote just and equitable terms of trade for them, in a manner which is remunerative for producers and equitable for producers and consumers.

III. COMMON RESPONSIBILITIES TOWARDS THE INTERNATIONAL COMMUNITY

ARTICLE 29

The sea-bed and ocean floor and the subsoil thereof, beyond the limits of national jurisdiction, as well as the resources of the area, are the common heritage of mankind. On the basis of the principles adopted by the General Assembly in resolution 2749 (XXV) of 17 December 1970, all States shall ensure that the exploration of the area and exploitation of its resources are carried out exclusively for peaceful purposes and that the benefits derived therefrom are shared equitably by all States, taking into account the particular interests and needs of developing countries; an international regime applying to the area and its resources and including appropriate international machinery to give effect to its provisions shall be established by an international treaty of a universal character, generally agreed upon.

ARTICLE 30

The protection, preservation and the enhancement of the environment for the present and future generations is the responsibility of all States. All States shall endeavour to establish their own environmental and developmental policies in conformity with such responsibility. The environmental policies of all States should enhance and not adversely affect the present and future development potential of developing countries. All States have the responsibility to ensure that activities within their jurisdiction or control do not cause damage to the environment of other States or of areas beyond the limits of national jurisdiction. All States should cooperate in evolving international norms and regulations in the field of the environment.

IV. FINAL PROVISIONS

ARTICLE 31

All States have the duty to contribute to the balanced expansion of the world economy, taking duly into account the close interrelationship between the well-being of the developed countries and the growth and development of the developing countries, and the fact that the prosperity of the international community as a whole depends upon the prosperity of its constituent parts.

ARTICLE 32

No State may use or encourage the use of economic, political, or any other type of measures to coerce another State in order to obtain from it the subordination of the exercise of its sovereign rights.

ARTICLE 33

1. Nothing in the present Charter shall be construed as impairing or derogating from the provisions of the Charter of the United Nations or actions taken in pursuance thereof.

2. In their interpretation and application, the provisions of the present Charter are interrelated and each provision should be construed in the context of the other provisions.

ARTICLE 34

An item on the Charter of Economic Rights and Duties of States shall be inscribed in the agenda of the General Assembly at its thirtieth session, and thereafter on the agenda of every fifth session. In this way a systematic and comprehensive consideration of the implementation of the Charter, covering both progress achieved and any improvements and additions which might become necessary, would be carried out and appropriate measures recommended. Such consideration should take into account the evolution of all the economic, social, legal, and other factors related to the principles upon which the present Charter is based and on its purpose.

18. Statute of the International Atomic Energy Agency

Signed at the Headquarters of the United Nations on October 26, 1956, the Statute came into force on July 29, 1957. U.S. Treaties and Other International Agreements, Vol. 8 (1957), Part I, pp. 1095–1113. Annex omitted.

ARTICLE I: ESTABLISHMENT OF THE AGENCY

The Parties hereto establish an International Atomic Energy Agency (hereinafter referred to as "the Agency") upon the terms and conditions hereinafter set forth.

ARTICLE II: OBJECTIVE

The Agency shall seek to accelerate and enlarge the contribution of atomic energy to peace, health and prosperity throughout the world. It shall ensure, so far as it is able, that assistance provided by it or at its request or under its supervision or control is not used in such a way as to further any military purpose.

ARTICLE III: FUNCTIONS

A. The Agency is authorized:

1. To encourage and assist research on, and development and practical application of, atomic energy for peaceful uses throughout the world; and, if requested to do so, to act as an intermediary for the purposes of securing the performance of services or the supplying of materials, equipment, or facilities by one member of the Agency for another; and to perform any operation or service useful in research on, or development or practical application of, atomic energy for peaceful purposes;

2. To make provision, in accordance with this Statute, for materials, services, equipment, and facilities to meet the needs of research on, and development and practical application of, atomic energy for peaceful purposes, including the production of electric power, with due consideration for the needs of the underdeveloped areas of the world;

3. To foster the exchange of scientific and technical information on peaceful uses of atomic energy;

4. To encourage the exchange and training of scientists and experts in the field of peaceful uses of atomic energy;

5. To establish and administer safeguards designed to ensure that special fissionable and other materials, services, equipment, facilities, and information made available by the Agency or at its request or under its supervision or control are not used in such a way as to further any military purpose; and to apply safeguards, at the request of the parties, to any bilateral or multlateral arrangement, or, at the request of a State, to any of that State's activities in the field of atomic energy;

6. To establish or adopt, in consultation and, where appropriate, in collaboration with the competent organs of the United Nations and with the specialized agencies concerned, standards of safety for protection of health and minimization of danger to life and property (including such standards for labour conditions), and to provide for the application of these standards to its own operations as well as to the operations making use of materials, services, equipment, facilities, and information made available by the Agency or at its request or under its control or supervision; and to provide for the application of these standards, at the request of the parties, to operations under any bilateral or multilateral arrangement, or, at the request of a State, to any of that State's activities in the field of atomic energy;

7. To acquire or establish any facilities, plant and equipment useful in carrying out its authorized functions, whenever the facilities, plant, and equipment otherwise available to it in the area concerned are inadequate or available only on terms it deems unsatisfactory.

B. In carrying out its functions, the Agency shall:

1. Conduct its activities in accordance with the purposes and principles of the United Nations to promote peace and international cooperation, and in conformity with policies of the United Nations furthering the establishment of safe-guarded world-wide disarmament and in conformity with any international agreements entered into pursuant to such policies;

2. Establish control over the use of special fissionable materials received by the Agency, in order to ensure that these materials are used only for peaceful purposes;

3. Allocate its resources in such a manner as to secure efficient utilization and the greatest possible general benefit in all areas of the world, bearing in mind the special needs of the underdeveloped areas of the world;

4. Submit reports on its activities annually to the General Assembly of the United Nations and, when appropriate, to the Security Council: if in connexion with the activities of the Agency there should arise questions that are within the competence of the Security Council, the Agency shall notify the Security Council, as the organ bearing the main responsibility for the maintenance of international peace and security, and may also take the measures open to it under this Statute, including those provided in paragraph C of article XII;

5. Submit reports to the Economic and Social Council and other organs of the United Nations on matters within the competence of these organs.

C. In carrying out its functions, the Agency shall not make assistance to members subject to any political, economic, military, or other conditions incompatible with the provisions of this Statute.

D. Subject to the provisions of this Statute and to the terms of agreements concluded between a State or a group of States and the Agency which shall be in accordance with the provisions of the Statute, the activities of the Agency shall be carried out with due observance of the sovereign rights of States.

ARTICLE IV: MEMBERSHIP

A. The initial members of the Agency shall be those States Members of the United Nations or of any of the specialized agencies which shall have signed this Statute within ninety days after it is opened for signature and shall have deposited an instrument of ratification.

B. Other members of the Agency shall be those States, whether or not Members of the United Nations or of any of the specialized agencies, which deposit an instrument of acceptance of this Statute after their membership has been approved by the General Conference upon the recommendation of the Board of Governors. In recommending and approving a State for membership, the Board of Governors and the General Conference shall determine that the State is able and willing to carry out the obligations of membership in the Agency, giving due consideration to its ability and willingness to act in accordance with the purposes and principles of the Charter of the United Nations.

C. The Agency is based on the principle of the sovereign equality of all its members, and all members, in order to ensure to all of them the rights and benefits resulting from membership, shall fulfil in good faith the obligations assumed by them in accordance with this Statute.

ARTICLE V: GENERAL CONFERENCE

A. A General Conference consisting of representatives of all members shall meet in regular annual session and in such special sessions as shall be convened by the Director General at the request of the Board of Governors or of a majority of members. The sessions shall take place at the headquarters of the Agency unless otherwise determined by the General Conference.

B. At such sessions, each member shall be represented by one delegate who may be accompanied by alternates and by advisers. The cost of attendance of any delegation shall be borne by the member concerned.

C. The General Conference shall elect a President and such other officers as may be required at the beginning of each session. They shall hold office for the duration of the session. The General Conference, subject to the provisions of this Statute, shall adopt its own rules of procedure. Each member shall have one vote. Decisions pursuant to paragraph H of article XIV, paragraph C of article XVIII and paragraph B of article XIX shall be made by a two-thirds majority of the members present and voting. Decisions on other questions, including the determination of additional questions or categories of questions to be decided by a two-thirds majority, shall be made by a majority of the members present and voting. A majority of members shall constitute a quorum.

D. The General Conference may discuss any questions or any matters within the scope of this Statute or relating to the powers and functions of any organs provided for in this Statute, and may make recommendations to the membership of the Agency or to the Board of Governors or to both on any such questions or matters.

E. The General Conference shall:

1. Elect members of the Board of Governors in accordance with article VI;

2. Approve States for membership in accordance with article IV;

3. Suspend a member from the privileges and rights of membership in accordance with article XIX;

4. Consider the annual report of the Board;

5. In accordance with article XIV, approve the budget of the Agency recommended by the Board or return it with recommendations as to its entirety or parts to the Board, for resubmission to the General Conference;

6. Approve reports to be submitted to the United Nations as required by the relationship agreement between the Agency and the United Nations, escept reports referred to in paragraph C of article XII, or return them to the Board with its recommendations;

7. Approve any agreement or agreements between the Agency and the United Nations and other organizations as provided in article XVI or return such agreements with its recommendations to the Board, for resubmission to the General Conference;

8. Approve rules and limitations regarding the exercise of borrowing powers by the Board, in accordance with paragraph G of article XIV; approve rules regarding the acceptance of voluntary contributions to the Agency; and approve, in accordance with paragraph F of article XIV, the manner in which the general fund referred to in that paragraph may be used;

9. Approve amendments to this Statute in accordance with paragraph C of article XVIII;

10. Approve the appointment of the Director General in accordance with paragraph A of article VII.

F. The General Conference shall have the authority:

1. To take decisions on any matter specifically referred to the General Conference for this purpose by the Board;

2. To propose matters for consideration by the Board and request from the Board reports on any matter relating to the functions of the Agency.

ARTICLE VI: BOARD OF GOVERNORS

A. The Board of Governors shall be composed as follows:

1. The outgoing Board of Governors (or in the case of the first Board, the Preparatory Commission referred to in Annex I) shall designate for membership on the Board the five members most advanced in the technology of atomic energy including the production of source materials and the member most advanced in the technology of atomic energy including the production of source materials in each of the following areas not represented by the aforesaid five:

(1) North America
(2) Latin America
(3) Western Europe
(4) Eastern Europe
(5) Africa and the Middle East
(6) South Asia
(7) South East Asia and the Pacific
(8) Far East.

2. The outgoing Board of Governors (or in the case of the first Board, the Preparatory Commission referred to in Annex I) shall designate for membership on the Board two members from among the following other producers of source materials: Belgium, Czechoslovakia, Poland, and Portugal; and shall also designate for membership on the Board one other member as a supplier of technical assistance. No member in this category in any one year will be eligible for redesignation in the same category for the following year.

3. The General Conference shall elect ten members to membership on the Board of Governors, with due regard to equitable representation on the Board as a whole of the members in the areas listed in subparagraph A-1 of this article, so that the Board shall at all times include in this category a representative of each of those areas except North America. Except for the five members chosen for a term of one year in accordance with paragraph D of this article, no member in this category in any one term of office will be eligible for re-election in the same category for the following term of office.

B. The designations provided for in subparagraphs A-1 and A-2 of this article shall take place not less than sixty days before each regular annual session of the General Conference. The elections provided for in subparagraph A-3 of this article shall take place at regular annual sessions of the General Conference.

C. Members represented on the Board of Governors in accordance with subparagraphs A-1 and A-2 of this article shall hold office from the end of the next regular annual session of the General Conference after their designation until the end of the following regular annual session of the General Conference.

D. Members represented on the Board of Governors in accordance with subparagraph A-3 of this article shall hold office from the end of the regular annual session of the General Conference at which they are elected until the end of the second regular annual session of the General Conference thereafter. In the election of these members for the first Board, however, five shall be chosen for a term of one year.

E. Each member of the Board of Governors shall have one vote. Decisions on the amount of the Agency's budget shall be made by a two-thirds majority of those present and voting, as provided in paragraph H of article XIV. Decisions on other questions, including the determination of additional questions or categories of questions to be decided by a two-thirds majority, shall be made by a majority of those present and voting. Two-thirds of all members of the Board shall constitute a quorum.

F. The Board of Governors shall have authority to carry out the functions of the Agency in accordance with this Statute, subject to its responsibilities to the General Conference as provided in this Statute.

G. The Board of Governors shall meet at such times as it may determine. The meetings shall take place at the headquarters of the Agency unless otherwise determined by the Board.

H. The Board of Governors shall elect a Chairman and other officers from among its members and, subject to the provisions of this Statute, shall adopt its own rules of procedure.

I. The Board of Governors may establish such committees as it deems advisable. The Board may appoint persons to represent it in its relations with other organizations.

J. The Board of Governors shall prepare an annual report of the General Conference concerning the affairs of the Agency and any projects approved by the Agency. The Board shall also prepare for submission to the General Conference such reports as the Agency is or may be required to make to the United Nations or to any other organization the work of which is related to that of the Agency. These reports, along with the annual reports, shall be submitted to members of the Agency at least one month before the regular annual session of the General Conference.

ARTICLE VII: STAFF

A. The staff of the Agency shall be headed by a Director General. The Director General shall be appointed by the Board of Governors with the approval of the General Conference for a term of four years. He shall be the chief administrative officer of the Agency.

B. The Director General shall be responsible for the appointment, organization, and functioning of the staff and shall be under the authority of and subject to the control of the Board of Governors. He shall perform his duties in accordance with regulations adopted by the Board.

C. The staff shall include such qualified scientific and technical and other personnel as may be required to fulfill the objectives and functions of the Agency. The Agency shall be guided by the principle that its permanent staff shall be kept to a minimum.

D. The paramount consideration in the recruitment and employment of the staff and in the determination of the conditions of service shall be to secure employees of the highest standards of efficiency, technical competence, and integrity. Subject to this consideration, due regard shall be paid to the contributions of members to the Agency and to the importance of recruiting the staff on as wide a geographical basis as possible.

E. The terms and conditions on which the staff shall be appointed, remunerated, and dismissed shall be in accordance with regulations made by the Board of Governors, subject to the provisions of this Statute and to general rules approved by the General Conference on the recommendation of the Board.

F. In the performance of their duties, the Director General and the staff shall not seek or receive instructions from any source external to the Agency. They shall refrain from any action which might reflect on their position as officials of the Agency; subject to their responsibilities to the Agency, they shall not disclose any industrial secret or other confidential information coming to their knowledge by reason of their official duties for the Agency. Each member undertakes to respect the international character of the responsibilities of the Director General and the staff and shall not seek to influence them in the discharge of their duties.

G. In this article the term "staff" includes guards.

ARTICLE VIII: EXCHANGE OF INFORMATION

A. Each member should make available such information as would, in the judgment of the member, be helpful to the Agency.

B. Each member shall make available to the Agency all scientific information developed as a result of assistance extended by the Agency pursuant to article XI.

C. The Agency shall assemble and make available in an accessible form the information made available to it under paragraphs A and B of this article. It shall take positive steps to encourage the exchange among its members of information relating to the nature and peaceful uses of atomic energy and shall serve as an intermediary among its members for this purpose.

ARTICLE IX: SUPPLYING OF MATERIALS

A. Members may make available to the Agency such quantities of special fissionable materials as they deem advisable and on such terms as shall be agreed with the Agency. The materials made available to the Agency may, at the discretion of the member making them available, be stored either by the member concerned or, with the agreement of the Agency, in the Agency's depots.

B. Members may also make available to the Agency source materials as defined in article XX and other materials. The Board of Governors shall determine the quantities of such materials which the Agency will accept under agreements provided for in article XIII.

C. Each member shall notify the Agency of the quantities, form, and composition of special fissionable materials, source materials, and other materials which that member is prepared, in conformity with its laws, to make available immediately or during a period specified by the Board of Governors.

D. On request of the Agency a member shall, from the materials which it has made available, without delay deliver to another member or group of members such quantities of such materials as the Agency may specify, and shall without delay deliver to the Agency itself such quantities of such materials as are really necessary for operations and scientific research in the facilities of the Agency.

E. The quantities, form and composition of materials made available by any member may be changed at any time by the member with the approval of the Board of Governors.

F. An initial notification in accordance with paragraph C of this article shall be made within three months of the entry into force of this Statute with respect to the member concerned. In the absence of a contrary decision of the Board of Governors, the materials initially made available shall be for the period of the calendar year succeeding the year when this Statute takes effect with respect to the member concerned. Subsequent notifications shall likewise, in the absence of a contrary action by the Board, relate to the period of the calendar year following the notification and shall be made no later than the first day of November of each year.

G. The Agency shall specify the place and method of delivery and, where appropriate, the form and composition, of materials which it has requested a member to deliver from the amounts which that member has notified the Agency it is prepared to make available. The Agency shall also verify the quantities of materials delivered and shall report those quantities periodically to the members.

H. The Agency shall be responsible for storing and protecting materials in its possession. The Agency shall ensure that these materials shall be safeguarded against (1) hazards of the weather, (2) unauthorized removal or diversion, (3) damage or destruction, including sabotage, and (4) forcible seizure. In storing special fissionable materials in its possession, the Agency shall ensure the geographical distribution of these materials in such a way as not to allow concentration of large amounts of such materials in any one country or region of the world.

I. The Agency shall as soon as practicable establish or acquire such of the following as may be necessary:

1. Plant, equipment, and facilities for the receipt, storage, and issue of materials;

2. Physical safeguards;

3. Adequate health and safety measures;

4. Control laboratories for the analysis and verification of materials received;

5. Housing and administrative facilities for any staff required for the foregoing.

J. The materials made available pursuant to this article shall be used as determined by the Board of Governors in accordance with the provisions of this Statute. No member shall have the right to require that the materials it makes available to the Agency be kept separately by the Agency or to designate the specific project in which they must be used.

ARTICLE X: SERVICES, EQUIPMENT, AND FACILITIES

Members may make available to the Agency services, equipment, and facilities which may be of assistance in . fulfilling the Agency's objectives and functions.

ARTICLE XI: AGENCY PROJECTS

A. Any member or group of members of the Agency desiring to set up any project for research on, or development or practical application of, atomic energy for peaceful purposes may request the assistance of the Agency in securing special fissionable and other materials, services, equipment, and facilities necessary for this purpose. Any such request shall be accompanied by an explanation of the purpose and extent of the project and shall be considered by the Board of Governors.

B. Upon request, the Agency may also assist any member or group of members to make arrangements to secure necessary financing from outside sources to carry out such projects. In extending this assistance, the Agency will not be required to provide any guarantees or to assume any financial responsibility for the project.

C. The Agency may arrange for the supplying of any materials, services, equipment, and facilities necessary for the project by one or more members or may itself undertake to provide any or all of these directly, taking into consideration the wishes of the member or members making the request.

D. For the purpose of considering the request, the Agency may send into the territory of the member or group of members making the request a person or persons qualified to examine the project. For this purpose the Agency may, with the approval of the member or group of members making the request, use members of its own staff or employ suitably qualified nationals of any member.

E. Before approving a project under this article, the Board of Governors shall give due consideration to:

1. The usefulness of the project, including its scientific and technical feasibility;

2. The adequacy of plans, funds, and technical personnel to assure the effective execution of the project;

3. The adequacy of proposed health and safety standards for handling and storing materials and for operating facilities;

4. The inability of the member or group of members making the request to secure the necessary finances, materials, facilities, equipment, and services;

5. The equitable distribution of materials and other resources available to the Agency;

6. The special needs of the underdeveloped areas of the world; and

7. Such other matters as may be relevant.

F. Upon approving a project, the Agency shall enter into an agreement with the member or group of members submitting the project, which agreement shall:

1. Provide for allocation to the project of any required special fissionable or other materials;

2. Provide for transfer of special fissionable materials from their then place of custody, whether the materials be in the custody of the Agency or of the member making them available for use in Agency projects, to the member or group of members submitting the project, under conditions which ensure the safety of any shipment required and meet applicable health and safety standards;

3. Set forth the terms and conditions, including charges, on which any materials, services, equipment, and facilities are to be provided by the Agency itself, and, if any such materials, services, equipment, and facilities

are to be provided by a member, the terms and conditions as arranged for by the member or group of members submitting the project and the supplying member;

4. Include undertakings by the member or group of members submitting the project: (*a*) that the assistance provided shall not be used in such a way as to further any military purpose; and (*b*) that the project shall be subject to the safeguards provided for in article XII, the relevant safeguards being specified in the agreement;

5. Make appropriate provision regarding the rights and interests of the Agency and the member or members concerned in any inventions or discoveries or any patents therein, arising from the project;

6. Make appropriate provision regarding settlement of disputes;

7. Include such other provisions as may be appropriate.

G. The provisions of this article shall also apply where appropriate to a request for materials, services, facilities, or equipment in connexion with an existing project.

ARTICLE XII: AGENCY SAFEGUARDS

A. With respect to any Agency project, or other arrangement where the Agency is requested by the parties concerned to apply safeguards, the Agency shall have the following rights and responsibilities to the extent relevant to the project or arrangement:

1. To examine the design of specialized equipment and facilities, including nuclear reactors, and to approve it only from the viewpoint of assuring that it will not further any military purpose, that it complies with applicable health and safety standards, and that it will permit effective application of the safeguards provided for in this article;

2. To require the observance of any health and safety measures prescribed by the Agency;

3. To require the maintenance and production of operating records to assist in ensuring accountability for source and special fissionable materials used or produced in the project or arrangement;

4. To call for and receive progress reports;

5. To approve the means to be used for the chemical processing of irradiated materials solely to ensure that this chemical processing will not lend itself to diversion of materials for military purposes and will comply with applicable health and safety standards; to require that special fissionable materials recovered or produced as a by-product be used for peaceful purposes under continuing Agency safeguards for research or in reactors, existing or under construction, specified by the member or members concerned; and to require deposit with the Agency of any excess of any special fissionable materials recovered or produced as a by-product over what is needed for the above-stated uses in order to prevent stockpiling

of these materials, provided that thereafter at the request of the member or members concerned special fissionable materials so deposited with the Agency shall be returned promptly to the member or members concerned for use under the same provisions as stated above;

6. To send into the territory of the recipient State or States inspectors, designated by the Agency after consultation with the State or States concerned, who shall have access at all times to all places and data and to any person who by reason of his occupation deals with materials, equipment, or facilities which are required by this Statute to be safeguarded, as necessary to account for source and special fissionable materials supplied and fissionable products and to determine whether there is compliance with the undertaking against use in furtherance of any military purpose referred to in subparagraph F-4 of article XI, with the health and safety measures referred to in subparagraph A-2 of this article, and with any other conditions prescribed in the agreement between the Agency and the State or States concerned. Inspectors designated by the Agency shall be accompanied by representatives of the authorities of the State concerned, if that State so requests, provided that the inspectors shall not thereby be delayed or otherwise impeded in the exercise of their functions;

7. In the event of noncompliance and failure by the recipient State or States to take requested corrective steps within a reasonable time, to suspend or terminate assistance and withdraw any materials and equipment made available by the Agency or a member in furtherance of the project.

B. The Agency shall, as necessary, establish a staff of inspectors. The staff of inspectors shall have the responsibility of examining all operations conducted by the Agency itself to determine whether the Agency is complying with the health and safety measures prescribed by it for application to projects subject to its approval, supervision or control, and whether the Agency is taking adequate measures to prevent the source and special fissionable materials in its custody or used or produced in its own operations from being used in furtherance of any military purpose. The Agency shall take remedial action forthwith to correct any noncompliance or failure to take adequate measures.

C. The staff of inspectors shall also have the responsibility of obtaining and verifying the accounting referred to in subparagraph A-6 of this article and of determining whether there is compliance with the undertaking referred to in subparagraph F-4 of article XI, with the measures referred to in subparagraph A-2 of this article, and with all other conditions of the project prescribed in the agreement between the Agency and the State or States concerned. The inspectors shall report any noncompliance to the Director General who shall thereupon transmit the report to the Board of Governors. The Board shall call upon the recipient State or States to remedy forthwith any noncompliance which it finds to have occurred. The Board shall report the noncompliance to all members and to the Security Council and General Assembly of the United Nations. In the event of failure of the recipient State or States to take fully corrective action within a reasonable time, the Board may take one or both of the following measures: direct curtailment or suspension of assistance being provided by the Agency or by a member, and call for the return of materials and equipment made available to the recipient member or group of members. The Agency may also, in accordance with article XIX, suspend any noncomplying member from the exercise of the privileges and rights of membership.

ARTICLE XIII: REIMBURSEMENT OF MEMBERS

Unless otherwise agreed upon between the Board of Governors and the member furnishing to the Agency materials, services, equipment, or facilities, the Board shall enter into an agreement with such member providing for reimbursement for the items furnished.

ARTICLE XIV: FINANCE

A. The Board of Governors shall submit to the General Conference the annual budget estimates for the expenses of the Agency. To facilitate the work of the Board in this regard, the Director General shall initially prepare the budget estimates. If the General Conference does not approve the estimates, it shall return them together with its recommendations to the Board. The Board shall then submit further estimates to the General Conference for its approval.

B. Expenditures of the Agency shall be classified under the following categories:

1. Administrative expenses: these shall include:

(*a*) Costs of the staff of the Agency other than the staff employed in connexion with materials, services, equipment, and facilities referred to in subparagraph B-2 below; costs of meetings; and expenditures required for the preparation of Agency projects and for the distribution of information;

(*b*) Costs of implementing the safeguards referred to in article XII in relation to Agency projects or, under subparagraphs A-5 of article III, in relation to any bilateral or multilateral arrangement, together with the costs of handling and storage of special fissionable material by the Agency other than the storage and handling charges referred to in paragraph E below;

2. Expenses, other than those included in subparagraph 1 of this paragraph, in connexion with any materials, facilities, plant, and equipment acquired or established by the Agency in carrying out its authorized functions, and the costs of materials, services, equipment, and facilities provided by it under agreements with one or more members.

C. In fixing the expenditures under subparagraph B-1 (*b*) above, the Board of Governors shall deduct such amounts as are recoverable under agreements regarding the application of safeguards between the Agency and parties to bilateral or multilateral arrangements.

D. The Board of Governors shall apportion the expenses referred to in subparagraph B-1 above, among members in accordance with a scale to be fixed by the General Conference. In fixing the scale the General Conference shall be guided by the principles adopted by the United Nations in assessing contributions of Member States to the regular budget of the United Nations.

E. The Board of Governors shall establish periodically a scale of charges, including reasonable uniform storage and handling charges, for materials, services, equipment, and facilities furnished to members by the Agency. The scale shall be designed to produce revenues for the Agency adequate to meet the expenses and costs referred to in subparagraph B-2 above, less any voluntary contributions which the Board of Governors may, in accordance with paragraph F, apply for this purpose. The proceeds of such charges shall be placed in a separate fund which shall be used to pay members for any materials, services, equipment, or facilities furnished by them and to meet other expenses referred to in subparagraph B-2 above which may be incurred by the Agency itself.

F. Any excess of revenues referred to in paragraph E over the expenses and costs there referred to, and any voluntary contributions to the Agency, shall be placed in a general fund which may be used as the Board of Governors, with the approval of the General Conference, may determine.

G. Subject to rules and limitations approved by the General Conference, the Board of Governors shall have the authority to exercise borrowing powers on behalf of the Agency without, however, imposing on members of the Agency any liability in respect of loans entered into pursuant to this authority, and to accept voluntary contributions made to the Agency.

H. Decisions of the General Conference on financial questions and of the Board of Governors on the amount of the Agency's budget shall require a two-thirds majority of those present and voting.

ARTICLE XV: PRIVILEGES AND IMMUNITIES

A. The Agency shall enjoy in the territory of each member such legal capacity and such privileges and immunities as are necessary for the exercise of its functions.

B. Delegates of members together with their alternates and advisers, Governors appointed to the Board together with their alternates and advisers, and the Director General and the staff of the Agency, shall enjoy such privileges and immunities as are necessary in the independent exercise of their functions in connexion with the Agency.

C. The legal capacity, privileges, and immunities referred to in this article shall be defined in a separate agreement or agreements between the Agency, represented for this purpose by the Director General acting under instructions of the Board of Governors, and the members.

ARTICLE XVI: RELATIONSHIP WITH OTHER ORGANIZATIONS

A. The Board of Governors, with the approval of the General Conference, is authorized to enter into an agreement or agreements establishing an appropriate relationship between the Agency and the United Nations and any other organizations the work of which is related to that of the Agency.

B. The agreement or agreements establishing the relationship of the Agency and the United Nations shall provide for:

1. Submission by the Agency of reports as provided for in subparagraphs B-4 and B-5 of article III;

2. Consideration by the Agency of resolutions relating to it adopted by the General Assembly or any of the Councils of the United Nations and the submission of reports, when requested, to the appropriate organ of the United Nations on the action taken by the Agency or by its members in accordance with this Statute as a result of such consideration.

ARTICLE XVII: SETTLEMENT OF DISPUTES

A. Any question or dispute concerning the interpretation or application of this Statute which is not settled by negotiation shall be referred to the International Court of Justice in conformity with the Statute of the Court, unless the parties concerned agree on another mode of settlement.

B. The General Conference and the Board of Governors are separately empowered, subject to authorization from the General Assembly of the United Nations, to request the International Court of Justice to give an advisory opinion on any legal question arising within the scope of the Agency's activities.

ARTICLE XVIII: AMENDMENTS AND WITHDRAWALS

A. Amendments to this Statute may be proposed by any member. Certified copies of the text of any amendment proposed shall be prepared by the Director General and communicated by him to all members at least ninety days in advance of its consideration by the General Conference.

B. At the fifth annual session of the General Conference following the coming into force of this Statute, the question of a general review of the provisions of this Statute shall be placed on the agenda of that session. On approval by a majority of the members present and voting, the review will take place at the following General Conference. Thereafter, proposals on the question of a general review of this Statute may be submitted for decision by the General Conference under the same procedure.

C. Amendments shall come into force for all members when:

(i) Approved by the General Conference by a two-thirds majority of those present and voting after consideration of observations submitted by the Board of Governors on each proposed amendment, and

(ii) Accepted by two-thirds of all the members in accordance with their respective constitutional processes. Acceptance by a member shall be effected by the deposit of an instrument of acceptance with the depositary Government referred to in paragraph C of article XXI.

D. At any time after five years from the date when this Statute shall take effect in accordance with paragraph E of article XXI or whenever a member is unwilling to accept an amendment to this Statute, it may withdraw from the Agency by notice in writing to that effect given to the depositary Government referred to in paragraph C of article XXI, which shall promptly inform the Board of Governors and all members.

E. Withdrawal by a member from the Agency shall not affect its contractual obligations entered into pursuant to article XI or its budgetary obligations for the year in which it withdraws.

ARTICLE XIX: SUSPENSION OF PRIVILEGES

A. A member of the Agency which is in arrears in the payment of its financial contributions to the Agency shall have no vote in the Agency if the amount of its arrears equals or exceeds the amount of the contributions due from it for the preceeding two years. The General Conference may, nevertheless, permit such a member to vote if it is satisfied that the failure to pay is due to conditions beyond the control of the member.

B. A member which has persistently violated the provisions of this Statute or of any agreement entered into by it pursuant to this Statute may be suspended from the exercise of the privileges and rights of membership by the General Conference acting by a two-thirds majority of the members present and voting upon recommendation by the Board of Governors.

ARTICLE XX: DEFINITIONS

As used in this Statute:

1. The term "special fissionable material" means plutonium-239; uranium-233; uranium enriched in the isotopes 235 or 233; any material containing one or or more of the foregoing; and such other fissionable material as the Board of Governors shall from time to time determine; but the term "special fissionable material" does not include source material.

2. The term "uranium enriched in the isotopes 235 or 233" means uranium containing the isotopes 235 or 233 or both in an amount such that the abundance ratio of the sum of these isotopes to the isotope 238 is greater than the ratio of the isotope 235 to the isotope 238 occurring in nature.

3. The term "source material" means uranium containing the mixture of isotopes occurring in nature; uranium depleted in the isotope 235; thorium; any of the foregoing in the form of metal, alloy, chemical compound, or concentrate; any other material containing one or more of the foregoing in such concentration as the Board of Governors shall from time to time determine; and such other material as the Board of Governors shall from time to time determine.

ARTICLE XXI: SIGNATURE, ACCEPTANCE, AND ENTRY INTO FORCE

A. This Statute shall be open for signature on 26 October 1956 by all States Members of the United Nations or of any of the specialized agencies and shall remain open for signature by those States for a period of ninety days.

B. The signatory States shall become parties to this Stature by deposit of an instrument of ratification.

C. Instruments of ratification by signatory States and instruments of acceptance by States whose membership has been approved under paragraph B of article IV of this Statute shall be deposited with the Government of the United States of America, hereby designated as depositary Government.

D. Ratification or acceptance of this Statute shall be effected by States in accordance with their respective constitutional processes.

E. This Statute, apart from the Annex, shall come into force when eighteen States have deposited instruments of ratification in accordance with paragraph B of this article, provided that such eighteen Stttes shall include at least three of the following States: Canada, France, the Union of Soviet Socialist Republics, the United Kingdom of Great Britain and Northern Ireland, and the United States of America. Instruments of ratification and instruments of acceptance deposited thereafter shall take effect on the date of their receipt.

F. The depositary Government shall promptly inform all States signatory to this Statute of the date of each deposit of ratification and the date of entry into force of the Statute. The depositary Government shall promptly inform all signatories and members of the dates on which States subsequently become parties thereto.

G. The Annex to this Statute shall come into force on the first day this Statute is open for signature.

ARTICLE XXII: REGISTRATION WITH THE UNITED NATIONS

A. This Statute shall be registered by the depositary Government pursuant to Article 102 of the Charter of the United Nations.

B. Agreements between the Agency and any member or members, agreements between the Agency and any other organization or organizations, and agreements between members subject to approval of the Agency, shall be registered with the Agency. Such agreements shall be registered by the Agency with the United Nations if registration is required under Article 102 of the Charter of the United Nations.

ARTICLE XXIII: AUTHENTIC TEXTS AND CERTIFIED COPIES

This Statute, done in the Chinese, English, French, Russian and Spanish languages, each being equally authentic, shall be deposited in the archives of the depositary Government. Duly certified copies of this Statute shall be transmitted by the depositary Government to the Governments of the other signatory States and to the Governments of States admitted to membership under paragraph B of article IV.

In witness whereof the undersigned, duly authorized, have signed this Statute.

Done at the Headquarters of the United Nations, this twenty-sixth day of October, one thousand nine hundred and fifty-six.

Part II
Documents for Regional Application

19. The North Atlantic Treaty

Signed at Washington by Belgium, Canada, Denmark, France, Iceland, Italy, Luxembourg, the Netherlands, Norway, Portugal, the United Kingdom and the United States on April 4, 1949, the Treaty came into force on Aug. 24, 1949. Greece and Turkey acceded to the Treaty in 1951, and West Germany did the same in 1954. 34 U.N. Treaty Series, pp. 244–250.

The Parties to this Treaty reaffirm their faith in the purposes and principles of the Charter of the United Nations and their desire to live in peace with all peoples and all governments.

They are determined to safeguard the freedom, common heritage, and civilization of their peoples, founded on the principles of democracy, individual liberty, and the rule of law.

They seek to promote a stability and well-being in the North Atlantic area.

They are resolved to unite their efforts for collective defense and for the preservation of peace and security.

They therefore agree to this North Atlantic Treaty:

ARTICLE 1

The Parties undertake, as set forth in the Charter of the United Nations, to settle any international disputes in which they may be involved by peaceful means in such a manner that international peace and security, and justice, are not endangered, and to refrain in their international relations from the threat or use of force in any manner inconsistent with the purposes of the United Nations.

ARTICLE 2

The Parties will contribute toward the further development of peaceful and friendly international relations by strengthening their free institutions, by bringing about a better understanding of the principles upon which these institutions are founded, and by promoting conditions of stability and well-being. They will seek to eliminate conflict in their international economic policies and will encourage economic collaboration between any or all of them.

ARTICLE 3

In order more effectively to achieve the objectives of this Treaty, the Parties, separately and jointly, by means of continuous and effective self-help and mutual aid, will maintain and develop their individual and collective capacity to resist armed attack.

ARTICLE 4

The Parties will consult together whenever, in the opinion of any of them, the territorial integrity, political independence, or security of any of the Parties is threatened.

ARTICLE 5

The Parties agree that an armed attack against one or more of them in Europe or North America shall be considered an attack against them all; and consequently they agree that, if such an armed attack occurs, each of them, in exercise of the right of individual or collective self-defense recognized by Article 51 of the Charter of the United Nations, will assist the Party or Parties so attacked by taking forthwith, individually and in concert with the other Parties, such action as it deems necessary, including the use of armed force, to restore and maintain the security of the North Atlantic area.

Any such armed attack and all measures taken as a result thereof shall immediately be reported to the Security Council. Such measures shall be terminated when the Security Council has taken the measures necessary to restore and maintain international peace and security.

ARTICLE 6

For the purpose of Article 5, an armed attack on one or more of the Parties is deemed to include an armed attack:

(*i*) on the territory of any of the Parties in Europe or North America, on the Algerian Departments of France, on the territory of Turkey, or on the islands under the jurisdiction of any of the Parties in the North Atlantic area north of the Tropic of Cancer;

(*ii*) on the forces, vessels, or aircraft of any of the Parties, when in or over these territories or any other area in Europe in which occupation forces of any of the Parties were stationed on the date when the Treaty entered into force or the Mediterranean Sea or the North Atlantic area north of the Tropic of Cancer.

ARTICLE 7

This Treaty does not affect, and shall not be interpreted as affecting, in any way the rights and obligations under the Charter of the Parties which are members of the United Nations, or the primary responsibility of the Security Council for the maintenance of international peace and security.

ARTICLE 8

Each Party declares that none of the international engagements now in force between it and any other of the Parties or any third state is in conflict with the provisions of this Treaty, and undertakes not to enter into any international engagement in conflict with this Treaty.

ARTICLE 9

The Parties hereby establish a council, on which each of them shall be represented, to consider matters concerning the implementation of this Treaty. The council shall be so organized as to be able to meet promptly at any time. The council shall set up such subsidiary bodies as may be necessary; in particular it shall establish immediately a defense committee which shall recommend measures for the implementation of Articles 3 and 5.

ARTICLE 10

The Parties may, by unanimous agreement, invite any other European state in a position to further the principles of this Treaty and to contribute to the security of the North Atlantic area to accede to this Treaty. Any state so invited may become a party to the Treaty by depositing its instrument of accession with the Government of the United States of America. The Government of the United States of America will inform each of the Parties of the deposit of each such instrument of accession.

ARTICLE 11

This Treaty shall be ratified and its provisions carried out by the Parties in accordance with their respective constitutional processes. The instruments of ratification shall be deposited as soon as possible with the Government of the United States of America, which will notify all the other signatories of each deposit. The Treaty shall enter into force between the states which have ratified it as soon as the ratifications of the majority of the signatories, including the ratifications of Belgium, Canada, France, Luxembourg, the Netherlands, the United Kingdom, and the United States, have been deposited and shall come into effect with respect to other states on the date of the deposit of their ratifications.

ARTICLE 12

After the Treaty has been in force for ten years, or at any time thereafter, the Parties shall, if any of them so requests, consult together for the purpose of reviewing the Treaty, having regard for the factors then affecting peace and security in the North Atlantic area, including the development of universal as well as regional arrangements under the Charter of the United Nations for the maintenance of international peace and security.

ARTICLE 13

After the Treaty has been in force for twenty years, any Party may cease to be a party one year after its notice of denunciation has been given to the Government of the United States of America, which will inform the Governments of the other Parties of the deposit of each notice of denunciation.

ARTICLE 14

This Treaty, of which the English and French texts are equally authentic, shall be deposited in the archives of the Government of the United States of America. Duly certified copies thereof will be transmitted by that Government to the Governments of the other signatories.

In witness whereof, the undersigned plenipotentiaries have signed this Treaty.

Done at Washington, the fourth day of April, 1949.

20. Statute of the Council of Europe

Signed at London by Belgium, Denmark, France, Ireland, Italy, Luxembourg, the Netherlands, Norway, Sweden and the United Kingdom on May 5, 1949, the Statute came into force on August 3, 1949. Austria (1958), Cyprus (1961), German Federal Republic (1951), Greece (1949), Iceland (1950), Portugal (1977), and Turkey (1950) acceded to the Treaty in the years as indicated. The attached Statutory Texts adopted by the Committee of Ministers have the effect of amendments.

The [signatory] Governments . . .;

Convinced that the pursuit of peace based upon justice and international cooperation is vital for the preservation of human society and civilization;

Reaffirming their devotion to the spiritual and moral values which are the common heritage of their peoples and the true source of individual freedom, political liberty, and the rule of law, principles which form the basis of all genuine democracy;

Believing that, for the maintenance and further realization of these ideals and in the interests of economic and social progress, there is need of a closer unity between all like-minded countries of Europe;

Considering that, to respond to this need and to the expressed aspirations of their peoples in this regard, it is necessary forthwith to create an organization which will bring European States into closer association;

Have in consequence decided to set up a Council of Europe consisting of a Committee of representatives of Governments and of a Consultative Assembly, and have for this purpose adopted the following Statute:

I. AIM OF THE COUNCIL OF EUROPE

ARTICLE 1

(*a*) The aim of the Council of Europe is to achieve a greater unity between its Members for the purpose of safeguarding and realizing the ideals and principles which are their common heritage and facilitating their economic and social progress.

(*b*) This aim shall be pursued through the organs of the Council by discussion of questions of common concern and by agreements and common action in economic, social, cultural, scientific, legal, and administrative matters and in the maintenance and further realization of human rights and fundamental freedoms.

(*c*) Participation in the Council of Europe shall not affect the collaboration of its Members in the work of the United Nations and of other international organizations or unions to which they are parties.

(*d*) Matters relating to National Defense do not fall within the scope of the Council of Europe.

II. MEMBERSHIP
ARTICLE 2
The Members of the Council of Europe are the Parties to this Statute.

ARTICLE 3
Every Member of the Council of Europe must accept the principles of the rule of law and of the enjoyment by all persons within its jurisdiction of human rights and fundamental freedoms, and collaborate sincerely and effectively in the realization of the aim of the Council as specified in Chapter I.

ARTICLE 4
Any European State which is deemed to be able and willing to fulfill the provisions of Article 3 may be invited to become a Member of the Council of Europe by the Committee of Ministers. Any State so invited shall become a Member on the deposit on its behalf with the Secretary-General of an instrument of accession to the present Statute.

ARTICLE 5
(*a*) In special circumstances, a European country which is deemed to be able and willing to fulfill the provisions of Article 3 may be invited by the Committee of Ministers to become an Associate Member of the Council of Europe. Any country so invited shall become an Associate Member on the deposit on its behalf with the Secretary-General of an instrument accepting the present Statute. An Associate Member shall be entitled to be represented in the Consultative Assembly only.

(*b*) The expression "Member" in this Statute includes an Associate Member except when used in connection with representation on the Committee of Ministers.

ARTICLE 6
Before issuing invitations under Article 4 or 5 above, the Committee of Ministers shall determine the number of representatives on the Consultative Assembly to which the proposed Mamber shall be entitled and its proportionate financial contribution.

ARTICLE 7

Any Member of the Council of Europe may withdraw by formally notifying the Secretary-General of its intention to do so. Such withdrawal shall take effect at the end of the financial year in which it is notified, if the notification is given during the first nine months of that financial year. If the notification is given in the last three months of the financial year, it shall take effect at the end of the next financial year.

ARTICLE 8

Any Member of the Council of Europe which has seriously violated Article 3 may be suspended from its rights of representation and requested by the Committee of Ministers to withdraw under Article 7. If such Member does not comply with this request, the Committee may decide that it has ceased to be a Member of the Council as from such date as the Committee may determine.

ARTICLE 9

The Committee of Ministers may suspend the right of representation on the Committee and on the Consultative Assembly of a Member which has failed to fulfill its financial obligation, during such period as the obligation remains unfulfilled.

III. GENERAL

ARTICLE 10

The organs of the Council of Europe are: (*i*) the Committee of Ministers; (*ii*) the Consultative Assembly.

Both these organs shall be served by the Secretariat of the Council of Europe.

ARTICLE 11

The seat of the Council of Europe is at Strasbourg.

ARTICLE 12

The official languages of the Council are English and French. The rules of procedure of the Committee of Ministers and of the Consultative Assembly shall determine in what circumstances and under what conditions other languages may be used.

IV. COMMITTEE OF MINISTERS

ARTICLE 13

The Committee of Ministers is the organ which acts on behalf of the Council of Europe in accordance with Articles 15 and 16.

ARTICLE 14

Each Member shall be entitled to one representative on the Committee of Ministers and each representative shall be entitled to one vote. Representatives on the Committee shall be the Ministers for Foreign Affairs. When a Minister for Foreign Affairs is unable to be present or in other circumstances where it may be desirable, an alternate may be nominated to act for him, who shall, whenever possible, be a member of his Government.

ARTICLE 15

(*a*) On the recommendation of the Consultative Assembly or on its own initiative, the Committee of Ministers shall consider the action required to further the aim of the Council of Europe, including the conclusion of conventions or agreements and the adoption by Governments of a common policy with regard to particular matters. Its conclusions shall be communicated to Members by the Secretary-General.

(*b*) In appropriate cases, the conclusions of the Committee may take the form of recommendations to the Governments of Members, and the Committee may request the Governments of Members to inform it of the action taken by them with regard to such recommendations.

ARTICLE 16

The Committee of Ministers shall, subject to the provisions of Articles 24, 28, 30, 32, 33, and 35, relating to the powers of the Consultative Assembly, decide with binding effect all matters relating to the internal organization and arrangements of the Council of Europe. For this purpose the Committee of Ministers shall adopt such financial and administrative regulations as may be necessary.

ARTICLE 17

The Committee of Ministers may set up advisory and technical committees or commissions for such specific purposes as it may deem desirable.

ARTICLE 18

The Committee of Ministers shall adopt its rules of procedure which shall determine amongst other things: (*i*) the quorum; (*ii*) the method of appointment and term of office of its President; (*iii*) the procedure for the admission of items to its agenda, including the giving of notice of proposals for resolutions; and (*iv*) the notifications required for the nomination of alternates under Article 14.

ARTICLE 19

At each session of the Consultative Assembly the Committee of Ministers shall furnish the Assembly with statements of its activities, accompanied by appropriate documentation.

ARTICLE 20

(*a*) Resolutions of the Committee of Ministers relating to the following important matters, namely: (*i*) recommendations under Article 15*b;* (*ii*) questions under Article 19; (*iii*) questions under Article 21*a* (*i*) and 21*b*; (*iv*) questions under Article 33; (*v*) recommendations for the amendment of Articles 1*d,* 7, 15, 20, and 22; and (*iv*) any other question which the Committee may, by a resolution passed under (*d*) below, decide should be subject to a unanimous vote on account of its importance; require the unanimous vote of the representatives casting a vote, and of a majority of the representatives entitled to sit on the Committee.

(*b*) Questions arising under the rules of procedure or under the financial and administrative regulations may be decided by a simple majority vote of the representatives entitled to sit on the Committee.

(*c*) Resolutions of the Committee under Articles 4 and 5 require a two-thirds majority of all the representatives entitled to sit on the Committee.

(*d*) All other resolutions of the Committee, including the adoption of the budget, of rules of procedure, and of financial and administrative regulations, recommendations for the amendment of articles of this Statute, other than those mentioned in paragraph (*a*) (*v*) above, and deciding in case of doubt which paragraph of this Article applies, require a two-thirds majority of the representatives casting a vote and of a majority of the representatives entitled to sit on the Committee.

ARTICLE 21

(*a*) Unless the Committee decides otherwise, meetings of the Committee of Ministers shall be held: (*i*) in private, and (*ii*) at the seat of the Council.

(*b*) The Committee shall determine what information shall be published regarding the conclusions and discussions of a meeting held in private.

(*c*) The Committee shall meet before and during the beginning of every session of the Consultative Assembly and at such other times as it may decide.

V. CONSULTATIVE ASSEMBLY

ARTICLE 22

The Consultative Assembly is the deliberative organ of the Council of Europe. It shall debate matters within its competence under this Statute and present its conclusions, in the form of recommendations, to the Committee of Ministers.

ARTICLE 23

(*a*) The Consultative Assembly may discuss and make recommendations upon any matter within the aim and scope of the Council of Europe as defined in Chapter I. It shall also discuss and may make recommendations upon any matter referred to it by the Committee of Ministers with a request for its opinion.

(*b*) The Assembly shall draw up its Agenda in accordance with the provisions of paragraph (*a*) above. In so doing, it shall have regard to the work of other European intergovernmental organizations to which some or all of the Members of the Council are parties.

(*c*) The President of the Assembly shall decide, in case of doubt, whether any question raised in the course of the Session is within the Agenda of the Assembly.

ARTICLE 24

The Consultative Assembly may, with due regard to the provisions of Article 38*d,* establish committees or commissions to consider and report to it on any matter which falls within its competence under Article 23, to examine and prepare questions on its agenda and to advise on all matters of procedure.

ARTICLE 25

(*a*) The Consultative Assembly shall consist of Representatives of each Member elected by its Parliament or appointed in such manner as that Parliament shall decide, subject, however, to the right of each Member Government to make any additional appointments necessary when the Parliament is not in session and has not laid down the procedure to be followed in that case. Each representative must be a national of the Member whom he represents, but shall not at the same time be a member of the Committee of Ministers.

The term of office of Representatives thus appointed will date from the opening of the Ordinary Session following their appointment; it will expire at opening of the next Ordinary Session or of a latter Ordinary Session, except that, in the event of elections to their Parliaments having taken place, Members shall be entitled to make new appointments.

If a Member fills vacancies due to death or resignation, or proceeds to make new appointments as a result of elections to its Parliament, the term of office of the new Representatives shall date from the first Sitting of the Assembly following their appointment.

(*b*) No representative shall be deprived of his position as such during a session of the Assembly without the agreement of the Assembly.

(*c*) Each representative may have a substitute who may, in the absence of the representative, sit, speak, and vote in his place. The provisions of paragraph (*a*) above apply to the appointment of substitutes.

ARTICLE 26
Members shall be entitled to the number of Representatives given below:

Austria	6	Italy	18
Belgium	7	Luxembourg	3
Cyprus	3	Netherlands	7
Denmark	5	Norway	5
France	18	Sweden	6
Germany (Federal Republic)	18	Turkey	10
Greece	7	United Kingdom of Great	
Iceland	3	Britain and Northern	
Ireland	4	Ireland	18

ARTICLE 27
The conditions under which the Committee of Ministers collectively may be represented in the debates of the Consultative Assembly, or individual representatives on the Committee or their alternates may address the Assembly, shall be determined by such rules of procedure on this subject as may be drawn up by the Committee after consultation with the Assembly.

ARTICLE 28
(*a*) The Consultative Assembly shall adopt its rules of procedure and shall elect from its members its President, who shall remain in office until the next ordinary session.

(*b*) The President shall control the proceedings but shall not take part in the debate or vote. The substitute of the Representative who is President may sit, speak, and vote in his place.

(*c*) The rules of procedure shall determine *inter alia:* (*i*) the quorum; (*ii*) the manner of the election and terms of office of the President and other officers; (*iii*) the manner in which the agenda shall be drawn up and be communicated to Representatives; and (*iv*) the time and manner in which the names of Representatives and their Substitutes shall be notified.

ARTICLE 29
Subject to the provisions of Article 30, all resolutions of the Consultative Assembly, including resolutions: (*i*) embodying recommendations to the Committee of Ministers; (*ii*) proposing to the Committee matters for

discussion in the Assembly; (*iii*) establishing committees or commissions; (*iv*) determining the date of commencement of its sessions; [and] (*v*) determining what majority is required for resolutions in cases not covered by (*i*) to (*iv*) above or determining cases of doubt as to what majority is required, shall require a two-thirds majority of the Representatives casting a vote.

ARTICLE 30

On matters relating to its internal procedure, which includes the election of officers, the nomination of persons to serve on committees and commissions and the adoption of rules of procedure, resolutions of the Consultative Assembly shall be carried by such majorities as the Assembly may determine in accordance with Article 29 (*v*).

ARTICLE 31

Debates on proposals to be made to the Committee of Ministers that a matter should be placed on the Agenda of the Consultative Assembly shall be confined to an indication of the proposed subject matter and the reasons for and against its inclusion in the Agenda.

ARTICLE 32

The Consultative Assembly shall meet in ordinary session once a year, the date and duration of which shall be determined by the Assembly so as to avoid as far as possible overlapping with parliamentary sessions of Members and with sessions of the General Assembly of the United Nations. In no circumstances shall the duration of an ordinary session exceed one month unless both the Assembly and the Committee of Ministers concur.

ARTICLE 33

Ordinary sessions of the Consultative Assembly shall be held at the seat of the Council unless both the Assembly and the Committee of Ministers concur that it should be held elsewhere.

ARTICLE 34

The Consultative Assembly may be convened in extraordinary sessions upon the initiative either of the Committee of Ministers or of the President of the Assembly after agreement between them, such agreement also to determine the date and place of the sessions.

ARTICLE 35

Unless the Consultative Assembly decides otherwise, its debates shall be conducted in public.

VI. SECRETARIAT

ARTICLE 36

(*a*) The Secretariat shall consist of a Secretary-General, a Deputy Secretary-General and such other staff as may be required.

(*b*) The Secretary-General and Deputy Secretary-General shall be appointed by the Consultative Assembly on the recommendation of the Committee of Ministers.

(*c*) The remaining staff of the Secretariat shall be appointed by the Secretary-General, in accordance with the administrative regulations.

(*d*) No member of the Secretariat shall hold any salaried office from any Government or be a member of the Consultative Assembly or of any national legislature or engage in any occupation incompatible with his duties.

(*e*) Every member of the staff of the Secretariat shall make a solemn declaration affirming that his duty is to the Council of Europe and that he will perform his duties conscientiously, uninfluenced by any national considerations, and that he will not seek or receive instructions in connection with the performance of his duties from any Government or any authority external to the Council and will refrain from any action which might reflect on his position as an international official responsible only to the Council. In the case of the Secretary-General and the Deputy Secretary-General this declaration shall be made before the Committee, and in the case of all other members of the staff, before the Secretary-General.

(*f*) Every Member shall respect the exclusively international character of the responsibilities of the Secretary-General and the staff of the Secretariat and not seek to influence them in the discharge of their responsibilities.

ARTICLE 37

(*a*) The Secretariat shall be located at the seat of the Council.

(*b*) The Secretary-General is responsible to the Committee of Ministers for the work of the Secretariat. Amongst other things, he shall, subject to Article 38*d,* provide such secretariat and other assistance as the Consultative Assembly may require.

VII. FINANCE

ARTICLE 38

(*a*) Each Member shall bear the expenses of its own representation in the Committee of Ministers and in the Consultative Assembly.

(*b*) The expenses of the Secretariat and all other common expenses shall be shared between all Members in such proportions as shall be determined by the Committee on the basis of the population of Members.

The contributions of an Associate Member shall be determined by the Committee.

(*c*) In accordance with the financial regulations, the budget of the Council shall be submitted annually by the Secretary-General for adoption by the Committee.

(*d*) The Secretary-General shall refer to the Committee requests from the Assembly which involve expenditure exceeding the amount already allocated in the Budget for the Assembly and its activities.

(*e*) The Secretary-General shall also submit to the Committee of Ministers an estimate of the expenditure to which the implementation of each of the recommendations presented to the Committee would give rise. Any resolution the implementation of which requires additional expenditure shall not be considered as adopted by the Committee of Ministers unless the Committee has also approved the corresponding estimates for such additional expenditure.

ARTICLE 39

The Secretary-General shall each year notify the Government of each Member of the amount of its contribution, and each Member shall pay to the Secretary-General the amount of its contribution, which shall be deemed to be due on the date of its notification, not later than six months after that date.

VIII. PRIVILEGES AND IMMUNITIES
ARTICLE 40

(*a*) The Council of Europe, Representatives of Members and the Secretariat shall enjoy in the territories of its Members such privileges and immunities as are reasonably necessary for the fulfillment of their functions. These immunities shall include immunity for all Representatives in the Consultative Assembly from arrest and all legal proceedings in the territories of all Members, in respect of words spoken and votes cast in the debates of the Assembly or its committees or commissions.

(*b*) The Members undertake as soon as possible to enter into agreement for the purpose of fulfilling the provisions of paragraph (*a*) above. For this purpose the Committee of Ministers shall recommend to the Governments of Members the acceptance of an Agreement defining the privileges and immunities to be granted in the territories of all Members. In addition a special Agreement shall be concluded with the Government of the French Republic defining the privileges and immunities which the Council shall enjoy at its seat.

IX. AMENDMENTS

ARTICLE 41

(*a*) Proposals for the amendments of this Statute may be made in the Committee of Ministers or, in the conditions provided for in Article 23, in the Consultative Assembly.

(*b*) The Committee shall recommend and cause to be embodied in a Protocol those amendments which it considers to be desirable.

(*c*) An amending Protocol shall come into force when it has been signed and ratified on behalf of two-thirds of the Members.

(*d*) Notwithstanding the provisions of the preceding paragraphs of this Article, amendments to Articles 23–35, 38, and 39 which have been approved by the Committee and by the Assembly shall come into force on the date of the certificate of the Secretary-General, transmitted to the Governments of Members, certifying that they have been so approved. This paragraph shall not operate until the conclusion of the second ordinary session of the Assembly.

X. FINAL PROVISIONS

ARTICLE 42

(*a*) This Statute shall be ratified. Ratifications shall be deposited with the Government of the United Kingdom of Great Britain and Northern Ireland.

(*b*) The present Statute shall come into force as soon as seven instruments of ratification have been deposited. The Government of the United Kingdom shall transmit to all signatory Governments a certificate declaring that the Statute has entered into force, and giving the names of the Members of the Council of Europe on that date.

(*c*) Thereafter each other signatory shall become a party to this Statute as from the date of the deposit of its instrument of ratification.

In witness whereof the undersigned, being duly authorized thereto, have signed the present Statute.

Done at London, this fifth day of May, 1949, in English and French, both texts being equally authentic, in a single copy which shall remain deposited in the archives of the Government of the United Kingdom which shall transmit certified copies to the other signatory Governments.

I: TEXTS OF A STATUTORY CHARACTER

The Committee of Ministers,

Having regard to certain proposals made by the Consultative Assembly for the revision of the Statute of the Council of Europe;

Considering that the provisions hereinafter set out are not inconsistent with the present Statute;

Declares its intention of putting into effect the following provisions:

Admission of New Members

The Committee of Ministers, before inviting a State to become a Member or Associate Member of the Council of Europe, in accordance with Articles 4 and 5 of the Statute, or inviting a Member of the Council of Europe to withdraw, in accordance with Article 8, shall first consult the Consultative Assembly in accordance with existing Practice.

Powers of the Committee of Ministers (Article 15 of the Statute)

The conclusions of the Committee may, where appropriate, take the form of a convention or agreement. In that event the following provisions shall be applied:

(*i*) The convention or agreement shall be submitted by the Secretary-General to all Members for ratification;

(*ii*) Each Member undertakes that within one year of such submission, or, where this is impossible owing to exceptional circumstances, within eighteen months, the question of ratification of the convention or agreement shall be brought before the competent authority or authorities in its country;

(*iii*) The instruments of ratification shall be deposited with the Secretary-General;

(*iv*) The convention or agreement shall be binding only on such Members as have ratified it.

Joint Committee

(*i*) The Joint Committee is the organ of coordination of the Council of Europe. Without prejudice to the respective rights of the Committee of Ministers and the Consultative Assembly, the functions of the Joint Committee shall be, in particular: (*a*) to examine the problems which are common to those two organs; (*b*) to draw the attention of those two organs to questions which appear to be of particular interest to the Council of Europe; (*c*) to make proposals for the draft Agenda of the sessions of the Committee of Ministers and of the Consultative Assembly; (*d*) to examine and promote means of giving practical effect to the recommendations adopted by one or other of these two organs.

(*ii*) (*a*) The Joint Committee shall be composed in principle of twelve members, five representing the Committee of Ministers and seven representing the Consultative Assembly, the latter number to include the President of the Consultative who shall be a member ex officio.

The number of members may be increased by agreement between the Committee of Ministers and the Assembly. Nevertheless, the Committee of Ministers shall, at its discretion, be entitled to increase the number of its representatives by one or two.

(*b*) The Committee of Ministers and the Consultative Assembly shall each be free to choose its own method of selecting its representatives on the Joint Committee.

(*c*) The Secretary-General shall be entitled to attend the meetings of the Joint Committee in an advisory capacity.

(*iii*) (*a*) The President of the Consultative Assembly shall be the Chairman of the Joint Committee.

(*b*) No proceedings of the Committee shall be regarded as valid unless there is a quorum consisting of three of the representatives of the Committee of Ministers and five of the representatives of the Consultative Assembly.

(*c*) The conclusions of the Joint Committee shall be reached without voting.

(*d*) The meetings of the Joint Committee shall be convened by the Chairman and shall take place as often as is necessary and, in particular, before and after the sessions of the Committee of Ministers and of the Consultative Assembly.

(*e*) Subject to the foregoing provisions, the Joint Committee may adopt its own Rules of Procedure.

Specialized Authorities

(*i*) (*a*) The Council of Europe may take the initiative of instituting negotiations between Members with a view to the creation of European Specialized Authorities, each with its own competence in the economic, social, cultural, legal, administrative, or other related fields.

(*b*) Each Member shall remain free to adhere or not to adhere to any such European Specialized Authority.

(*ii*) If Member States set up European Specialized Authorities among themselves on their own initiative, the desirability of bringing these Authorities into relationship with the Council of Europe shall be considered, due account being taken of the interests of the European community as a whole.

(*iii*) (*a*) The Committee of Ministers may invite each Authority to submit to it a periodical report on its activities.

(*b*) Insofar as any agreement setting up a Specialized Authority provides for a parliamentary body, this body may be invited to submit a periodical report to the Consultative Assembly of the Council of Europe.

(*iv*) (*a*) The conditions under which a Specialized Authority shall be brought into relationship with the Council may be determined by special agreements concluded between the Council and the Specialized Authority concerned. Such agreements may cover, in particular:

1)   reciprocal representation and, if the question arises, appropriate forms of integration between the organs of the Council of Europe and those of the Specialized Authority;
2)   the exchange of information, documents, and statistical data;
3)   the presentation of reports by the Specialized Authority to the Council of Europe and of recommendations of the Council of Europe to the Specialized Authority;
4)   arrangements concerning staff and administrative, technical, budgetary and financial services.

(*b*) Such agreements shall be negotiated and concluded on behalf of the Council of Europe by the Committee of Ministers after an opinion has been given by the Consultative Assembly.

(*v*) The Council of Europe may coordinate the work of the Specialized Authorities brought into relationship with the Council of Europe in accordance with the foregoing provisions by holding joint discussions and by submitting recommendations to them, as well as by submitting recommendations to Member Governments.

Relations with Intergovernmental and Nongovernmental International Organizations

(*i*) The Committee of Ministers may, on behalf of the Council of Europe, conclude with any intergovernmental organization agreements on matters which are within the competence of the Council. These agreements shall, in particular, define the terms on which such an organization shall be brought into relationship with the Council of Europe.

(*ii*) The Council of Europe, or any of its organs, shall be authorized to exercise any functions coming within the scope of the Council of Europe which may be entrusted to it by other European intergovernmental organizations. The Committee of Ministers shall conclude any agreements necessary for this purpose.

(*iii*) The agreement referred to in paragraph (*i*) may provide, in particular: (*a*) that the Council shall take appropriate steps to obtain from, and furnish to, the organizations in question regular reports and information, either in writing or orally; (*b*) that the Council shall give opinions and render such services as may be requested by these organizations.

(*iv*) The Committee of Ministers may, on behalf of the Council of Europe, make suitable arrangements for consultation with international nongovernmental organizations which deal with matters that are within the competence of the Council of Europe.

II: PARTIAL AGREEMENTS

The Committee of Ministers,

Having regard to Article 20a of the Statute, which provides that recommendations by the Committee of Ministers to Member Governments require the unanimous vote of the representatives casting a vote and of a majority of the representatives entitled to sit on the Committee;

Having regard to Recommendation 3 adopted by the Consultative Assembly in August, 1950;

Desirous, whenever possible, of reaching agreement by unanimous decision, but recognizing, nevertheless, that in certain circumstances individual Members may wish to abstain from participating in a course of action advocated by other Members;

Considering that it is desirable for this purpose that the procedure of abstention already recognized under Article 20a of the Statute should be so defined that the individual representatives on the Committee of Ministers should be able, by abstaining from voting for a proposal, to avoid committing their Governments to the decision taken by their colleagues,

Resolves:

1. If the Committee, by the unanimous vote of the representatives casting a vote and of a majority of the representatives entitled to sit on the Committee, decides that abstention from participation in any proposal before it shall be permitted, that proposal shall be put to the Committee; it shall be considered as adopted only by the representatives who then vote in favor of it, and its application shall be limited accordingly.

2. Any additional expenditure incurred by the Council in connection with a proposal adopted under the above procedure shall be borne exclusively by the Members whose representatives have voted in favor of it.

21. Treaty Establishing the European Economic Community (Common Market)

Signed at Rome by Belgium, France, German Federal Republic, Italy, Luxembourg and the Netherlands on March 25, 1957, the Treaty came into force on January 1, 1958. Membership of the Common Market has been expanded to include Denmark, Ireland, and the United Kingdom now. Because of space limitation, some parts of the text are omitted. For full text, see 298 U.N. Treaty Series, 11.

I. PRINCIPLES

ARTICLE 1

By the present Treaty, the HIGH CONTRACTING PARTIES establish among themselves a EUROPEAN ECONOMIC COMMUNITY.

ARTICLE 2

It shall be the aim of the Community, by establishing a Common Market and progressively approximating the economic policies of Member States, to promote throughout the Community a harmonious development of economic activities, a continuous and balanced expansion, an increased stability, an accelerated raising of the standard of living and closer relations between its Member States.

ARTICLE 3

For the purposes set out in the preceding Article, the activities of the Community shall include, under the conditions and with the timing provided for in this Treaty:

(*a*) the elimination, as between Member States, of customs duties and of quantitative restrictions in regard to the importation and exportation of goods, as well as of all other measures with equivalent effect;

(*b*) the establishment of a common customs tariff and a common commercial policy towards third countries;

(*c*) the abolition, as between Member States, of the obstacles to the free movement of persons, services and capital;

(*d*) the inauguration of a common agricultural policy;

(*e*) the inauguration of a common transport policy;

(*f*) the establishment of a system ensuring that competition shall not be distorted in the Common Market;

(*g*) the application of procedures which shall make it possible to coordinate the economic policies of Member States and to remedy disequilibria in their balance of payments;

(*h*) the approximation of their respective municipal law to the extent necessary for the functioning of the Common Market;

(*i*) the creation of a European Social Fund in order to improve the possibilities of employment for workers and to contribute to the raising of their standard of living;

(*j*) the establishment of a European Investment Bank intended to facilitate the economic expansion of the Community through the creation of new resources; and

(*k*) the association of overseas countries and territories with the Community with a view to increasing trade and to pursuing jointly their effort towards economic and social development.

ARTICLE 4

1. The achievement of the tasks entrusted to the Community shall be ensured by:

—an ASSEMBLY,

—a COUNCIL,

—a COMMISSION, and

—a COURT OF JUSTICE.

Each of these institutions shall act within the limits of the powers conferred upon it by this Treaty.

2. The Council and the Commission shall be assisted by an Economic and Social Committee acting in a consultative capacity.

ARTICLE 5

Member States shall take all general or particular measures which are appropriate for ensuring the carrying out of the obligations arising out of this Treaty or resulting from the acts of the institutions of the Community. They shall facilitate the achievement of the Community's aims.

They shall abstain from any measures likely to jeopardise the attainment of the objectives of this Treaty.

ARTICLE 6

1. Member States, acting in close collaboration with the institutions of the Community, shall coordinate their respective economic policies to the extent that is necessary to attain the objectives of this Treaty.

2. The institutions of the Community shall take care not to prejudice the internal and external financial stability of Member States.

ARTICLE 7

Within the field of application of this Treaty and without prejudice to the special provisions mentioned therein, any discrimination on the grounds of nationality shall hereby be prohibited.

The Council may, acting by means of a qualified majority vote on a proposal of the Commission and after the Assembly has been consulted, lay down rules in regard to the prohibition of any such descrimination.

ARTICLE 8

1. The Common Market shall be progressively established in the course of a transitional period of twelve years.

The transitional period shall be divided into three stages of four years each; the length of each stage may be modified in accordance with the provisions set out below.

2. To each stage there shall be allotted a group of actions which shall be undertaken and pursued concurrently.

.   .   .

5. The second and third stages may not be extended or curtailed except pursuant to a decision of the Council acting by means of a unanimous vote on a proposal of the Commission.

6. The provisions of the preceding paragraphs shall not have the effect of extending the transitional period beyond a total duration of fifteen years after the date of the entry into force of this Treaty.

7. Subject to the exceptions or deviations provided for in this Treaty, the expiry of the transitional period shall constitute the final date for the entry into force of all the rules laid down and for the completion of all the measures required for the establishment of the Common Market.

II. BASES OF THE COMMUNITY

Title I: Free Movement of Goods

ARTICLE 9

1. The Community shall be based upon a customs union covering the exchange of all goods and comprising both the prohibition, as between Member States, of customs duties on importation and exportation and all charges with equivalent effect and the adoption of a common customs tariff in their relations with third countries.

.   .   .

ARTICLE 11

The Member States shall take all appropriate measures to enable Governments to carry out, within the time-limits laid down, the obligations with regard to customs duties which are incumbent on them pursuant to this Treaty.

ARTICLE 12

Member States shall refrain from introducing, as between themselves, any new customs duties on importation or exportation or charges with equivalent effect and from increasing such duties or charges as they apply in their commercial relations with each other.

ARTICLE 13

1. Customs duties on importation in force between Member States shall be progressively abolished by them in the course of the transitional period under the conditions laid down in Articles 14 and 15.

. . .

ARTICLE 14

1. In respect of each product, the basic duty which shall be subject to the successive reductions shall be the duty applied on 1 January 1957.

. . .

ARTICLE 16

Member States shall abolish as between themselves, not later than at the end of the first stage, the customs duties on exportation and charges with equivalent effect.

ARTICLE 19

1. Under the conditions and within the limits laid down below, the duties under the common customs tariff shall be at the level of the arithmetical average of the duties applied in the four customs territories covered by the Community.

2. The duties taken into account for calculating this average shall be those applied by Member States on 1 January 1957.

. . .

ARTICLE 23

. . .

3. The common customs tariff shall be applied in its entirety not later than at the date of the expiry of the transitional period.

ARTICLE 26

The Commission may authorise any Member State encountering special difficulties to postpone the lowering or the raising, in accordance with the provisions of Article 23, of the duties on certain headings of its tariff.

Such authorization may only be granted for a limited period and for tariff headings which together represent for such State not more than 5 percent of the value of its total imports coming from third countries in the course of the latest year for which statistical data are available.

ARTICLE 29

In carrying out the tasks entrusted to it under this Section, the Commission shall be guided by:

(*a*) the need for promoting commercial exchanges between the Member States and third countries;

(*b*) the development of competitive conditions within the Community to the extent to which such development will result in the increase of the competitive capacity of the enterprises;

(*c*) the Community's requirements of supply in raw materials and semifinished goods, while at the same time taking care not to distort competitive conditions between Member States with regard to finished goods; and

(*d*) the need for avoiding serious disturbances in the economic life of Member States and for ensuring a rational development of production and an expansion of consumption within the Community.

ARTICLE 30

Quantitative restrictions on importation and all measures with equivalent effect shall, without prejudice to the following provisions, hereby be prohibited between Member States.

ARTICLE 36

The provisions of Articles 30 to 34 inclusive shall not be an obstacle to prohibitions or restrictions in respect of importation, exportation or transit which are justified on grounds of public morality, public order, public safety, the protection of human or animal life or health, the preservation of plant life, the protection of national treasures of artistic, historical of archeological value or the protection of industrial and commercial property. Such prohibitions or restrictions shall not, however, constitute either a means of arbitrary discrimination or a disguised restriction on trade between Member States.

ARTICLE 37

1. Member States shall progressively adjust any State monopolies of a commercial character in such a manner as will ensure the exclusion, at the date of the expiry of the transitional period, of all discrimination between the nationals of Members States in regard to conditions of supply or marketing of goods.

The provisions of this Article shall apply to any body by means of which a Member State shall *de jure* or *de facto* either directly or indirectly control, direct or appreciably influence importation or exportation between Member States. These provisions shall apply also to monopolies assigned by the State.

2. Member States shall abstain from any new measure which is contrary to the principles laid down in paragraph 1 or which may limit the scope of the Articles relating to the abolition, as between Member States, of customs duties and quantitative restrictions.

.   .   .

Title III: Free Movement of Persons, Services, and Capital
Chap. 1: Workers

ARTICLE 48

1. The free movement of workers shall be ensured within the Community not later than at the date of the expiry of the transitional period.

2. This shall involve the abolition of any discrimination based on nationality between workers of the Member States as regards employment, remuneration and other working conditions.

3. It shall include the right, subject to limitations justified by reasons of public order, public safety, and public health:

(*a*) to accept offers of employment actually made:

(*b*) to move about freely for this purposes within the territory of Member States;

(*c*) to stay in any Member State in order to carry on an employment in conformity with the legislative and administrative provisions governing the employment of the workers of that State; and

(*d*) to live, on conditions which shall be the subject of implementing regulations to be laid down by the Commission, in the territory of a Member State after having been employed there.

4. The provisions of this Article shall not apply to employment in the public administration.

ARTICLE 49

Upon the entry into force of this Treaty, the Council, acting on a proposal of the Commission and after the Economic and Social Committee has been consulted, shall, by means of directives or regulations, lay down the measures necessary to effect progressively the free movement of workers, as defined in the preceding Article, in particular:

(*a*) by ensuring close collaboration between national labour administrations;

(*b*) by progressively abolishing according to a plan any such administrative procedures and practices and also any such time-limits in respect of eligibility for available employment as are applied as a result either of municipal law or of agreements previously concluded between Member States and the maintenance of which would be an obstacle to the freeing of the movement of workers;

(*c*) by progressively abolishing according to a plan all such time-limits and other restrictions provided for either under municipal law or under agreements previously concluded between Member States as impose on workers of other Member States conditions for the free choice of employment different from those imposed on workers of the State concerned; and

(*d*) by setting up appropriate machinery for connecting offers of employment and requests for employment, with a view to equilibrating them in such a way as to avoid serious threats to the standard of living and employment in the various regions and industries.

ARTICLE 50
Member States shall, under a common programme, encourage the exchange of young workers.

ARTICLE 51
The Council, acting by means of a unanimous vote on a proposal of the Commission, shall, in the field of social security, adopt the measures necessary to effect the free movement of workers, in particular, by introducing a system which permits an assurance to be given to migrant workers and their beneficiaries:

(*a*) that, for the purposes of qualifying for and retaining the right to benefits and of the calculation of these benefits, all periods taken into consideration by the respective municipal law of the countries concerned, shall be added together; and

(*b*) that these benefits will be paid to persons resident in the territories of Member States.

Chapter 2: The Right of Establishment
ARTICLE 52
Within the framework of the provisions set out below, restrictions on the freedom of establishment of nationals of a Member State in the territory of another Member State shall be progressively abolished in the course of the transitional period. Such progressive abolition shall also extend to restrictions on the setting up of agencies, branches or subsidiaries by nationals of any Member State established in the territory of any Member State.

Freedom of establishment shall include the right to engage in and carry on non-wage-earning activities, and also to set up and manage enterprises and, in particular, companies within the meaning of Article 58, second paragraph, under the conditions laid down by the law of the contry of establishment for its own nationals, subject to the provisions of the Chapter relating to capital.

ARTICLE 53

Member States shall not, subject to the provisions of this Treaty, introduce any new restrictions on the establishment in their territories of nationals of other Member States.

ARTICLE 54

1. Before the expiry of the first stage, the Council, acting by means of a unanimous vote on a proposal of the Commission and after the Economic and Social Committee and the Assembly have been consulted, shall lay down a general programme for the abolition of restrictions existing within the Community on freedom of establishment. The Commission shall submit such proposal to the Council in the course of the first two years of the first stage.

The programme shall, in respect of each category of activities, fix the general conditions for achieving freedom of establishment and, in particular, the stages by which it shall be attained.

2. In order to implement the general programme or, if no such programme exists, to complete one stage towards the achievement of freedom of establishment for a specific activity, the Council, on a proposal of the Commission and after the Economic and Social Committee and the Assembly have been consulted, shall, until the end of the first stage by means of a unanimous vote and subsequently by means of a qualified majority vote, act by issuing directives.

3. The Council and the Commission shall exercise the functions entrusted to them by the above provisions, in particular:

(*a*) by according, as a general rule, priority treatment to activities in regard to which freedom of establishment constitutes a specially valuable contribution to the development of production and trade;

(*b*) by ensuring close collaboration between the competent national authorities with a view to ascertaining the special situation within the Community of the various activities concerned;

(*c*) by abolishing any such administrative procedures and practice whether resulting from municipal law or from agreements previously concluded between Member States as would, if maintained, be an obstacle to freedom of establishment;

(*d*) by ensuring that wage-earning workers of one Member State employed in the territory of another Member State may remain in that territory for the purpose of undertaking a non-wage-earning activity there, provided that they satisfy the conditions which they would be required to satisfy if they came to that State at the time when they wish to engage in such activity;

(*e*) by enabling a national of one Member State to acquire and exploit real property situated in the territory of another Member State, to the extent that no infringement of the principles laid down in Article 39, paragraph 2 in thereby caused;

(*f*) by applying the progressive abolition of restrictions on freedom of establishment, in each branch of activity under consideration, both in respect of the conditions for setting up agencies, branches or subsidiaries in the territory of a Member State and in respect of the conditions governing the entry of personnel of the main establishment into the managerial or supervisory organs of such agencies, branches, and subsidiaries;

(*g*) by coordinating, to the extent that is necessary and with a view to making them equivalent, the guarantees demanded in Member States from companies within the meaning of Article 58, second paragraph, for the purpose of protecting the interests both of the members of such companies and of third parties; and

(*h*) by satisfying themselves that conditions of establishment shall not be impaired by any aids granted by Member States.

ARTICLE 55

Activities which in any State include, even incidentally, the exercise of public authority shall, in so far as that State is concerned, by excluded from the application of the provisions of this Chapter.

The Council, acting by means of a qualified majority vote on a proposal of the Commission, may exclude certain activities from the application of the provisions of this Chapter.

ARTICLE 56

1. The provisions of this Chapter and the measures taken in pursuance thereof shall not prejudice the applicability of legislative and administrative provisions which lay down special treatment for foreign nationals and which are justified by reasons of public order, public safety, and public health.

2. Before the expiry of the transitional period, the Council, acting by means of a unanimous vote on a proposal of the Commission and after the Assembly has been consulted, shall issue directives for the coordination of the above-mentioned legislative and administrative provisions. After the end of the second stage, however, the Council, acting by means of a

qualified majority vote on a proposal of the Commission, shall issue directives for coordinating such provisions as, in each Member State, fall within the administrative field.

ARTICLE 57

1. In order to facilitate the engagement in and exercise of non-wage-earning activities, the Council, on a proposal of the Commission and after the Assembly has been consulted, shall, in the course of the first stage by meany of a unanimous vote and subsequently by means of a qualified majority vote, act by issuing directives regarding mutual recognition of diplomas, certificates and other qualifications.

2. For the same purpose, the Council, acting on a proposal of the Commission and after the Assembly has been consulted, shall, before the expiry of the transitional period, issue directives regarding the coordination of legislative and administrative provisions of Member States concerning the engagement in and exercise of non-wage-earning activities. A unanimous vote shall be required on matters which, in at least one Member State, are subject to legislative provisions, and on measures concerning the protection of savings, in particular the allotment of credit and the banking profession, and concerning the conditions governing the exercise in the various Member States of the medical, para-medical and pharmaceutical professions. In all other cases, the Council shall act in the course of the first stage by means of a unanimous vote and subsequently by means of a qualified majority vote.

3. In the case of the medical, para-medical and pharmaceutical professions, the progressive removal of restrictions shall be subject to the coordination of conditions for their exercise in the various Member States.

ARTICLE 58

Companies constituted in accordance with the law of a Member State and having their registeed office, central management or main establishment within the Community shall, for the purpose of applying the provisions of this Chapter, be assimilated to natural persons being nationals of Member States.

The term "companies" shall mean companies under civil or commercial law including cooperative companies and other legal persons under public or private law, with the exception of non-profit-making companies.

Chap. 4: Capital

ARTICLE 67

1. Member States shall, in the course of the transitional period and to the extent necessary for the proper functioning of the Common Market, progressively abolish as between themselves restrictions on the movement of

capital belonging to persons resident in Member States and also any discriminatory treatment based on the nationality or place of residence of the parties or on the place in which such capital is invested.

2. Current payments connected with movements of capital between Member States shall be freed from all restrictions not later than at the end of the first stage.

III: POLICY OF THE COMMUNITY

Title I: Common Rules

Chap. 1: Rules Governing Competition

ARTICLE 85

1. The following shall be deemed to be incompatible with the Common Market and shall hereby be prohibited: any agreements between enterprises, any decisions by associations of enterprises and any concerted practices which are likely to affect trade between the Member States and which have as their object or result the prevention, restriction or distortion of competition within the Common Market, in particular those consisting in:

(*a*) the direct or indirect fixing of purchase or selling prices or of any other trading conditions;

(*b*) the limitation or control of production, markets, technical development or investment;

(*c*) market-sharing or the sharing of sources of supply;

(*d*) the application to parties to transactions of unequal terms in respect of equivalent supplies, thereby placing them at a competitive disadvantage; or

(*e*) the subjecting of the conclusion of a contract to the acceptance by a party of additional supplies which, either by their nature or according to commercial usage, have no connection with the subject of such contract.

2. Any agreements or decisions prohibited pursuant to this Article shall be null and void.

3. Nevertheless, the provisions of paragraph 1 may be declared inapplicable in the case of:

—any agreements or classes of agreements between enterprises,

—any decisions or classes of decisions by associations of enterprises, and

—any concerted practices or classes of concerted practices which contribute to the improvement of the production or distribution of goods or to the promotion of technical or economic progress while reserving to users an equitable share in the profit resulting therefrom, and which:

(*a*) neither impose on the enterprises concerned any restrictions not indispensable to the attainment of the above objectives;

(*b*) nor enable such enterprises to eliminate competition in respect of a substantial proportion of the goods concerned.

ARTICLE 86

To the extent to which trade between any Member States may be affected thereby, action by one or more enterprises to take improper advantage of a dominant position within the Common Market or within a substantial part of it shall be deemed to be incompatible with the Common Market and shall hereby be prohibited.

Such improper practices may, in particular, consist in:

(*a*) the direct or indirect imposition of any inequitable purchase or selling prices or of any other inequitable trading conditions;

(*b*) the limitation of production, markets or technical development to the prejudice of consumers;

(*c*) the application to parties to transactions of unequal terms in respect of equivalent supplies, thereby placing them at a competitive disadvantage: or

(*d*) the subjecting of the conclusion of a contract to the acceptance, by a party, of additional supplies which, either by their nature or according to commercial usage, have no connection with the subject of such contract.

ARTICLE 87

1. Within a period of three years after the date of the entry into force of this Treaty, the Council, acting by means of a unanimous vote on a proposal of the Commission and after the Assembly has been consulted, shall lay down any appropriate regulations or directives with a view to the application of the principles set out in Articles 85 and 86.

If such provisions have not been adopted within the above-mentioned time-limit, they shall be laid down by the Council acting by means of a qualified majority vote on a proposal of the Commission and after the Assembly has been consulted.

2. The provisions referred to in paragraph 1 shall be designed, in particular:

(*a*) to ensure observance, by the institution of fines or penalties, of the prohibitions referred to in Article 85, paragraph 1, and in Article 86:

(*b*) to determine the particulars of the application of Article 85, paragraph 3, taking due account of the need, on the one hand, of ensuring effective supervision and, on the other hand, of simplifying administrative control to the greatest possible extent;

(*c*) to specify, where necessary, the scope of application in the various economic sectors of the provisions contained in Articles 85 and 86;

(*d*) to define the respective responsibilities of the Commission and of the Court of Justice in the application of the provisions referred to in this paragraph; and

(*e*) to define the relations between, on the one hand, municipal law and, on the other hand, the provisions contained in this Section or adopted in application of this Article.

ARTICLE 88

Until the date of the entry into force of the provisions adopted in application of Article 87, the authorities of Member States shall, in accordance with their respective municipal law and with the provisions of Article 85, particularly paragraph 3, and of Article 86, rule upon the admissibility of any understanding and upon any improper advantage taken of a dominant position in the Common Market.

ARTICLE 89

1. Without prejudice to the provisions of Article 88, the Commission shall, upon taking up its duties, ensure the application of the principles laid down in Articles 85 and 86. It shall, at the request of a Member State or *ex officio,* investigate, in conjunction with the competent authorities of the Member States which shall lend it their assistance, any alleged infringement of the above-mentioned principles. If it finds that such infringement has taken place, it shall propose appropriate means for bringing it to an end.

2. If such infringement continues, the Commission shall, by means of a reasoned decision, confirm the existence of such infringement of the principles. The Commission may publish its decision and may authorize Member States to take the necessary measures, of which it shall determine the conditions and particulars, to remedy the situation.

ARTICLE 90

1. Member States shall, in respect of public enterprises and enterprises to which they grant special or exclusive rights, neither enact nor maintain in force any measure contrary to the rules contained in this Treaty, in particular, to those rules provided for in Article 7 and in Articles 85 to 94 inclusive.

2. Any enterprise charged with the management of services of general economic interest or having the character of a fiscal monopoly shall be subject to the rules contained in this Treaty, in particular to those governing competition, to the extent that the application of such rules does not obstruct the *de jure* or *de facto* fulfilment of the specific tasks entrusted to

such enterprise. The development of trade may not be affected to such a degree as would be contrary to the interest of the Community.

3. The Commission shall ensure the application of the provisions of this Article and shall, where necessary, issue appropriate directives or decisions to Member States.

Chap. 3: Approximation of Laws
ARTICLE 100

The Council, acting by means of a unanimous vote on a proposal of the Commission, shall issue directives for the approximation of such legislative and administrative provisions of the Member States as have a direct incidence on the establishment or functioning of the Common Market.

The Assembly and the Economic and Social Committee shall be consulted concerning any directives whose implementation in one or more of the Member States would involve amendment of legislative provisions.

ARTICLE 101

Where the Commission finds that a disparity existing between the legislative or administrative provisions of the Member States distorts the conditions of competition in the Common Market and thereby causes a state of affairs which must be eliminated, it shall enter into consultation with the interested Member States.

If such consultation does not result in an agreement which eliminates the particular distortion, the Council, acting during the first stage by means of a unanimous vote and subsequently by means of a qualified majority vote on a proposal of the Commission, shall issue the directives necessary for this purpose. The Commission and the Council may take any other appropriate measures as provided for in this Treaty.

ARTICLE 102

1. Where there is reason for fear that the enactment or amendment of a legislative or administrative provision will cause a distortion within the meaning of the preceding Article, the Member State desiring to proceed therewith shall consult the Commission. After consulting the Member States, the Commission shall recommend to the States concerned such measures as may be appropriate to avoid the particular distortion.

2. If the State desiring to enact or amend its own provisions does not comply with the recommendation made to it by the Commission, other Member States may not be requested, in application of Article 101 to amend their own provisions in order to eliminate such distortion. If the Member State which has ignored the Commission's recommendation causes a distortion to its own detriment only, the provisions of Article 101 shall not apply.

Title II: Ecomomic Policy

Chap. 3: Commercial Policy

ARTICLE 110

By establishing a customs union between themselves the Member States intend to contribute, in conformity with the common interest, to the harmonious development of world trade, the progressive abolition of restrictions on international exchanges and the lowering of customs barriers.

The common commercial policy shall take into account the favourable incidence which the abolition of customs duties as between Member States may have on the increase of the competitive strength of the enterprises in those States.

ARTICLE 111

In the course of the transitional period and without prejudice to Articles 115 and 116, the following provisions shall apply:

1. Member States shall coordinate their commercial relations with third countries in such a way as to bring about, not later than at the expiry of the transitional period, the conditions necessary to the implementation of a common policy in the matter of external trade.

The Commission shall submit to the Council proposals regarding the procedure to be applied, in the course of the transitional period, for the establishment of common action and regarding the achievement of a uniform commercial policy.

2. The Commission shall submit to the Council recommendations with a view to tariff negotiations with third countries concerning the common customs tariff.

The Council shall authorize the Commission to open such negotiations.

The Commission shall conduct these negotiations in consultation with a special Committee appointed by the Council to assist the Commission in this task and within the framework of such directives as the Council may issue to it.

3. The Council shall, when exercising the powers conferred upon it under this Article, act during the first two stages by means of a unanimous vote and subsequently by means of a qualified majority vote.

4. Member States shall, in consultation with the Commission, take all necessary measures with the object, in particular, of adjusting their tariff agreements in force with third countries in order that the entry into force of the common customs tariff may not be delayed.

.   .   .

ARTICLE 112

1. Without prejudice to obligations undertaken by Member States within the framework of other international organizations, their measures to aid exports to third countries shall be progressively harmonized before the end of the transitional period to the extent necessary to ensure that competition between enterprises within the Community shall not distorted.

On a proposal of the Commission, the Council, acting until the end of the second stage by means of a unanimous vote and subsequently by means of a qualified majority vote, shall issue the directives necessary for this purpose.

. . .

ARTICLE 113

1. After the expiry of the transitional period, the common commercial policy shall be based on uniform principles, particularly in regard to tariff amendments, the conclusion of tariff or trade agreements, the alignment of measures of 7 liberalisation, export policy and protective commercial measures including measures to be taken in cases of dumping or subsidies.

2. The Commission shall submit proposals to the Council for the putting into effect of this common commercial policy.

3. Where agreements with third countries require to be negotiated, the Commission shall make recommendations to the Council, which will authorize the Commission to open the necessary negotiations.

The Commission shall conduct these negotiations in consultation with a special Committee appointed by the Council to assist the Commission in this task and within the framework of such directives as the Council may issue to it.

4. The Council shall, when exercising the powers conferred upon it by this Article, act by means of a qualified majority vote.

ARTICLE 114

The agreements referred to in Article III, paragraph 2, and in Article 113 shall be concluded on behalf of the Community by the Council acting during the first two stages by means of a unanimous vote and subsequently by means of a qualified majority vote.

ARTICLE 115

In order to ensure that the execution of measures of commercial policy taken in conformity with this Treaty by any Member State shall not be prevented by diversions of commercial traffic, or where disparities between such measures lead to economic difficulties in one or more of the Member

States, the Commission shall recommend the methods whereby the other Member States shall provide the necessary cooperation. Failing this, the Commission shall authorize the Member States to take the necessary protective measures of which it shall determine the conditions and particulars.

In cases of emergency and during the transitional period, Member States may themselves take such necessary measures and shall notify them to the other Member States and also to the Commission which may decide that the State concerned shall amend or revoke such measures.

In choosing such measures, priority shall be given to those which cause the least disturbance to the functioning of the Common Market and which take due account of the necessity for expediting, as far as possible, the introduction of the common customs tariff.

ARTICLE 116

As from the end of the transitional period, Member States shall in respect of all matters of particular interest in regard to the Common Market, within the framework of any international organizations of an economic character, only proceed by way of common action. The Commission shall for this purpose submit to the Council, which shall act by means of a qualified majority vote, proposals concerning the scope and implementation of such common action.

During the transitional period, Member States shall consult with each other with a view to concerting their action and, as far as possible, adopting a uniform attitude.

Title III: Social Policy
Chap. 2: The European Social Fund
ARTICLE 123

In order to improve opportunities of employment of workers in the Common Market and thus contribute to raising the standard of living, a European Social Fund shalt hereby be established in accordance with the provisions set out below; it shall have the task of promoting within the Community employment facilities and the geographical and occupational mobility of workers.

ARTICLE 124

The administration of the Fund shall be incumbent on the Commission.

The Commission shall be assisted in this task by a Committee presided over by a member of the Commission and composed of representatives of Governments, trade unions and employers' associations.

ARTICLE 125

1. At the request of a Member State, the Fund shall, within the framework of the rules provided for in Article 127, cover 50 percent of expenses incurred after the entry into force of this Treaty by that State or by a body under public law for the purpose of:

(*a*) ensuring productive reemployment of workers by means of:
—occupational retraining,
—resettlement allowances; and

(*b*) granting aids for the benefit of workers whose employment is temporarily reduced or wholly or partly suspended as a result of the conversion of their enterprise to other productions, in order that they may maintain the same wage-level pending their full reemployment.

Title IV: The European Investment Bank

ARTICLE 129

A European Investment Bank having legal personality shall hereby be established.

The members of the European Investment Bank shall be the Member States.

The statute of the European Investment Bank shall form the subject of a Protocol annexed to this Treaty.

ARTICLE 130

The task of the European Investment Bank shall be to contribute, by calling on the capital markets and its own resources, to the balanced and smooth development of the Common Market in the interest of the Community. For this purpose, the Bank shall by granting loans and guarantees on a non-profit-making basis facilitate the financing of the following projects in all sectors of the economy:

(*a*) projects for developing less developed regions,

(*b*) projects for modernising or converting enterprises or for creating new activities which are called for by the progressive establishment of the Common Market where such projects by their size or nature cannot be entirely financed by the various means available in each of the Member States; and

(*c*) projects of common interest to several Member States which by their size or nature cannot be entirely financed by the various means available in each of the Member States.

V. INSTITUTIONS OF THE COMMUNITY

Title I: Provisions Governing Institutions

Chap. I: Institutions

Section 1: The Assembly

ARTICLE 137

The Assembly, which shall be composed of representatives of the peoples of the States united within the Community, shall exercise the powers of deliberation and of control which are conferred upon it by this Treaty.

ARTICLE 138

1. The Assembly shall be composed of delegates whom the Parliaments shall be called upon to appoint from among their members in accordance with the procedure laid down by each Member State.

2. The number of these delegates shall be fixed as follows:

Belgium 14
Germany 36
France 36
Italy 36
Luxembourg 6
Netherlands 14

3. The Assembly shall draw up proposals for elections by direct universal suffrage in accordance with a uniform procedure in all Member States.

The Council, acting by means of a unanimous vote, shall determine the provisions which it shall recommend to Member States for adoption in accordance with their respective constitutional rules.

ARTICLE 139

The Assembly shall hold an annual session. It shall meet as of right on the third Tuesday in October.

The Assembly may meet in extraordinary session at the request of a majority of its members or at the request of the Council or of the Commission.

ARTICLE 140

The Assembly shall appoint its President and its officers from among its members.

Members of the Commission may attend all meetings and shall at their request, be heard on behalf of the Commission.

The Commission shall reply orally or in writing to questions put to it by the Assembly or its members.

The Council shall be heard by the Assembly under the conditions which the Council shall lay down in its rules of procedure.

ARTICLE 141

Except where otherwise provided for in this Treaty, the Assembly shall act by means of an absolute majority of the votes cast.

The quorum shall be laid down in the rules of procedure.

ARTICLE 144

If a motion of censure concerning the activities of the Commission is introduced in the Assembly, a vote may be taken thereon only after a period of not less than three days following its introduction, and such vote shall be by open ballot.

If the motion of censure is adopted by a two-thirds majority of the votes cast, representing a majority of the members of the Assembly, the members of the Commission shall resign their office in a body. They shall continue to carry out current business until their replacement in accordance with the provisions of Article 158 has taken place.

Section 2: The Council

ARTICLE 145

With a view to ensuring the achievement of the objectives laid down in this Treaty, and under the conditions provided for therein, the Council shall:

—ensure the coordination of the general economic policies of the Member States, and

—Dispose of a power of decision.

ARTICLE 146

The Council shall be composed of representatives of the Member States. Each Government shall delegate to it one of its members.

The office of President shall be exercised for a term of six months by each member of the Council in rotation according to the alphabetical order of the Member States.

ARTICLE 148

1. Except where otherwise provided for in this Treaty, the conclusions of the Council shall be reached by a majority vote of its members.

2. Where conclusions of the Council require a qualified majority, the votes of its members shall be weighted as follows:

Belgium 2
Germany 4
France 4
Italy 4
Luxembourg 1
Netherlands 2

Majorities shall be required for the adoption of any conclusions as follows:

—twelve votes in cases where this Treaty requires a previous proposal of the Commission, or

—twelve votes including a favourable vote by at least four members in all other cases.

3. Abstentions by members either present or represented shall not prevent the adoption of Council conclusions requiring unanimity.

ARTICLE 149

When, pursuant to this Treaty, the Council acts on a proposal of the Commission, it shall, where the amendment of such proposal is involved, act only by means of a unanimous vote.

As long as the Council has not so acted, the Commission may amend its original proposal, particularly in cases where the Assembly has been consulted on the proposal concerned.

Section 3: The Commission

ARTICLE 155

With a view to ensuring the functioning and development of the Common Market, the Commission shall:

—ensure the application of the provisions of this Treaty and of the provisions enacted by the institutions of the Community in pursuance thereof;

—formulate recommendations or opinions in matters which are the subject of this Treaty, where the latter expressly so provides or where the Commission considers it necessary;

—under the conditions laid down in this Treaty dispose of a power of decision of its own and participate in the preparation of acts of the Council and of the Assembly; and

—exercise the competence conferred on it by the Council for the implementation of the rules laid down by the latter.

ARTICLE 156

The Commission shall annually, not later than one month before the opening of the Assembly session, publish a general report on the activities of the Community.

ARTICLE 157

1. The Commission shall be composed of nine members chosen for their general competence and of indisputable independence.

The number of members of the Commission may be amended by a unanimous vote of the Council.

Only nationals of Member States may be members of the Commission.

The Commission may not include more than two members having the nationality of the same State.

2. The members of the Commission shall perform their duties in the general interest of the Community with complete independence.

In the performance of their duties, they shall not seek or accept instructions from any Government or other body. They shall refrain from any action incompatible with the character of their duties. Each Member State undertakes in respect this character and not to seek to influence the members of the Commission in the performance of their duties.

.   .   .

ARTICLE 158

The Members of the Commission shall be appointed by the Governments of Member States acting in common agreement.

Their term of office shall be for a period of four years. It shall be renewable.

ARTICLE 161

The President and the two Vice-Presidents of the Commission shall be appointed from among its members for a term of two years in accordance with the same procedure as that laid down for the appointment of members of the Commission. Their term of office shall be renewable.

.   .   .

ARTICLE 162

The Council and the Commission shall consult each other and shall settle by mutual agreement the particulars of their collaboration.

.   .   .

ARTICLE 163

The conclusions of the Commission shall be reached by a majority of the number of members provided for in Article 157.

A meeting of the Commission shall only be valid if the number of members laid down in its rules of procedure are present.

Section 4: The Court of Justice

ARTICLE 164

The Court of Justice shall ensure observance of law and justice in the interpretation and application of this Treaty.

ARTICLE 165

The Court of Justice shall be composed of seven judges.

.   .   .

ARTICLE 166

The Court of Justice shall be assisted by two advocates-general.

The duty of the advocate-general shall be to present publicly, with complete impartiality and independence, reasoned conclusions on cases submitted to the Court of Justice, with a view to assisting the latter in the performance of its duties as laid down in Article 164.

.   .   .

ARTICLE 167

The judges and the advocates-general shall be chosen from among persons of indisputable independence who fulfil the conditions required for the holding of the highest judicial office in their respective countries or who are jurists of a recognised competence; they shall be appointed for a term of six years by the Governments of Member States acting in common agreement.

A partial renewal of the Court of Justice shall take place every three years. It shall affect three and four judges alternately. The three judges whose terms of office are to expire at the end of the first period of three years shall be chosen by lot.

.   .   .

ARTICLE 169

If the Commission considers that a Member State has failed to fulfill any of its obligations under this Treaty, it shall give a reasoned opinion on the matter after requiring such State to submit its comments.

If such State does not comply with the terms of such opinion within the period laid down by the Commission, the latter may refer the matter to the Court of Justice.

ARTICLE 170

Any Member State which considers that another Member State has failed to fulfill any of its obligations under this Treaty may refer the matter to the Court of Justice.

Before a Member State institutes, against another Member State, proceedings relating to an alleged infringement of the obligations under this Treaty, it shall refer the matter to the Commission.

The Commission shall give a reasoned opinion after the States concerned have been required to submit their comments in written and oral pleadings.

If the Commission, within a period of three months after the date of reference of the matter ot it, has not given an opinion, reference to the Court of Justice shall not hereby be prevented.

ARTICLE 171

If the Court of Justice finds that a Member State has failed to fulfil any of its obligations under this Treaty, such State shall take the measures required for the implementation of the judgment of the Court.

ARTICLE 172

The regulations laid down by the Council pursuant to the provisions of this Treaty may confer on the Court of Justice full jurisdiction in respect of penalties provided for in such regulations.

ARTICLE 173

The Court of Justice shall review the lawfulness of acts other than recommendations or opinions of the Council and the Commission. For this purpose, it shall be competent to give judgment on appeals by a Member State, the Council or the Commission on grounds of incompetence, of errors of substantial form, of infringement of this Treaty or of any legal provision relating to its application, or of abuse of power.

Any natural or legal person may, under the same conditions, appeal against a decision addressed to him or against a decision which, although in the form of a regulation or a decision addressed to another person, is of direct and specific concern to him.

The appeals provided for in this Article shall be lodged within a period of two months dating, as the case may be, either from the publication of the act concerned or from its notification to the appellant or, failing that, from the day on which the latter had knowledge of that act.

ARTICLE 174

If the appeal is well founded, the Court of Justice shall declare the act concerned to be null and void.

In the case of regulations, however, the Court of Justice shall, if it considers it necessary, indicate those effects of the regulation annulled which shall be deemed to remain in force.

ARTICLE 176

An institution originating an act subsequently declared null and void or an institution whose failure to act has been declared contrary to the provisions of this Treaty shall take the measures required for the implementation of the judgment of the Court of Justice.

. . .

ARTICLE 177
The Court of Justice shall be competent to make a preliminary decision concerning:

(*a*) The interpretation of this Treaty;

(*b*) the validity and interpretation of acts of the institutions.of the Community; and

(*c*) the interpretation of the statutes of any bodies set up by an act of the Council, where such statutes so provide.

Where any such question is raised before a court or tribunal of one of the Member States, such court or tribunal may, if it considers that its judgment depends on a preliminary decision on this question, request the Court of Justice to give a ruling thereon.

Where any such question is raised in a case pending before a domestic court or tribunal from whose decisions no appeal lies under municipal law, such court or tribunal shall refer the matter to the Court of Justice.

ARTICLE 182
The Court of Justice shall be competent to decide in any dispute between Member States in connection with the object of this Treaty, where such dispute is submitted ot it under the terms of a compromise.

ARTICLE 183
Subject to the powers conferred on the Court of Justice by this Treaty, cases to which the Community is a party shall not for that reason alone be excluded from the competence of domestic courts or tribunals.

ARTICLE 184
Where a regulation of the Council or of the Commission is the subject of a dispute in legal proceedings, any of the parties concerned may, notwithstanding the expiry of the period laid down in Article 173, third paragraph invoke the grounds set out in Article 173, first paragraph in order to allege before the Court of Justice that the regulation concerned is inapplicable.

ARTICLE 185
Appeals submitted to the Court of Justice shall not have any staying effect. The Court of Justice may, however, if it considers that circumstances so require, order the suspension of the execution of the act appealed against.

ARTICLE 186

The Court of Justice may, in any cases referred to it, make any necessary interim order.

ARTICLE 187

The judgments of the Court of Justice shall be enforceable under the conditions laid down in Article 192.

Chap. 2: Provisions Common to Several Institutions

ARTICLE 189

For the achievement of their aims and under the conditions provided for in this Treaty, the Council and the Commission shall adopt regulations and directives, make decisions and formulate recommendations or opinions.

Regulations shall have a general application. They shall be binding in every respect and directly applicable in each Member State.

Directives shall bind any Member State to which they are addressed, as to the result to be achieved, while leaving to domestic agencies a competence as to form and means.

Decisions shall be binding in every respect for the addressees named therein.

Recommendations and opinions shall have no binding force.

ARTICLE 190

The regulations, directives, and decisions of the Council and of the Commission shall be supported by reasons and shall refer to any proposals or opinions which are to be obtained pursuant to this Treaty.

ARTICLE 191

The regulations shall be published in the *Official Journal of the Community*. They shall enter into force on the date fixed in them or, failing this, on the twentieth day following their publication.

Directives and decisions shall be notified to their addressees and shall take effect upon such notification.

ARTICLE 192

Decisions of the Council or of the Commission which contain a pecuniary obligation on persons other than States shall be enforceable.

Forced execution shall be governed by the rules of civil procedure in force in the State in whose territory it takes place. The writ of execution shall be served, without other formality than the verification of the authenticity of the written act, by the domestic authority which the Government of each Member State shall designate for this purpose and of which it shall give notice to the Commission and to the Court of Justice.

After completion of these formalities at the request of the party concerned, the latter may, in accordance with municipal law, proceed with such forced execution by applying directly to the authority which is competent.

Forced execution may only be suspended pursuant to a decision of the Court of Justice. Supervision as to the regularity of the measures of execution shall, however, be within the competence of the domestic courts or tribunals.

Chap. 3: The Economic and Social Committee
ARTICLE 193

There shall hereby be established an Economic and Social Committee with consultative status.

The Committee shall be composed of representatives of the various categories of economic and social life, in particular, representatives of producers, agriculturists, transport operators, workers, merchants, artisans, the liberal professions and of the general interest.

ARTICLE 194

The number of members of the Committee shall be fixed as follows:

Belgium   12
Germany   24
France   24
Italy . . . .~ 24
Luxembourg   5
Netherlands   12

The members of the Committee shall be appointed for a term of four years by the Council acting by means of a unanimous vote. This term shall be renewable.

The members of the Committee shall be appointed in their personal capacity and shall not be bound by any mandatory instructions.

ARTICLE 198

The Committee shall be consulted by the Council or by the Commission in the cases provided for in this Treaty. The Committee may be consulted by these institutions in all cases in which they deem it appropriate.

. . .

Title II: Financial Provisions
ARTICLE 199

Estimates shall be drawn up for each financial year for all revenues and expenditures of the Community, including those relating to the European Social Fund, and shall be shown in the budget.

The budget shall be in balance as to revenues and expenditures.

ARTICLE 200

1. The revenues of the budget shall comprise, apart from any other revenues, the financial contributions of Member States fixed according to the following scale:

Belgium	7.9
Germany	28
France	28
Italy	28
Luxembourg	0.2
Netherlands	7.9

2. The financial contributions of Member States, however, which are intended to meet the expenses of the European Social Fund, shall be fixed according to the following scale:

Belgium	8.8
Germany	32
France	32
Italy	20
Luxembourg	0.2
Netherlands	7

3. The scales may be amended by the Council acting by means of a unanimous vote.

VI. GENERAL AND FINAL PROVISIONS
ARTICLE 210

The Community shall have legal personality.

ARTICLE 211

The Community shall in each of the Member States possess the most extensive legal capacity accorded to legal persons under their respective municipal law; it may, in particular, acquire or transfer movable and immovable property and may sue and be sued in its own name. For this purpose the Community shall be represented by the Commission.

ARTICLE 215

The contractual liability of the Community shall be governed by the law applying to the contract concerned.

As regards noncontractual liability, the Community shall, in accordance with the general principles common to the laws of Member States, make reparation for any damage caused by its institutions or by its employees in the performance of their duties.

.   .   .

ARTICLE 218

The Community shall, under conditions defined in a separate Protocol, enjoy in the territories of the Member States the privileges and immunities necessary for the achievement of its aims.

ARTICLE 219

Member States undertake not to submit a dispute concerning the interpretation or application of this Treaty to any method of settlement other than those provided for in this Treaty.

ARTICLE 220

Member States shall, in so far as necessary, engage in negotiations with each other with a view to ensuring for the benefit of their nationals:

—the protection of persons as well as the enjoyment and protection of rights under the conditions granted by each State to its own nationals;

—the elimination of double taxation within the Community;

—the mutual recognition of companies within the meaning of Article 58, second paragraph, the maintenance of their legal personality in cases where the registered office is transferred from one country to another, and the possibility for companies subject to the municipal law of different Member States to form mergers; and

—the simplification of the formalities governing the reciprocal recognition and execution of judicial decisions and of arbitral awards.

ARTICLE 221

Within a period of three years after the date of the entry into force of this Treaty, Member States shall treat nationals of other Member States in the same manner, as regards financial participation by such nationals in the capital of companies within the meaning of Article 58, as they treat their own nationals, without prejudice to the application of the other provisions of this Treaty.

ARTICLE 222

This Treaty shall in no way prejudice the system existing in Member States in respect of property.

ARTICLE 223

1. The provisions of this Treaty shall not detract from the following rules:

(*a*) No Member State shall be obliged to supply information the disclosure of which it considers contrary to the essential interests of its security;

(*b*) Any Member State may take the measures which it considers necessary for the protection of the essential interests of its security, and which are connected with the production of or trade in arms, ammunition and war material; such measures shall not, however, prejudice conditions of competition in the Common Market in respect of products not intended for specifically military purposes.

2. In the course of the first year after the date of the entry into force of this Treaty, the Council, acting by means of a unanimous vote, shall determine the list of products to which the provisions of paragraph 1 (*b*) shall apply.

3. The Council, acting by means of a unanimous vote on a proposal of the Commission, may amend the said list.

ARTICLE 224

Member States shall consult one another for the purpose of enacting in common the necessary provisions to prevent the functioning of the Common Market from being affected by measures which a Member State may be called upon to take in case of serious internal disturbances affecting public order, in case of war or of serious international tension constituting a threat of war or in order to carry out undertakings into which it has entered for the purpose of maintaining peace and international security.

ARTICLE 225

If measures taken in the cases mentioned in Articles 223 and 224 have the effect of distorting conditions of competition in the Common Market, the Commission shall together with the State concerned, examine the conditions under which these measures may be adapted to the rules established by this Treaty.

Notwithstanding the procedure provided for in Articles 169 and 170, the Commission or any Member State may make direct reference to the Court of Justice if it considers that another Member State is making an improper use of the powers provided for under Articles 223 and 224. The Court of Justice shall sit *in camera*.

ARTICLE 226

1. In the course of the transitional period, where there are serious difficulties which are likely to persist in any sector of economic activity or difficulties which may seriously impair the economic situation in any region, a Member State may ask for authorization to take measures of safeguard in order to restore the situation and adapt the sector concerned to the Common Market economy.

2. At the request of the State concerned, the Commission shall by an expedited procedure immediately determine the measures of safeguard which it considers necessary, specifying the conditions and particulars of application.

3. The measures authorized under paragraph 2 may include derogations from the provisions of this Treaty, to the extent and for the periods strictly necessary for the achievement of the objects referred to in paragraph 1. Priority shall be given in the choice of such measures to those which will least disturb the functioning of the Common Market.

ARTICLE 228

1. Where this Treaty provides for the conclusion of agreements between the Community and one or more States or an international organization, such agreements shall be negotiated by the Commission. Subject to the powers conferred upon the Commission in this field, such agreements shall be concluded by the Council after the Assembly has been consulted in the cases provided for by this Treaty.

The Council, the Commission or a Member State may, as a preliminary, obtain the opinion of the Court of Justice as to the compatibility of the contemplated agreements with the provisions of this Treaty. An agreement which is the subject of a negative opinion of the Court of Justice may only enter into force under the conditions laid down, according to the case concerned, in Article 236.

2. Agreements concluded under the conditions laid down above shall be binding on the institutions of the Community and on Member States.

ARTICLE 229

The Commission shall be responsible for ensuring all suitable contacts with the organs of the United Nations, of their Specialized Agencies and of the General Agreement on Tariffs and Trade.

The Commission shall also ensure appropriate contacts with all international organizations.

ARTICLE 230

The Community shall establish all suitable cooperation with the Council of Europe.

ARTICLE 231

The Community shall establish with the Organization for European Economic Cooperation close collaboration, the particulars of which shall be determined by common agreement.

ARTICLE 233

The provisions of this Treaty shall not be an obstacle to the existence or completion of regional unions between Belgium and Luxembourg, and between Belgium, Luxembourg and the Netherlands, in so far as the objectives of these regional unions are not achieved by application of this Treaty.

Article 234

The rights and obligations resulting from conventions concluded prior to the entry into force of this Treaty between one or more Member States, on the one hand, and one or more third countries, on the other hand, shall not be affected by the provisions of this Treaty.

In so far as such conventions are not compatible with this Treaty, the Member State or States concerned shall take all appropriate steps to eliminate any incompatibility found to exist. Member States shall, if necessary, assist each other in order to achieve this purpose and shall, where appropriate, adopt a common attitude.

Member States shall, in the application of the conventions referred to in the first paragraph, take due account of the fact that the advantages granted under this Treaty by each Member State form an integral part of the establishment of the Community and are therefore inseparably linked with the creation of common institutions, the conferring of competences upon such institutions and the granting of the same advantages by all other Member States.

ARTICLE 235

If any action by the Community appears necessary to achieve, in the functioning of the Common Market, one of the aims of the Community in cases where this Treaty has not provided for the requisite powers of action, the Council, acting by means of a unanimous vote on a proposal of the Commission and after the Assembly has been consulted, shall enact the appropriate provisions.

ARTICLE 236

The Government of any Member State or the Commission may submit to the Council proposals for the revision of this Treaty.

If the Council, after consulting the Assembly and, where appropriate, the Commission, expresses an opinion in favour of the calling of a conference of representatives of the Governments of Member States, such conference be convened by the President of the Council for the purpose of determining in common agreement the amendments to be made to this Treaty.

Such amendments shall enter into force after being ratified by all Member States in accordance with their respective constitutional rules.

ARTICLE 237

Any European [State] may apply to become a member of the Community. It shall address its application to the Council which, after obtaining the opinion of the Commission, shall act by means of a unanimous vote.

The conditions of admission and the amendments to this Treaty necessitated thereby shall be the subject of an agreement between the Member States and the applicant State. Such agreement shall be submitted to all the contracting States for ratification in accordance with their respective constitutional rules.

ARTICLE 238

The Community may conclude with a third country, a union of States or an international organization agreements creating an association embodying reciprocal rights and obligations, joint actions and special procedures.

Such agreements shall be concluded by the Council acting by means of a unanimous vote and after consulting the Assembly.

Where such agreements involve amendments to this Treaty, such amendments shall be subject to prior adoption in accordance with the procedure laid down in Article 236.

ARTICLE 239

The Protocols which are to be annexed to this Treaty by common agreement between the Member States shall form an integral part thereof.

ARTICLE 240

This Treaty shall be concluded for an unlimited period.

22. Treaty of Friendship, Cooperation and Mutual Assistance

Signed at Warsaw by Albania, Bulgaria, Czechoslovakia, Hungary, Poland, Romania and the Soviet Union on May 14, 1955, the Treaty came into force on June 6, 1955. The German Democratic Republic adhered to the Treaty in 1956, but Albania became inactive in recent years.

The Contracting Parties,

Reaffirming their desire to create a system of collective security in Europe based on the participation of all European States, irrespective of their social and political structure, whereby the said States may be enabled to combine their efforts in the interests of ensuring peace in Europe.

Taking into consideration, at the same time, the situation that has come about in Europe as a result of the ratification of the Paris Agreements, which provide for the constitution of a new military group in the form of a "West European Union," with the participation of a remilitarized West Germany and its inclusion in the North Atlantic bloc, thereby increasing the danger of a new war and creating a threat to the national security of peace-loving States;

Being convinced that in these circumstances the peace-loving States of Europe must take the necessary steps to safeguard their security and to promote the maintenance of peace in Europe;

Being guided by the purposes and principles of the Charter of the United Nations;

In the interests of the further strengthening and development of friendship, cooperation, and mutual assistance in accordance with the principles of respect for the independence and sovereignty of States and of nonintervention in their domestic affairs;

Have resolved to conclude the present Treaty of Friendship, Cooperation, and Mutual Assistance and . . . have agreed as follows:

ARTICLE 1

The Contracting Parties undertake, in accordance with the Charter of the United Nations, to refrain in their international relations from the threat or use of force and to settle their international disputes by peaceful means in such a manner that international peace and security are not endangered.

ARTICLE 2

The Contracting Parties declare that they are prepared to participate, in a spirit of sincere cooperation, in all international action for ensuing international peace and security and will devote their full efforts to the realization of these aims.

In this connection, the Contracting Parties shall endeavor to secure, in agreement with other States desiring to cooperate in this manner, the adoption of effective measures for the general reduction of armaments and the prohibition of atomic, hydrogen, and other weapons of mass destruction.

ARTICLE 3

The Contracting Parties shall consult together on all important international questions involving their common interests, with a view to strengthening international peace and security.

Whenever any one of the Contracting Parties considers that a threat of armed attack on one or more of the States Parties to the Treaty has arisen, they shall consult together immediately with a view to providing for their joint defense and maintaining peace and security.

ARTICLE 4

In the event of an armed attack in Europe on one or more of the States Parties to the Treaty by any State or group of States, each State Party to the Treaty shall, in the exercise of the right of individual or collective self-defense, in accordance with Article 51 of the United Nations Charter, afford the State or States so attacked immediate assistance, individually and in agreement with the other States Parties to the Treaty, by all the means it considers necessary, including the use of armed force. The States Parties to the Treaty shall consult together immediately concerning the joint measures necessary to restore and maintain international peace and security.

Measures taken under this article shall be reported to the Security Council in accordance with the provisions of the United Nations Charter. These measures shall be discontinued as soon as the Security Council takes the necessary action to restore and maintain international peace and security.

ARTICLE 5

The Contracting Parties have agreed to establish a Unified Command, to which certain elements of their armed forces shall be allocated by agreement between the Parties, and which shall act in accordance with jointly established principles. The Parties shall likewise take such other concerted action as may be necessary to reinforce their defensive strength, in order to defend the peaceful labor of their peoples, guarantee the inviolability of their frontiers and territories, and afford protection against possible aggression.

ARTICLE 6

For the purpose of carrying out the consultations provided for in the present Treaty between the States Parties thereto, and for the consideration of matters arising in connection with the application of the present Treaty, a Political Consultative Committee shall be established, in which each State Party to the Treaty shall be represented by a member of the Government or by some other specially appointed representative.

The Committee may establish such auxiliary organs as may prove to be necessary.

ARTICLE 7

The Contracting Parties undertake not to participate in any coalitions or alliances, and not to conclude any agreements, the purposes of which are incompatible with the purposes of the present Treaty.

The Contracting Parties declare that their obligations under international treaties at present in force are not incompatible with the provisions of the present Treaty.

ARTICLE 8

The Contracting Parties declare that they will act in a spirit of friendship and cooperation to promote the further development and strengthening of the economic and cultural ties among them, in accordance with the principles of respect for each other's independence and sovereignty and of nonintervention in each other's domestic affairs.

ARTICLE 9

The present Treaty shall be open for accession by other States, irrespective of their social and political structure, which express their readiness, by participating in the present Treaty, to help in combining the efforts of the peace-loving States to ensure the peace and security of the peoples. Such accessions shall come into effect with the consent of the States Parties to the Treaty after the instruments of accession have been deposited with the Government of the Polish People's Republic.

ARTICLE 10

The present Treaty shall be subject to ratification, and the instruments of ratification shall be deposited with the Government of the Polish People's Republic.

The Treaty shall come in force on the date of deposit of the last instrument of ratification. The Government of the Polish People's Republic shall inform the other States Parties to the Treaty of the deposit of each instrument of ratification.

ARTICLE 11

The present Treaty shall remain in force for twenty years. For Contracting Parties which do not, one year before the expiration of that term, give notice of termination of the Treaty to the Government of the Polish People's Republic, the Treaty shall remain in force for a further ten years.

In the event of the establishment of a system of collective security in Europe and the conclusion for that purpose of a General European Treaty concerning collective security, a goal which the contracting Parties shall steadfastly strive to achieve, the present Treaty shall cease to have effect as from the date on which the General European Treaty comes into force.

Done at Warsaw, this fourteenth day of May, nineteen hundred fifty-five, in one copy, in the Russian, Polish, Czech, and German languages, all the texts being equally authentic. Certified copies of the present Treaty shall be transmitted by the Government of the Polish People's Republic to all the other Parties to the Treaty. . . .

23. Charter of the Council for Mutual Economic Assistance

As a response to United States' Marshall Plan, the Soviet Union informally set up COMECON with Bulgaria, Czechoslovakia, Hungary, Poland and Romania in January 1949. The Charter was formally signed at Sofia on December 14, 1959, and it came into force on April 13, 1960. Albania and East Germany had joined COMECON in 1949 and 1950 respectively, but Albania became inactive ever since 1962.

[The signatory Governments] . . . taking into consideration that successful economic cooperation between their countries promotes a more rational development of the national economy, a higher standard of living, and a stronger unity and solidarity; determined to accelerate the development of many sided economic cooperation on the basis of the successive realization of the international socialist division of labor in the interest of building socialism and Communism in their countries and ensuring a stable peace throughout the whole world; convinced that the development of economic cooperation between their countries contributes to the attainment of the goals defined by the United Nations; confirming their readiness to develop economic ties with all countries, regardless of existing social and governmental systems, on the principles of equality, mutual benefit, and noninterference in one another's internal affairs; and recognizing the constantly expanding role of the Council for Mutual Economic Assistance in the organization of economic cooperation between their countries; hereby agree, with these aims, to adopt the following Charter.

ARTICLE 1: AIMS AND PRINCIPLES

1. The Council for Mutual Economic Assistance shall have as its aim contributing, through the union and coordination of the forces of the member countries of the Council, to the planned development of the national economy and an acceleration of the economic and technical progress of these countries; raising the level of industrialization of the underdeveloped countries; an uninterrupted growth in labor productivity; and a steady rise in the well-being of the peoples of the member countries.

2. The Council for Mutual Economic Assistance shall be based on the principles of the sovereign equality of all the member countries of the Council.

The economic and scientific-technical cooperation of the member countries shall be accomplished in accordance with the principles of complete equality of rights, respect for sovereignty and national interests, mutual benefit, and comradely mutual aid.

ARTICLE 2: MEMBERSHIP

1. The charter members of the Council for Mutual Economic Assistance shall be the countries signing and ratifying this Charter.

2. Admission to the Council shall be open to such other countries of Europe as share the aims and principles of the Council and agree to accept the obligations contained in this Charter.

The admission of new members to the Council shall be effected by decision of a Session of the Council upon the receipt of official requests from the relevant countries for such admission.

3. Any member country of the Council shall be permitted to withdraw from the Council after notifying the depositary of the Charter of its intention to do so. Such withdrawal shall come into force six months after receipt of the relevant notification by the depositary. Upon the receipt of such withdrawal notification, the depositary shall notify thereof the member countries of the Council.

4. The member countries of the Council agree: (*a*) to ensure the fulfillment of the recommendations made by the organs of the Council; (*b*) to render the necessary assistance to the Council and its officials in their fulfillment of the functions stipulated by the present Charter; (*c*) to provide the Council with such materials and information as are necessary for the accomplishment of its tasks; (*d*) to inform the Council as to the progress of the fulfillment of the recommendations made by the Council.

ARTICLE 3: FUNCTIONS AND POWERS

1. In accordance with the aims and principles enumerated in Article 1 of this Charter, the Council for Mutual Economic Assistance: (*a*) shall organize:

[*i*] the many-sided economic and scientific-technical cooperation of the member countries of the Council with an aim to a more economical utilization of their natural resources and an acceleration of the growth of the productive forces;

[*ii*] the preparation of recommendations regarding the most important questions of economic relations resulting from the respective plans for the development of the national economy of the member countries of the Council, with a view to coordinating these plans;

[*iii*] the study of those economic problems encompassing the interests of the member countries of the Council;

(*b*) shall assist the member countries of the Council in working out and accomplishing joint measures in the following areas:

[*i*] the development of the industry and agriculture of the member countries of the Council on the basis of successive realization of the international socialist division of labor, specialization, and cooperation in production;

[*ii*] the development of transport with the aim, first and foremost, of ensuring an increase in the export-import and transit freight of the member countries of the Council;

[*iii*] a more effective utilization of the capital investments allotted by the member countries of the Council for the construction of projects to be accomplished on the basis of joint participation;

[*iv*] the development of commodity turnover and trade between the member countries of the Council themselves and with other countries;

[*v*] the exchange of scientific-technical achievements and advanced production experience;

(*c*) shall undertake such other activities as are necessary for the achievement of the aims of the Council.

2. In the person of its organs acting within the limits of their competence, the Council for Mutual Economic Assistance shall be empowered to make recommendations and decisions in accordance with this Charter.

ARTICLE 4: RECOMMENDATIONS AND DECISIONS

1. Recommendations shall be made on questions of economic and scientific-technical collaboration. The recommendations shall be communicated to the member countries of the Council for their consideration.

Realization by the member countries of the Council of the recommendations adopted by them shall be carried out according to the decisions of the Governments, or the competent organs, of the said countries in accordance with the relevant legislation.

2. Decisions shall be made on organizational and procedural questions. These decisions shall come into force, if not otherwise stipulated in the decisions themselves, on the day of the signing of the protocol of the session of the corresponding organ of the Council.

3. All recommendations and decisions of the Council shall be made only with the concurrence of those member countries of the Council concerned, each country having the right to express itself regarding its interests on each question considered in the Council.

Recommendations and decisions shall not extend to those countries expressing disinterest in the given question. However, any of these countries may subsequently concur in the recommendations and decisions made by other member countries of the Council.

ARTICLE 5: ORGANS

1. For execution of the functions and plenary powers specified in Article 3 of this Charter, the Council for Mutual Economic Assistance shall have the following basic organs: the Session of the Council, the Consultative Body of Representatives of the member countries of the Council, the Permanent Commissions, the Secretariat.

2. Such other organs as may be found necessary shall be established in conformity with this Charter.

ARTICLE 6: THE SESSION OF THE COUNCIL

1. The Session of the Council shall represent the highest organ of the Council for Mutual Economic Assistance. It shall have full power to consider all questions falling within the competence of the Council, and to make recommendations and decisions in accordance with this Charter.

2. The Session of the Council shall consist of the delegations from all the member countries of the Council. The composition of the delegation of each country shall be determined by the government of the respective country.

3. Under the chairmanship of the head of the delegation of the country in which such Session is conducted, regular Sessions of the Council shall be convoked two times in successive capitals of the member countries of the Council.

4. An extraordinary Session of the Council shall be convoked upon the request of, or with the concurrence of, not less than one third of the member countries of the Council.

5. The Session of the Council:

(*a*) shall examine: [*i*] proposals on questions of economic and scientific-technical cooperation submitted by the member countries, and also by the Consultative Body of Representatives of the member countries of the Council, the Permanent Commissions and the Secretariat of the Council; [*ii*] the report of the Secretariat of the Council on the activities of the Council;

(*b*) shall determine the basic direction of the activities of the other organs of the Council, and the basic questions of the agenda for the next Session of the Council;

(*c*) shall carry out such other functions as prove necessary for achieving the aims of the Council.

6. The Session of the Council shall be empowered to establish such organs as it considers necessary for carrying out the functions entrusted to the Council.

7. The Session of the Council shall establish its own rules of procedure.

ARTICLE 7: THE CONSULTATIVE BODY OF REPRESENTATIVES OF MEMBER COUNTRIES OF THE COUNCIL

1. The Consultative Body of Representatives of the member countries of the Council for Mutual Economic Assistance shall consist of representatives of all the member countries of the Council: specifically, one from each country.

At the seat of the Secretariat of the Council, the representative of each member country of the Council shall have a deputy, the necessary staff of advisers, and other coworkers. Upon authorization of the representative in the Consultative Body.

2. The Consultative Body shall conduct its sessions as necessary.

3. Within the limits of its competence, the Consultative Body shall have the right to make recommendations and decisions in conformity with this Charter. The Consultative Body shall also introduce proposals for consideration by the Session of the Council.

4. The Consultative Body:

(a) shall consider the proposals of the member countries of the Council, the Permanent Commissions, and the Secretariat as regards ensuring the execution of the recommendations and decisions of the Session of the Council, as well as other questions of economic and scientific cooperation requiring decisions in the period between Sessions of the Council;

(b) shall consider ahead of time, when necessary, proposals of the member countries of the Council, the Permanent Commissions, and the Secretariat of the Council regarding questions for the agenda of the next Session of the Council;

(c) shall coordinate the work of the Permanent Commissions of the Council; shall examine their reports concerning the performance of the work, and further activities;

(d) shall approve [i] the staffs and budget of the Secretariat of the Council, as well as the accounts of the Secretariat of the Council concerning the execution of the budget; [ii] the status of the Permanent Commissions and Secretariat of the Council;

(e) shall create control organs for the verification of the financial activities of the Secretariat of the Council;

(f) shall perform such other functions as arise from the present Charter, as well as from the recommendations and decisions of the Session of the Council.

5. The Consultative Body shall create when necessary auxiliary organs for the preliminary working up of questions.

6. The Consultative Body shall establish its own rules of procedure.

ARTICLE 8: THE PERMANENT COMMISSIONS

1. The Permanent Commissions of the Council for Mutual Economic Assistance shall be formed by the Session of the Council with an aim to contributing to the further development of the economic relations between the member countries of the Council, and to organizing many-sided economic and scientific-technical cooperation in the various sectors of the national economy of the said countries.

The status of the Permanent Commissions shall be approved by the Consultative Body of Representatives of the member countries of the Council.

2. Each member country of the Council shall name its representatives to the Permanent Commissions.

3. The Permanent Commissions shall have the right to make recommendations and decisions, within the limits of their competence, in accordance with the present Charter. The Commissions may also introduce proposals for the consideration of the Session of the Council and the Consultative Body of Representatives of the member countries of the Council.

4. The Permanent Commissions shall elaborate measures and prepare proposals for the realization of the economic-technical cooperation indicated in paragraph 1 of this article. They shall also carry out such other functions as arise from this Charter, the recommendations and decisions of the Session of the Council, and the Consultative Body of Representatives of the member countries of the Council.

The Permanent Commissions shall present to the Consultative Body of Representatives of the member countries of the Council annual reports on the progress of their work and further activities.

5. The sessions of the Permanent Commissions shall be conducted, as a rule, at the place of their permanent abode, which shall be determined by the Session of the Council.

6. The Permanent Commissions shall form auxiliary organs when necessary. The composition and competence of these organs, as well as their place of meeting, shall be determined by the parent Commission.

7. Each Permanent Commission shall have a secretariat headed by the secretary of the Commission. The staff of the secretariat of such Commission shall become a constituent part of the Secretariat of the Council, and shall be maintained at the expense of its budget.

8. The Permanent Commissions shall establish their own rules of procedure.

ARTICLE 9: THE SECRETARIAT

1. The Secretariat of the Council for Mutual Economic Assistance shall consist of the Secretary of the Council, his deputies, and such person-

nel as may be required for carrying out the functions entrusted to the Secretariat.

The Secretary and his deputies shall be named by the Session of the Council, and shall direct the work of the Secretariat of the Council. The personnel of the Secretariat shall be recruited from among the citizens of the member countries of the Council, in accordance with the Regulations applicable to the Secretariat of the Council.

The Secretary shall be the head official of the Council. He shall represent the Council before the officials and organizations of the member countries of the Council and other countries, as well as before international organizations. The Secretary of the Council shall, where necessary, empower his deputies, as well as other employees of the Secretariat, to appear in his behalf.

The Secretary and his deputies shall be permitted to take part in all sessions of the organs of the Council.

2. The Secretariat of the Council:

(*a*) shall present a report on the activities of the Council to the regular Session of the Council;

(*b*) shall assist in the preparation and conduct of the Session of the Council, the Consultative Body of Representatives of the member countries of the Council, the sessions of the Permanent Commissions of the Council, and the Consultative bodies formed by the decisions of these organs of the Council;

(*c*) shall prepare, under the authority of the Session of the Council or the Consultative Body of Representatives of the member countries of the Council, economic surveys and analyses according to the materials of the member countries of the Council, and shall also publish materials on questions of the economic and scientific-technical cooperation of these countries;

(*d*) [shall] prepare: [*i*] proposals on questions of the work of the Council for the consideration of the corresponding organs of the Council; [*ii*] informational and reference materials on questions of the economic and scientific-technical cooperation of the member countries of the Council;

(*e*) shall organize, jointly with the Permanent Commissions of the Council, the preparation of projects in relation to questions of economic and scientific-technical cooperation on the basis of the recommendations and decisions of the Session of the Council and the Consultative Body of Representatives of the member countries of the Council;

(*f*) shall undertake other activities arising from this Charter, the recommendations and decisions made by the Council, and the regulations applicable to the Secretariat of the Council.

3. The Secretary of the Council, his deputies, and the personnel of the Secretariat shall act in the capacity of international officials in the performance of their official duties.

4. The seat of the Secretariat of the Council shall be Moscow.

ARTICLE 10: PARTICIPATION OF OTHER COUNTRIES IN THE WORK OF THE COUNCIL

The Council of Mutual Economic Assistance shall be permitted to invite countries which are not members of the Council to take part in the work of the organs of the Council.

The conditions under which representatives of these countries may participate in the work of the organs of the Council shall be determined by the Council, in agreement with the respective countries concerned.

ARTICLE 11: RELATIONS WITH INTERNATIONAL ORGANIZATIONS

The Council of Mutual Economic Assistance shall be permitted to establish and maintain relations with the economic organizations of the United Nations and with other international organizations.

The character and form of these relations shall be determined by the Council, in agreement with the respective international organizations concerned.

ARTICLE 12: QUESTIONS OF FINANCE

1. The member countries of the Council of Mutual Economic Assistance shall bear the expenses incurred in the maintenance of the Secretariat and the execution of its activities. Each member country's share of these expenses shall be established by the Session of the Council; other financial questions shall be resolved by the Consultative Body of Representatives of the member countries of the Council.

2. The Secretariat of the Council shall present to the Consultative Body of Representatives of the member countries of the Council a report on the execution of the budget for each calendar year.

3. The expenses incurred by the participants in the Session of the Council, the Consultative Body of Representatives of the member countries of the Council, the Permanent Commissions of the Council, and the consultations conducted within the framework of the Council, shall be borne by the countries represented at these meetings and consultations.

4. The expenses incurred in connection with the meetings and consultations mentioned in paragraph 3 of this article shall be borne by the country in which the meetings and consultations are conducted.

ARTICLE 13: VARIOUS ENACTMENTS

1. The Council of Mutual Economic Assistance shall enjoy within the territory of each member country of the Council such capacities as are necessary for carrying out its functions and achieving its aims.

2. The Council, as well as the representatives of the member countries of the Council and the officials of the Council, shall enjoy, within the territory of each of these countries, such privileges and immunities as are necessary for carrying out the functions and achieving the aims foreseen by this Charter.

3. The capacities, privileges, and immunities mentioned in this Article shall be specified in a special Convention.

4. The regulations of this Charter shall not affect such rights and obligations of the member countries of the Council as arise from membership in other international organizations, or from the conclusion of international treaties.

ARTICLE 14: LANGUAGES

The official languages of the Council for Mutual Economic Assistance shall be the languages of all the member countries.

The working language of the Council shall be Russian.

ARTICLE 15: THE RATIFICATION AND PROMULGATION OF THE CHARTER

1. This Charter shall be subject to ratification by the signatures of the respective countries in accordance with their constitutional procedures.

2. Instruments of ratification shall be deposited with the depositary of this Charter.

3. The Charter shall come into force immediately upon the deposit of the instruments of ratification by all the countries signatory to this Charter, which fact the depositary shall communicate to the respective countries.

4. In regard to any country which, in accordance with paragraph 2, Article 2, shall in the future be admitted into the Council for Mutual Economic Assistance, and which ratifies this Charter, the Charter shall enter into force as regards such country on the day said country deposits the document attesting its ratification of the Charter, which fact the depository shall communicate to the other member countries of the Council.

ARTICLE 16: PROCEDURE FOR AMENDING THE CHARTER

Any member country of the Council for Mutual Economic Assistance may introduce proposals for amendments to this Charter.

Such amendments to the Charter as are approved by a Session of the Council shall come into force immediately upon deposition by the respective member countries with the depositary of their ratifications of such amendments.

ARTICLE 17: CONCLUDING ENACTMENTS

The present Charter shall be drawn up in one copy in the Russian language. The Charter shall be placed in the custody of the Government of the Union of Soviet Socialist Republics, which shall distribute certified copies thereof to the Governments of all the member countries of the Council. The Government of the U.S.S.R. shall also communicate to said Governments and to the Secretariat of the Council information concerning the receipt of instruments of ratification. . . .

Concluded in Sofia, December 14, 1959.

24. Pact of the League of Arab States

Signed at Cairo by Egypt, Iraq, Lebanon, Saudi Arabia, Syria, Transjordan on March 22, 1945, and by Yemen on May 5, 1945, the Pact came into force on May 10, 1945. Subsequent adherents included Algeria, Bahrain, Democratic Yemen, Djibouti, Kuwait, Libya, Mauritania, Morocco, Oman, Qatar, Somalia, Sudan and Tunisia, United Arab Emirates, and PLO.

[The High Contracting Parties]. . .

Desirous of strengthening the close relations and numerous ties which link the Arab States;

And anxious to support and stabilize these ties upon a basis of respect for the independence and sovereignty of these states, and to direct their efforts toward the common good of all the Arab countries, the improvement of their status, the security of their future, the realization of their aspirations and hopes;

And responding to the wishes of Arab public opinion in all Arab lands;

Have agreed to conclude a Pact to that end and have . . . agreed upon the following provisions:

ARTICLE 1

The League of Arab States is composed of the independent Arab States which have signed this Pact.

Any independent Arab State has the right to become a member of the League. If it desires to do so, it shall submit a request which will be deposited with the Permanent Secretariat-General and submitted to the Council at the first meeting after submission of the request.

ARTICLE 2

The League has as its purpose the strengthening of the relations between the member states; the coordination of then policies in order to achieve cooperation between them and to safeguard their independence and sovereignty; and a general concern with the affairs and interests of the Arab countries. It has also as its purpose the close cooperation of the member states, with due regard to the organization and circumstances of each state, on the following matters:

(*a*) economic and financial affairs, including commercial relations, customs, currency, and questions of agriculture and industry.

(*b*) communications; this includes railroads, roads, aviation, navigation, telegraph, and post.

(*c*) cultural affairs.

(*d*) nationality, passports, visas, execution of judgments, and extradition of criminals.

(*e*) social affairs.

(*f*) health problems.

ARTICLE 3

The League shall possess a Council composed of the representatives of the member states of the League; each state shall have a single vote, irrespective of the number of its representatives.

It shall be the task of the Council to achieve the realization of the objectives of the League and to supervise the execution of agreements which the member states have concluded on the questions enumerated in the preceding article, or on any other questions.

It likewise shall be the Council's task to decide upon the means by which the League is to cooperate with the international bodies to be created in the future in order to guarantee security and peace and regulate economic and social relations.

ARTICLE 4

For each of the questions listed in Article 2 there shall be set up a special committee in which the member states of the League shall be represented. These committees shall be charged with the task of laying down the principles and extent of cooperation. Such principles shall be formulated as draft agreements, to be presented to the Council for examination preparatory to their submission to the aforesaid states.

Representatives of the other Arab countries may take part in the work of the aforesaid committees. The Council shall determine the conditions under which these representatives may be permitted to participate and the rules governing such representation.

ARTICLE 5

Any resort to force in order to resolve disputes arising between two or more member states of the League is prohibited. If there should arise among them a difference which does not concern a state's independence, sovereignty, or territorial integrity, and if the parties to the dispute have recourse to the Council for the settlement of this difference, the decision of the Council shall then be enforceable and obligatory.

In such a case, the states between whom the difference has arisen shall not participate in the deliberations and decisions of the Council.

The Council shall mediate in all differences which threaten to lead to war between two member states, or a member state and a third state, with a view to bringing about their reconciliation.

Decisions of arbitration and mediation shall be taken by majority vote.

ARTICLE 6

In case of aggression or threat of aggression by one state against a member state, the state which has been attacked or threatened with aggression may demand the immediate convocation of the Council.

The Council shall by unanimous decision determine the measures necessary to repulse the aggression. If the aggressor is a member state, his vote shall not be counted in determining unanimity

If, as a result of the attack, the government of the state attacked finds itself unable to communicate with the Council, that state's representative in the Council shall have the right to request the convocation of the Council for the purpose indicated in the foregoing paragraph. In the event that this representative is unable to communicate with the Council, any member state of the League shall have the right to request the convocation of the Council.

ARTICLE 7

Unanimous decisions of the Council shall be binding upon all member states of the League, majority decisions shall be binding only upon those states which have accepted them.

In either case, the decisions of the Council shall be enforced in each member state according to its respective basic laws.

ARTICLE 8

Each member state shall respect the systems of government established in the other member states and regard them as exclusive concerns of those states. Each shall pledge to abstain from any action calculated to change established system of government.

ARTICLE 9

States of the League which desire to establish closer cooperation and stronger bonds than are provided by this Pact may conclude agreements to that end.

Treaties and agreements already concluded or to be concluded in the future between a member state and another state shall not be binding or restrictive upon other members.

ARTICLE 10

The permanent seat of the League of Arab States is established in Cairo. The Council may, however, assemble at any other place it may designate.

ARTICLE 11

The Council of the League shall convene in ordinary session twice a year, in March and in September. It shall convene in extraordinary session upon the request of two member states of the League whenever the need arises.

ARTICLE 12

The League shall have a permanent Secretariat-General which shall consist of a Secretary-General, Assistant Secretaries, and an appropriate number of officials.

The Council of the League shall appoint the Secretary-General by a majority of two-thirds of the states of the League. The Secretary-General, with the approval of the Council shall appoint the Assistant Secretaries and the principal officials of the League.

The Council of the League shall establish an administrative regulation for the functions of the Secretariat-General and matters relating to the Staff.

The Secretary-General shall have the rank of Ambassador and the Assistant Secretaries that of Ministers Plenipotentiary.

The first Secretary-General of the League is named in an Annex to this Pact.

ARTICLE 13

The Secretary-General shall prepare the draft of the budget of the League and shall submit it to the Council for approval before the beginning of each fiscal year.

The Council shall fix the share of the expenses to be borne by each state of the League. This share may be reconsidered if necessary.

ARTICLE 14

The members of the Council of the League as well as the members of the committees and the officials who are to be designated in the administrative regulation shall enjoy diplomatic privileges and immunity when engaged in the exercise of their functions.

The buildings occupied by the organs of the League shall be inviolable.

ARTICLE 15

The first meeting of the Council shall be convened at the invitation of the head of the Egyptian Government. Thereafter it shall be convened at the invitation of the Secretary-General.

The representatives of the member states of the League shall alternately assume the presidency of the Council at each of its ordinary sessions.

ARTICLE 16

Except in cases specifically indicated in this Pact, a majority vote of the Council shall be sufficient to make enforceable decisions on the following matters:

(*a*) matters relating to personnel.

(*b*) adoption of the budget of the League.

(*c*) establishment of the administrative regulations for the Council, the committees, and the Secretariat-General.

(*d*) decisions to adjourn the sessions.

ARTICLE 17

Each member state of the League shall deposit with the Secretariat-General one copy of every treaty or agreement concluded or to be concluded in the future between itself and another member state of the League or a third state.

ARTICLE 18

If a member state contemplates withdrawal from the League, it shall inform the Council of its intention one year before such withdrawals is to go into effect.

The Council of the League may consider any state which fails to fulfill its obligations under this Pact as having become separated from the League, this to go into effect upon a unanimous decision of the states, not counting the state concerned.

ARTICLE 19

This Pact may be amended with the consent of two-thirds of the states belonging to the League, especially in order to make firmer and stronger the ties between the member states, to create an Arab Tribunal of Arbitration, and to regulate the relations of the League with any international bodies to be created in the future to guarantee security and peace.

Final action on an amendment cannot be taken prior to the session following the session in which the motion was initiated.

If a state does not accept such an amendment it may withdraw at such time as the amendment goes into effect, without being bound by the provisions of the preceding article.

ARTICLE 20

This Pact and its Annexes shall be ratified according to the basic laws in force among the High Contracting Parties.

The instruments of ratification shall be deposited with the Secretariat-General of the Council and the Pact shall become operative as regards each ratifying state fifteen days after the Secretary-General has received the instruments of ratification from four states.

This Pact has been drawn up in Cairo in the Arabic language on this eighth day of Rabi' II, thirteen hundred and sixty-four (March 22, 1945), in one copy which shall be deposited in the safe keeping of the Secretariat-General.

An identical copy shall be delivered to each state of the League.

25. Pact of Baghdad (CENTO)

Signed at Baghdad by Iraq and Turkey on February 24, 1955, the Pact came into force on April 15, 1955. Adherents included the United Kingdom (April 5, 1955), Pakistan (September 23, 1955), and Iran (November 3, 1955). However, after a revolution in 1958, Iraq withdrew from CENTO on March 24, 1959. The United States is not a member of CENTO, but cooperates with it as an observer because of its commitments to Turkey, Pakistan, and Iran through bilateral agreements.

Whereas the friendly and brotherly relations existing between Iraq and Turkey are in constant progress, and in order to complement the contents of the Treaty of friendship and good neighborhood concluded between His Majesty the King of Iraq and His Excellency the President of the Turkish Republic signed in Ankara on March 29, 1946, which recognized the fact that peace and security between the two countries is an integral part of the peace and security of all the Nations of the world and in particular the Nations of the Middle East, and that it is the basis for their foreign policies;

Whereas Article 11 of the Treaty of Joint Defense and Economic Cooperation between the Arab League States provides that no provision of that Treaty shall in any way affect, or is designed to affect, any of the rights and obligations according to the Contracting Parties from the United Nations Charter;

And having realized the great responsibilities borne by them in their capacity as members of the United Nations concerned with the maintenance of peace and security in the Middle East region which necessitate taking the required measures in accordance with Article 51 of the United Nations Charter.

They have been fully convinced of the necessity of concluding a pact fulfilling these aims and for that purpose have . . . agreed as follows:

ARTICLE 1
Consistent with Article 51 of the United Nations Charter the High Contracting Parties will cooperate for their security and defense. Such measures as they agree to take to give effect to this cooperation may form the subject of special agreements with each other.

ARTICLE 2

In order to ensure the realization and effect application of the cooperation provided for in Article 1 above, the competent authorities of the High Contracting Parties will determine the measures to be taken as soon as the present Pact enters into force. These measures will become operative as soon as they have been approved by the Governments of the High Contracting Parties.

ARTICLE 3

The High Contracting Parties undertake to refrain from any interference whatsoever in each other's internal affairs. They will settle any dispute between themselves in a peaceful way in accordance with the United Nations Charter.

ARTICLE 4

The High Contracting Parties declare that the dispositions of the present Pact are not in contradiction with any of the international obligations contracted by either of them with any third state or states. They do not derogate from, and cannot be interpreted as derogating from, the said international obligations. The High Contracting Parties undertake not to enter into any international obligation incompatible with the present Pact.

ARTICLE 5

This Pact shall be open for accession to any member of the Arab League or any other state actively concerned with the security and peace in this region and which is fully recognized by both of the High Contracting Parties. Accession shall come into force from the date of which the instrument of accession of the state concerned is deposited with the Ministry for Foreign Affairs of Iraq.

Any acceding state Party to the present Pact may conclude special agreements, in accordance with Article 1, with one or more states Parties to the present Pact. The competent authority of any acceding state may determine measures in accordance with Article 2. These measures will become operative as soon as they have been approved by the Governments of the Parties concerned.

ARTICLE 6

A Permanent Council at Ministerial level will be set up to function within the framework of the purposes of this Pact when at least four Powers become parties to the Pact.

The Council will draw up its own rules of procedure.

ARTICLE 7

This Pact remains in force for a period of five years renewable for other five-year periods. Any Contracting Party may withdraw from the Pact by notifying the other Parties in writing of its desire to do so, six months before the expiration of any of the above-mentioned periods, in which case the Pact remains valid for the other Parties.

ARTICLE 8

This Pact shall be ratified by the Contracting Parties and ratifications shall be exchanged at Ankara as soon as possible. Thereafter it shall come into force from the date of the exchange of ratifications.

In witness whereof, the said plenipotentiaries have signed the present Pact in Arabic, Turkish, and English, all three texts being equally authentic except in the case of doubt when the English text shall prevail.

Done in duplicate at Baghdad this second day of Rajab 1374 Hijri corresponding to the twenty-fourth day of February, 1955.

26. Charter of the Organization of African Unity

Adopted by the Conference of the Heads of African States and Governments in Addis Ababa, the Charter was signed by 32 African States on May 25, 1963. 479 U.N. Treaty Series, pp. 70–86.

We, the Heads of African States and Governments assembled in the City of Addis Ababa, Ethiopia;

Convinced that it is the inalienable right of all people to control their own destiny;

Conscious of the fact that freedom, equality, justice and dignity are essential objectives for the achievement of the legitimate aspirations of the African peoples;

Conscious of our responsibility to harness the natural and human resources of our continent for the total advancement of our peoples in spheres of human endeavour;

Inspired by a common determination to promote understanding among our peoples and cooperation among our States in response to the aspirations of our peoples for brotherhood and solidarity, in a larger unity transcending ethnic and national differences;

Convinced that, in order to translate this determination into a dynamic force in the cause of human progress, conditions for peace and security must be established and maintained;

Determined to safeguard and consolidate the hard-won independence as well as the sovereignty and territorial integrity of our States, and to fight against neocolonialism in all its forms;

Dedicated to the general progress of Africa;

Persuaded that the Charter of the United Nations and the Universal Declaration of Human Rights, to the principles of which we reaffirm our adherence, provide a solid foundation for peaceful and positive cooperation among states;

Desirous that all African States should henceforth unite so that the welfare and well-being of their peoples can be assured;

Resolved to reinforce the links between our states by establishing and strengthening common institutions;

Have agreed to the present Charter.

ESTABLISHMENT
ARTICLE I

1. The High Contracting Parties do by the present Charter establish an Organization to be known as the *Organization of African Unity*.

2. The Organization shall nclude the Continental African States, Madagascar and other Islands surrounding Africa.

PURPOSES
ARTICLE II

1. The Organization shall have the following purposes:

a. to promote the unity and solidarity of the African States;

b. to coordinate and intensify their cooperation and efforts to achieve a better life for the peoples of Africa;

c. to defend their sovereignty, their territorial integrity and independence;

d. to eradicate all forms of colonialism from Africa; and

e. to promote international cooperation, having due regard to the Charter of the United Nations and the Universal Declaration of Human Rights.

2. To these ends, the Member States shall coordinate and harmonise their general policies, especially in the following fields:

a. political and diplomatic cooperation;

b. economic cooperation, including transport and communications;

c. educational and cultural cooperation;

d. health, sanitation, and nutritional cooperation;

e. scientific and technical cooperations; and

f. cooperation for defence and security.

PRINCIPLES
ARTICLE III

The Member States, in pursuit of the purposes stated in Article II, solemnly affirm and declare their adherence to the following principles:

1. the sovereign equality of all Member States;

2. noninterference in the internal affairs of States;

3. respect for the sovereignty and territorial integrity of each State and for its inalienable right to independent existence;

4. peaceful settlement of disputes by negotiation, mediation, conciliation or arbitration;

5. unreserved condemnation, in all its forms, of political assassination as well as of subversive activities on the part of neighbouring States or any other State;

6. absolute dedication to the total emancipation of the African territories which are still dependent;

7. affirmation of a policy of nonalignment with regard to all blocs.

MEMBERSHIP

ARTICLE IV

Each independent sovereign African State shall be entitled to become a Member of the Organization.

RIGHTS AND DUTIES OF MEMBER STATES

ARTICLE V

All Member States shall enjoy equal rights and have equal duties.

ARTICLE VI

The Member States pledge themselves to observe scrupulously the principles enumerated in Article III of the present Charter.

INSTITUTIONS

ARTICLE VII

The Organization shall accomplish its purposes through the following principal institutions:

1. the Assembly of Heads of State and Government;
2. the Council of Ministers;
3. the General Secretariat;
4. the Commission of Mediation, Conciliation and Arbitration.

THE ASSEMBLY OF HEADS OF STATE AND GOVERNMENT

ARTICLE VIII

The Assembly of Heads of State and Government shall be the supreme organ of the Organization. It shall, subject to the provisions of this Charter, discuss matters of common concern to Africa with a view to coordinating and harmonizing the general policy of the Organization. It may in addition review the structure, functions and acts of all the organs and any specialized agencies which may be created in accordance with the present Charter.

ARTICLE IX

The Assembly shall be composed of the Heads of State and Government or their duly accredited representatives and it shall meet at least once a year. At the request of any Member State and on approval by a two-thirds majority of the Member States, the Assembly shall meet in extraordinary session.

ARTICLE X

1. Each Member State shall have one vote.

2. All resolutions shall be determined by a two-thirds majority of the Members of the Organization.

3. Questions of procedure shall require a simple majority. Whether or not a question is one of procedure shall be determined by a simple majority of all Member States of the Organization.

4. Two-thirds of the total membership of the Organization shall form a quorum at any meeting of the Assembly.

ARTICLE XI

The Assembly shall have the power to determine its own rules of procedure.

THE COUNCIL OF MINISTERS

ARTICLE XII

1. The Council of Ministers shall consist of Foreign Ministers or such other Ministers as are designated by the Governments of Member States.

2. The Council of Ministers shall meet at least twice a year. When requested by any Member State and approved by two-thirds of all Member States, it shall meet in extraordinary session.

ARTICLE XIII

1. The Council of Ministers shall be responsible to the Assembly of Heads of State and Government. It shall be entrusted with the responsibility of preparing conferences of the Assembly.

2. It shall take cognisance of any matter referred to it by the Assembly. It shall be entrusted with the implementation of the decision of the Assembly, of Heads of State and Government. It shall coordinate inter-African cooperation in accordance with the instructions of the Assembly and in conformity with Article II (2) of the present Charter.

ARTICLE XIV

1. Each Member State shall have one vote.

2. All resolutions shall be determined by a simple majority of the members of the Council of Ministers.

3. Two-thirds of the total membership of the Council of Ministers shall form a quorum for any meeting of the Council.

ARTICLE XV

The Council shall have the power to determine its own rules of procedure.

GENERAL SECRETARIAT

ARTICLE XVI

There shall be an Administrative Secretary-General of the Organization, who shall be appointed by the Assembly of Heads of State and Government. The Administrative Secretary-General shall direct the affairs of the Secretariat.

ARTICLE XVII

There shall be one or more Assistant Secretaries-General of the Organization who shall be appointed by the Assembly of Heads of State and Government.

ARTICLE XVIII

The functions and conditions of services of the Secretary-General, of the Assistant Secretaries-General and other employees of the Secretariat shall be governed by the provisions of this Charter and the regulations approved by the Assembly of Heads of State and Government.

1. In the performance of their duties the Administrative Secretary-General and the staff shall not seek or receive instructions from any government or from any other authority external to the Organization. They shall refrain from any action which might reflect on their position as international officials responsible only to the Organization.

2. Each member of the Organization undertakes to respect the exclusive character of the responsibilities of the Administrative Secretary-General and the Staff and not to seek to influence them in the discharge of their responsibilities.

COMMISSION OF MEDIATION, CONCILIATION AND ARBITRATION

ARTICLE XIX

Member States pledge to settle all disputes among themselves by peaceful means and, to this end decide to establish a Commission of Mediation, Conciliation and Arbitration, the composition of which and conditions of service shall be defined by a separate Protocol to be approved by the Assembly of Heads of State and Government. Said Protocol shall be regarded as forming an integral part of the present Charter.

SPECIALIZED COMMISSIONS

ARTICLE XX

The Assembly shall establish such Specialized Commissions as it may deem necessary, including the following:

1. Economic and Social Commission;
2. Educational and Cultural Commission;
3. Health, Sanitation and Nutrition Commission;
4. Defence Commission;
5. Scientific, Technical and Research Commission.

ARTICLE XXI

Each Specialized Commission referred to in Article XX shall be composed of the Ministers concerned or other Ministers or Plenipotentiaries designated by the Governments of the Member States.

ARTICLE XXII

The functions of the Specialized Commissions shall be carried out in accordance with the provisions of the present Charter and of the regulations approved by the Council of Ministers.

THE BUDGET

ARTICLE XXIII

The budget of the Organization prepared by the Administrative Secretary-General shall be approved by the Council of Ministers. The budget shall be provided by contributions from Member States in accordance with the scale of assessment of the United Nations; provided, however, that no Member State shall be assessed an amount exceeding twenty percent of the yearly regular budget of the Organization. The Member States agree to pay their respective contributions regularly.

SIGNATURE AND RATIFICATION OF CHARTER

ARTICLE XXIV

1. This Charter shall be open for signature to all independent sovereign African States and shall be ratified by the signatory States in accordance with their respective constitutional processes.

2. The original instrument, done, if possible in African languages, in English and French, all texts being equally authentic, shall be deposited with the Government of Ethiopia which shall transmit certified copies thereof to all independent sovereign African States.

3. Instruments of ratification shall be deposited with the Government of Ethiopia, which shall notify all signatories of each such deposit.

ENTRY INTO FORCE

ARTICLE XXV

This Charter shall enter into force immediately upon receipt by the Government of Ethiopia of the instruments of ratification from two-thirds of the signatory States.

REGISTRATION OF THE CHARTER

ARTICLE XXVI

This Charter shall, after due ratification, be registered with the Secretariat of the United Nations through the Government of Ethiopia in conformity with Article 102 of the Charter of the United Nations.

INTERPRETATION OF THE CHARTER

ARTICLE XXVII

Any question which may arise concerning the interpretation of this Charter shall be decided by a vote of two-thirds of the Assembly of Heads of State and Government of the Organization.

ADHESION AND ACCESSION

ARTICLE XXVIII

1. Any independent sovereign African State may at any time notify the Administrative Secretary-General of its intention to adhere or accede to this Charter.

2. The Administrative Secretary-General shall, on receipt of such notification, communicate a copy of it to all the Member States. Admission shall be decided by a simple majority of the Member States. The decision of each Member State shall be transmitted to the Administrative Secretary-General, who shall, upon receipt of the required number of votes, communicate the decision to the State concerned.

MISCELLANEOUS

ARTICLE XXIX

The working languages of the Organization and all its institutions shall be, if possible African languages, English and French.

ARTICLE XXX

The Administrative Secretary-General may accept on behalf of the Organization gifts, bequests and other donations made to the Organization, provided that this is approved by the Council of Ministers.

ARTICLE XXXI

The Council of Ministers shall decide on the privileges and immunities to be accorded to the personnel of the Secretariat in the respective territories of the Member States.

CESSATION OF MEMBERSHIP

ARTICLE XXXII

Any State which desires to renounce its membership shall forward a written notification to the Administrative Secretary-General. At the end of one year from the date of such notification, if not withdrawn, the Charter shall cease to apply with respect to the renouncing State, which shall thereby cease to belong to the Organization.

AMENDMENT OF THE CHARTER

ARTICLE XXXIII

This Charter may be amended or revised if any Member States makes a written request to the Administrative Secretary-General to that effect; provided, however, that the proposed amendment is not submitted to the Assembly for consideration until all the Member States have been duly notified of it and a period of one year has elapsed. Such an amendment shall not be effective unless approved by at least two-thirds of all the Member States.

27. Charter of the Organization of American States

Signed at Bogota on April 30, 1948, the Charter came into force on December 13, 1951. As amended by the Protocol of Buenos Aires of February 27, 1967, the present text contains new provisions in italics to substitute the original text in brackets.

In the name of their Peoples, the States represented at the Ninth International Conference of American States

Convinced that the historic mission of America is to offer to man a land of liberty, and a favorable environment for the development of his personality and the realization of his just aspirations;

Conscious that that mission has already inspired numerous agreements, whose essential value lies in the desire of the American peoples to live together in peace, and, through their mutual understanding and respect for the sovereignty of each one, to provide for the betterment of all, in independence, in equality and under law;

Confident that the true significance of American solidarity and good neighborliness can only mean the consolidation on this continent, within the framework of democratic institutions, of a system of individual liberty and social justice based on respect for the essential rights of man;

Persuaded that their welfare and their contribution to the progress and the civilization of the world will increasingly require intensive continental cooperation;

Resolved to persevere in the noble undertaking that humanity has conferred upon the United Nations, whose principles and purposes they solemnly reaffirm;

Convinced that juridical organization is a necessary condition for security and peace founded on moral order and on justice; and

In accordance with Resolution IX of the Inter-American Conference on Problems of War and Peace, held at Mexico City,

Have agreed upon the following

PART ONE
CHARTER OF THE ORGANIZATION OF AMERICAN STATES

I. NATURE AND PURPOSES
ARTICLE 1

The American States establish by this Charter the international organization that they have developed to achieve an order of peace and justice, to promote their solidarity, to strengthen their collaboration, and to defend their sovereignty, their territorial integrity and their independence. Within the United Nations, the Organization of American States is a regional agency.

ARTICLE 2 [4]

The Organization of American States, in order to put into practice the principles on which it is founded and to fulfill its regional obligations under the Charter of the United Nations, proclaims the following essential purposes:

(a) To strengthen the peace and security of the continent;

(b) To prevent possible causes of difficulties and to ensure the pacific settlement of disputes that may arise among the Member States;

(c) To provide for common action on the part of those States in the event of aggression;

(d) To seek the solution of political, juridical and economic problems that may arise among them; and

(e) To promote, by cooperative action, their economic, social and cultural development.

II. PRINCIPLES
ARTICLE 3 [5]

The American States reaffirm the following principles:

(a) International law is the standard of conduct of States in their reciprocal relations;

(b) International order consists essentially of respect for the personality, sovereignty and independence of States, and the faithful fulfillment of obligations derived from treaties and other sources of international law.

(c) Good faith shall govern the relations between States;

(d) The solidarity of the American States and the high aims which are sought through it require the political organization of those States on the basis of the effective exercise of representative democracy;

(e) The American States condemn war of aggression: victory does not give rights;

(f) An act of aggression against one American State is an act of aggression against all the other American States;

(g) Controversies of an international character arising between two or more American States shall be settled by peaceful procedures;

(h) Social justice and social security are bases of lasting peace;

(i) Economic cooperation is essential to the common welfare and prosperity of the peoples of the continent;

(j) The American States proclaim the fundamental rights of the individual without distinction as to race, nationality, creed or sex;

(k) The spiritual unity of the continent is based on respect for the cultural values of the American countries and requires their close cooperation for the high purposes of civilization;

(l) The education of peoples should be directed toward justice, freedom and peace.

III. MEMBERS

ARTICLE 4 [2]

All American States that ratify the present Charter are Members of the Organization.

ARTICLE 5 [3]

Any new political entity that arises from the union of several Member States and that, as such, ratifies the present Charter, shall become a Member of the Organization. The entry of the new political entity into the Organization shall result in the loss of membership of each one of the States which constitute it.

ARTICLE 6

Any other independent American State that desires to become a Member of the Organization should so indicate by means of a note addressed to the Secretary-General, in which it declares that it is willing to sign and ratify the Charter of the Organization and to accept all the obligations inherent in membership, especially those relating to collective security expressly set forth in Articles 27 and 28 of the Charter.

ARTICLE 7

The General Assembly, upon the recommendation of the Permanent Council of the Organization, shall determine whether it is appropriate that the Secretary General be authorized to permit the applicant State to sign the Charter and to accept the deposit of the corresponding instrument of ratification. Both the recommendation of the Permanent Council and the decision of the General Assembly shall require the affirmative vote of two-thirds of the Member States.

ARTICLE 8

The Permanent Council shall not make any recommendation nor shall the General Assembly take any decision with respect to a request for admission on the part of a political entity whose territory became subject, in whole or in part, prior to December 18, 1964, the date set by the First Special Inter-American Conference, to litigation or claim between an extra-continental country and one or more Member States of the Organization, until the dispute has been ended by some peaceful procedure.

IV [III]. FUNDAMENTAL RIGHTS AND DUTIES OF STATES

ARTICLE 9 [6]

States are juridically equal, enjoy equal rights and equal capacity to exercise these rights, and have equal duties. The rights of each State depend not upon its power to ensure the exercise thereof, but upon the mere fact of its existence as a person under international law.

ARTICLE 10 [7]

Every American State has the duty to respect the rights enjoyed by every other State in accordance with international law.

ARTICLE 11 [8]

The fundamental rights of States may not be impaired in any manner whatsoever.

ARTICLE 12 [9]

The political existence of the State is independent of recognition by other States. Even before being recognized, the State has the right to defend its integrity and independence, to provide for its preservation and prosperity, and consequently to organize itself as it sees fit, to legislate concerning its interests, to administer its services, and to determine the jurisdiction and competence of its courts. The exercise of these rights is limited only by the exercise of the rights of other States in accordance with international law.

ARTICLE 13 [10]

Recognition implies that the State granting it accepts the personality of the new State, with all the rights and duties that international law prescribes for the two States.

ARTICLE 14 [11]

The right to each State to protect itself and to live its own life does not authorize it to commit unjust acts against another State.

ARTICLE 15 [12]

The jurisdiction of States within the limits of their national territory is exercised equally over all the inhabitants, whether nationals or aliens.

ARTICLE 16 [13]

Each State has the right to develop its cultural, political and economic life freely and natually. In this free development, the State shall respect the rights of the individual and the principles of universal morality.

ARTICLE 17 [14]

Respect for and the faithful observance of treaties constitute standards for the development of peaceful relations among States. International treaties and agreements should be public.

ARTICLE 18 [15]

No State or group of States has the right to intervene, directly or indirectly, for any reason whatever, in the internal or external affairs of any other State. The foregoing principle prohibits not only armed force but also any other form of interference or attempted threat against the personality of the State or against its political, economic and cultural elements.

ARTICLE 19 [16]

No State may use or encourage the use of coercive measures of an economic or political character in order to force the sovereign will of another State and obtain from it advantages of any kind.

ARTICLE 20 [17]

The territory of a State is inviolable; it may not be the object, even temporarily, of military occupation or of other measures of force taken by another State, directly or indirectly, on any grounds whatever. No territorial acquisitions or special advantages obtained either by force or by other means of coercion shall be recognized.

ARTICLE 21 [18]

The American States bind themselves in their international relations not to have recourse to the use of force, except in the case of self-defense in accordance with existing treaties or in fulfillment thereof.

ARTICLE 22 [19]

Measures adopted for the maintenance of peace and security in accordance with existing treaties do not constitute a violation of the principles set forth in Articles 18 and 20.

V [IV]. PACIFIC SETTLEMENT OF DISPUTES

ARTICLE 23 [20]

All international disputes that may arise between American States shall be submitted to the peaceful procedures set forth in this Charter, before being referred to the Security Council of the United Nations.

ARTICLE 24 [21]

The following are peaceful procedures: direct negotiation, good offices, mediation, investigation and conciliation, judicial settlement, arbitration, and those which the parties to the dispute may especially agree upon at any time.

ARTICLE 25 [22]

In the event that a dispute arises between two or more American States which, in the opinion of one of them, cannot be settled through the usual diplomatic channels, the Parties shall agree on some other peaceful procedure that will enable them to reach a solution.

ARTICLE 26 [23]

A special treaty will establish adequate procedures for the pacific settlement of disputes and will determine the appropriate means for their application, so that no dispute between American States shall fail of definitive settlement within a reasonable period.

VI [V]. COLLECTIVE SECURITY

ARTICLE 27 [24]

Every act of aggression by a State against the territorial integrity or the inviolability of the territory or against the sovereignty or political independence of an American State shall be considered an act of aggression against the other American States.

ARTICLE 28 [25]

If the inviolability or the integrity of the territory or the sovereignty or political independence of any American State should be affected by an armed attack or by an act of aggression that is not an armed attack, or by an extracontinental conflict, or by a conflict between two or more American States, or by any other fact or situation that might endanger the peace of America, the American States, in furtherance of the principles of continental solidarity or collective self-defense, shall apply the measures and procedures established in the special treaties on the subject.

VII [VI]. ECONOMIC STANDARDS

ARTICLE 29

The Member States, inspired by the principles of inter-American solidarity and cooperation, pledge themselves to a united effort to ensure social justice in the Hemisphere and dynamic and balanced economic development for their peoples, as conditions essential to peace and security.

ARTICLE 30

The Member States pledge themselves to mobilize their own national human and material resources through suitable programs, and recognize the importance of operating within an efficient domestic structure, as fundamental conditions for their economic and social progress and for assuring effective inter-American cooperation.

ARTICLE 31

To accelerate their economic and social development, in accordance with their own methods and procedures and within the framework of the democratic principles and the institutions of the inter-American system, the Member States agree to dedicate every effort to achieve the following basic goals:

(a) Substantial and self-sustained increase in the per capita national product;

(b) Equitable distribution of national income;

(c) Adequate and equitable systems of taxation;

(d) Modernization of rural life and reforms leading to equitable and efficient land-tenure systems, increased agricultural productivity, expanded use of undeveloped land, diversification of producttion; and improved processing and marketing systems for agricultural products; and the strengthening and expansion of facilities to attain these ends;

(e) Accelerated and diversified industrialization, especially of capital and intermediate goods;

(f) Stability in the domestic price levels, compatible with sustained economic development and the attainment of social justice;

(g) Fair wages, employment opportunities, and acceptable working conditions for all;

(h) Rapid eradication of illiteracy and expansion of educational opportunities for all;

(i) Protection of man's potential through the extension and application of modern medical science;

(j) Proper nutrition, especially through the acceleration of national efforts to increase the production and availability of food;

(k) Adequate housing for all sectors of the population;

(l) *Urban conditions that offer the opportunity for a healthful, productive, and full life;*

(m) *Promotion of private initiative and investment in harmony with action in the public sector; and*

(n) *Expansion and diversification of exports.*

ARTICLE 32

In order to attain the objectives set forth in this Chapter, the Member States agree to cooperate with one another, in the broadest spirit of inter-American solidarity, as far as their resources may permit and their laws may provide.

ARTICLE 33

To obtain balanced and sustained development as soon as feasible, the Member States agree that the resources made available from time to time by each, in accordance with the preceding Article, should be provided under flexible conditions and in support of the national and multinational programs and efforts undertaken to meet the needs of the assisted country, giving special attention to the relatively less-developed countries.

They will seek, under similar conditions and for similar purposes, financial and technical cooperation from sources outside the Hemisphere and from international institutions.

ARTICLE 34

The Member States should make every effort to avoid policies, actions, or measures that have serious adverse effects on the economic or social development of another Member State.

ARTICLE 35

The Member States agree to join together in seeking a solution to urgent or critical problems that may arise whenever the economic development or stability of any Member State is seriously affected by conditions that cannot be remedied through the efforts of that State.

ARTICLE 36

The Member States shall extend among themselves the benefits of science and technology by ecnouraging the exchange and utilization of scientific and technical knowledge in accordance with existing treaties and national laws.

ARTICLE 37

The Member States, recognizing the close interdependence between foreign trade and economic and social development, should make individual and united efforts to bring about the following:

(a) *Reduction or elimination, by importing countries, of tariff and nontariff barriers that affect the exports of the Members of the Organization, except when such barriers are applied in order to diversify the economic structure, to speed up the development of the less-developed Member States, or to intensify their process of economic integration, or when they are related to national security or to the needs for economic balance;*

(b) *Maintenance of continuity in their economic and social development by means of:*

i. *Improved conditions for trade in basic commodities through international agreements, where appropriate; orderly marketing procedures that avoid the disruption of markets; and other measures designed to promote the expansion of markets, and to obtain dependable incomes for producers, adequate and dependable supplies for consumers, and stable prices that are both remunerative to producers and fair to consumers.*

ii. *Improved international financial cooperation and the adoption of other means for lessening the adverse impact of sharp fluctuations in export earnings experienced by the countries exporting basic commodities; and*

iii. *Diversification of exports and expansion of export opportunities for manufactured and semimanufactured products from the developing countries by promoting and strengthening national and multinational institutions and arrangements established for these purposes.*

ARTICLE 38

The Member States reaffirm the principle that when the more-developed countries grant concessions in international trade agreements that lower or eliminate tariffs or other barriers to foreign trade so that they benefit the less-developed countries, they should not expect reciprocal concessions from those countries that are incompatible with their economic development, financial, and trade needs.

ARTICLE 39

The Member States, in order to accelerate their economic development, regional integration, and the expansion and improvement of the conditions of their commerce, shall promote improvement and coordination of transportation and communication in the developing countries and among the Member States.

ARTICLE 40

The Member States recognize that integration of the developing countries of the Hemisphere is one of the objectives of the inter-American system and, therefore, shall orient their efforts and take the necessary measures to accelerate the integration process, with a view to establishing a Latin American common market in the shortest possible time.

ARTICLE 41

In order to strengthen and accelerate integration in all its aspects, the Member States agree to give adequate priority to the preparation and carrying out of multinational projects and to their financing, as well as to encourage economic and financial institutions of the inter-American system to continue giving their broadest support to regional integration institutions and programs.

ARTICLE 42

The Member States agree that technical and financial cooperation that seeks to promote regional economic integration should be based on the principle of harmonious, balanced, and efficient development, with particular attention, to the relatively less-developed countries, so that it may be a decisive factor that will enable them to promote, with their own efforts, the improved development of their infrastructure programs, new lines of production, and export diversification.

VIII [VII]. SOCIAL STANDARDS

ARTICLE 43

The Member States, convinced that man can only achieve the full realization of his aspirations within a just social order, along with economic development and true peace, agree to dedicate every effort to the applicaton of the following principles and mechanisms:

(a) All human beings, without distinction as to race, sex, nationality, creed, or social condition, have a right to material well-being and to their spirtual development, under circumstances of liberty, dignity, equality of opportunity, and economic security;

(b) Work is a right and a social duty, it gives dignity to the one who performs it, and it should be performed under conditions, including a system of fair wages, that ensure life, health, and a decent standard of living for the worker and his family, both during his working years and in his old age, or when any circumstance deprives him of the possibility of working;

(c) Employers and workers, both rural and urban, have the right to associate themselves freely for the defense and promotion of their interests, including the right to collective bargaining and the workers' right to strike, and recognition of the juridical personality of associations and the protection of their freedom and independence, all in accordance with applicable laws;

(d) Fair and efficient systems and procedures for consultation and collaboration among the sectors of production, with due regard for safeguarding the interests of the entire society;

(e) *The operation of system of public administration, banking and credit, enterprise, and distribution and sales, in such a way, in harmony with the private sector, as to meet the requirements and interests of the community;*

(f) *The incorporation and increasing participation of the marginal sectors of the population, in both rural and urban areas, in the economic, social, civic, cultural, and political life of the nation, in order to achieve the full integration of the national community, acceleration of the process of social mobility, and the consolidation of the democratic system. The encouragement of all efforts of popular promotion and cooperation that have as their purpose the development and progress of the community;*

(g) *Recognition of the importance of the contribution of organizations such as labor unions, cooperatives and culutral, professional, business, neighborhood, and community associations to the life of the society and to the development process;*

(h) *Development of an efficient social security policy; and*

(i) *Adequate provision for all persons to have due legal aid in order to secure their rights.*

ARTICLE 44
The Member States recognize that, in order to facilitate the process of Latin American regional integration, it is necessary to harmonize the social legislation of the developing countries, especially in the labor and social security fields, so that the rights of the workers shall be equally protected, and they agree to make the greatest efforts possible to achieve this goal.

IX. EDUCATIONAL, SCIENTIFIC AND CULTURAL STANDARDS
[1948 Text: Chapter VIII. Cultural Standards]
ARTICLE 45
The Member States will give primary importance within their development plans to the encouragement of education, science, and culture, oriented toward the overall improvements of the individual, and as a foundation for democracy, social justice, and progress.

ARTICLE 46
The Member States will cooperate with one another to meet their educational needs, to promote scientific research, and to encourage technological progress. They consider themselves individually and jointly bound to preserve and enrich the cultural heritage of the American peoples.

ARTICLE 47

The Member States will exert the greatest efforts, in accordance with their constitutional processes, to ensure the effective exercise of the right to education, on the following bases:

(a) *Elementary education, compulsory for children of school age, shall also be offered to all others who can benefit from it. When provided by the State it shall be without charge;*

(b) *Middle-level education shall be extended progressively to as much of the population as possible, with a view to social improvement. It shall be diversified in such a way that it meets the development needs of each country without prejudice to providing a general education; and*

(c) *Higher education shall be available to all, provided that, in order to maintain its high level, the corresponding regulatory or academic standards are met.*

ARTICLE 48

The Member States will give special attention to the eradication of illiteracy, will strengthen adult and vocational education systems, and will ensure that the benefits of culture will be available to the entire population. They will promote the use of all information media to fulfill these aims.

ARTICLE 49

The Member States will develop science and technology through educational and research institutions and through expanded information programs. They will organize their cooperation in these fields efficiently and will substantially increase exchange of knowledge, in accordance with national objectives and laws and with treaties in force.

ARTICLE 50

The Member States, with due respect for the individuality of each of them, agree to promote cultural exchange as an effective means of consolidating inter-American understanding; and they recognize that regional integration programs should be strengthened by close ties in the fields of education, science, and culture.

PART TWO

X [IX]. THE ORGANS

ARTICLE 51

The Organization of American States accomplishes its purposes by means of:

(a) *The General Assembly;*

(b) *The Meeting of Consultation of Ministers of Foreign Affairs;*

(c) *The Councils;*

(d) The Inter-American Juridical Committee;

(e) *The Inter-American Commission on Human Rights;*

(f) *The General Secretariat;*

(g) *The Specialized Conferences; and*

(h) *The Specialized Organizations.*

There may be established, in addition to those provided for in the Charter and in accordance with the provisions thereof, such subsidiary organs, agencies, and other entities as are considered necessary.

XI. THE GENERAL ASSEMBLY

[1948 Text: Chapter X. The Inter-American Conference]
ARTICLE 52

The General Assembly is the supreme organ of the Organization of American States. It has as its principal powers, in addition to such others as are assigned to it by the Charter, the following:

(a) *To decide the general action and policy of the Organization, determine the structure and functions of its organs, and consider any matter relating to a friendly relations among the American States;*

(b) *To establish measures for coordinating the activities of the organs, agencies, and entities of the Organization among themselves and such activities with those of the other institutions of the inter-American system;*

(c) *To strengthen and coordinate cooperation with the United Nations and its specialized agencies;*

(d) *To promote collaboration, especially in the economic, social, and cultural fields, with other international organizations whose purposes are similar to those of the Organization of American States;*

(e) *To approve the program-budget of the Organization and determine the quotas of the Member States;*

(f) *To consider the annual and special reports that shall be presented to it by the organs, agencies, and entities of the inter-American system;*

(g) *To adopt general standards to govern the operations of the General Secretariat; and*

(h) *To adopt its own rules of procedure and, by a two-thirds vote, its agenda.*

The General Assembly shall exercise its powers in accordance with the provisions of the Charter and of other inter-American treaties.

ARTICLE 53 [54]

The *General Assembly* shall establish the bases for fixing the quota that each Government is to contribute to the maintenance of the *Organization,* taking into account the ability to pay of the respective countries and their determination to contribute in an equitable manner. Decisions on budgetary matters require the approval of two-thirds of the *Member States.*

ARTICLE 54
All Member States have the right to be represented *in the General Assembly.* Each State has the right to one vote.

ARTICLE 55
The General Assembly shall convene annually during the period deter-mined by the rules of procedure and at a place selected in accordance with the principle of rotation. At each regular session the date and place of the next regular session shall be determined, in accordance with the rules of procedure.

If for any reason the General Assembly cannot be held at the place chosen, it shall meet at the General Secretariat, unless one of the Member States should make a timely offer of a site in its territory, in which case the Permanent Council of the Organization may agree that the General Assembly will meet in that place.

ARTICLE 56
In special circumstances and with the approval of two-thirds of the Member States, the Permanent Council shall convoke a special session of the General Assembly.

ARTICLE 57
Decisions of the General Assembly shall be adopted by the affirmative vote of an absolute majority of the Member States, except in those cases that require a two-thirds vote as provided in the Charter or as may be pro-vided by the General Assembly in its rules of procedure.

ARTICLE 58
There shall be a Preparatory Committee of the General Assembly, composed of representatives of all the Member States, which shall:

(a) *Prepare the draft agenda of each session of the General Assembly;*

(b) *Review the proposed program-budget and the draft resolution on quotas, and present to the General Assembly a report thereon containing the recommendations it considers appropriate; and*

(c) *Carry out such other functions as the General Assembly may assign to it.*

The draft agenda and the report shall, in due course, be transmitted to the Governments of the Member States.

XII [XI]. THE MEETING OF CONSULTATION OF MINISTERS OF FOREIGN AFFAIRS

ARTICLE 59 [39]

The Meeting of Consultation of Ministers of Foreign Affairs shall be held in order to consider problems of an urgent nature and of common interest to the American States, and to serve as the Organ of Consultation.

ARTICLE 60 [40]

Any Member State may request that a Meeting of Consultation be called. The request shall be addressed to the *Permanent* Council of the Organization, which shall decide by an absolute majority whether a meeting should be held.

ARTICLE 61 [41]

The *agenda* and regulations of the Meeting of Consultation shall be prepared by the *Permanent* Council of the Organization and submitted to the Member States for consideration.

ARTICLE 62 [42]

If, for exceptional reasons, a Minister of Foreign Affairs is unable to attend the meeting, he shall be represented by a special delegate.

ARTICLE 63 [43]

In case of an armed attack within the territory of an American State or within the region of security delimited by treaties in force, a Meeting of Consultation shall be held without delay. Such Meeting shall be called immediately by the Chairman of the *Permanent* Council of the Organization, who shall at the same time call a meeting of the Council itself.

ARTICLE 64 [44]

An Advisory Defense Committee shall be established to advise the Organ of Consultation on problems of military cooperation that may arise in connection with the application of existing special treaties on collective security.

ARTICLE 65 [45]

The Advisory Defense Committee shall be composed of the highest military authorities of the American States participating in the Meeting of Consultation. Under exceptional circumstances the Governments may appoint substitutes. Each State shall be entitled to one vote.

ARTICLE 66 [46]

The Advisory Defense Committee shall be convoked under the same conditions as the Organ of Consultation, when the latter deals with matters relating to defense against aggression.

ARTICLE 67 [47]

The Committee shall also meet when the Conference or the Meeting of Consultation or the Governments, by a two-thirds majority of the Member States, assign to it technical studies or reports on specific subjects.

XIII. THE COUNCILS OF THE ORGANIZATION: COMMON PROVISIONS

ARTICLE 68

The Permanent Council of the Organization, the Inter-American Economic and Social Council, and the Inter-American Council for Education, Science, and Culture are directly responsible to the General Assembly and each has the authority granted to it in the Charter and other inter-American instruments, as well as the functions assigned to it by the General Assembly and the Meeting of Consultation of Ministers of Foreign Affairs.

ARTICLE 69

All Member States have the right to be represented on each of the Councils. Each State has the right to one vote.

ARTICLE 70

The Councils may, within the limits of the Charter and other inter-American instruments, make recommendations on matters within their authority.

ARTICLE 71

The Councils, on matters within their respective competence, may present to the General Assembly studies and proposals, drafts of international instruments, and proposals on the holding of specialized conferences, on the creation, modification, or elimination of specialized organizations and other inter-American agencies, as well as on the coordination of their activities. The Councils may also present studies, proposals, and drafts of international instruments to the Specialized Conferences.

ARTICLE 72

Each Council may, in urgent cases, convoke Specialized Conferences on matters within its competence, after consulting with the Member States and without having to resort to the procedure provided for in Article 128.

ARTICLE 73

The Councils, to the extent of their ability, and with the cooperation of the General Secretariat, shall render to the Governments such specialized services as the latter may request.

ARTICLE 74

Each Council has the authority to require the other Councils, as well as the subsidiary organs and agencies responsible to them, to provide it with information and advisory services on matters within their respective spheres of competence. The Councils may also request the same services from the other agencies of the inter-American system.

ARTICLE 75

With the prior approval of the General Assembly, the Councils may establish the subsidiary organs and the agencies that they consider advisable for the better performance of their duties. When the General Assembly is not in session, the aforesaid organs or agencies may be established provisionally by the corresponding Council. In constituting the membership of these bodies, the Councils, insofar as possible, shall follow the criteria of rotation and equitable geographic representation.

ARTICLE 76

The Councils may hold meetings in any Member State, when they find it advisable and with the prior consent of the Government concerned.

ARTICLE 77

Each Council shall prepare its own statutes and submit them to the General Assembly for approval. It shall approve its own rules of procedure and those of its subsidiary organs, agencies, and committees.

XIV. THE PERMANENT COUNCIL OF THE ORGANIZATION

[1948 Text: Chapter XII. The Council]

ARTICLE 78 [48]

The *Permanent* Council of the Organization is composed of one representative of each Member State, especially appointed by the respective Government, with the rank of *ambassador. Each Government may accredit an acting representative, as well as such alternates and advisers as it considers necessary.*

ARTICLE 79

The office of Chairman of the Permanent Council shall be held by each of the representatives, in turn, following the alphabetic order in Spanish, of the names of their respective countries. The office of Vice Chairman shall be filled in the same way, following reverse alphabetic order.

The Chairman and the Vice Chairman shall hold office for a term of not more than six months, which shall be determined by the statutes.

ARTICLE 80

Within the limits of the Charter and of inter-American treaties and agreements, the Permanent Council takes cognizance of any matter referred to it by the General Assembly or the Meeting of Consultation of Ministers of Foreign Affairs.

ARTICLE 81 [52]

The *Permanent* Council shall serve provisionally as the Organ of Consultation when the circumstances contemplated in Article 43 of this Charter arise.

ARTICLE 82

The Permanent Council shall keep vigilance over the maintenance of friendly relations among the Member States, and for that purpose shall effectively assist them in the peaceful settlement of their disputes, in accordance with the following provisions.

ARTICLE 83

To assist the Permanent Council in the exercise of these powers, an Inter-American Committee on Peaceful Settlement shall be established, which shall function as a subsidiary organ of the Council. The statutes of the Committee shall be prepare by the Council and approved by the General Assembly.

ARTICLE 84

The parties to a dispute may resort to the Permanent Council to obtain its good offices. In such a case the Council shall have authority to assist the parties and to recommend the procedures it considers suitable for the peaceful settlement of the dispute.

If the parties so wish, the Chairman of the Council shall refer the dispute directly to the Inter-American Committee on Peaceful Settlement.

ARTICLE 85

In the exercise of these powers, the Permanent Council, through the Inter-American Committee on Peaceful Settlement or by any other means, may ascertain the facts in the dispute, and may do so in the territory of any of the parties with the consent of the Government concerned.

ARTICLE 86

Any party to a dispute in which none of the peaceful procedures set forth in Article 24 of the Charter is being followed may appeal in the Permanent Council to take cognizance of the dispute.

The Council shall immediately refer the request to the Inter-American Committee on Peaceful Settlement, which shall consider whether or not the matter is within its competence and, if it deems it appropriate, shall offer its good offices to the other party or parties. Once these are accepted, the Inter-American Committee on Peaceful Settlement may assist the parties and recommend the procedures that it considers suitable for the peaceful settlement of the dispute.

In the exercise of these powers, the Committee may carry out an investigation of the facts in the dispute, and may do so in the territory of any of the parties with the consent of the Government concerned.

ARTICLE 87

If one of the parties should refuse the offer, the Inter-American Committee on Peaceful Settlement shall limit itself to informing the Permanent Council, without prejudice to its taking steps to restore relations between the parties, if they were interrupted, or to reestablish harmony between them.

ARTICLE 88

Once such a report is received, the Permanent Council may make suggestions for bringing the parties together for the purpose of Article 87 and, if it considers it necessary, it may urge the parties to avoid any action that might aggravate the dispute.

If one of the parties should continue to refuse the good offices of the Inter-American Committee on Peaceful Settlement or of the Council, the Council shall limit itself to submitting a report to the General Assembly.

ARTICLE 89

The Permanent Council, in the exercise of these functions, shall take its decisions by an affirmative vote of two-thirds of its members, excluding the parties to the dispute, except for such decisions as the rules of procedure provide shall be adopted by a simple majority.

ARTICLE 90

In performing their functions with respect to the peaceful settlement of disputes the Permanent Council and the Inter-American Committee on Peaceful Settlement shall observe the provisions of the Charter and the principles and standards of international law, as well as take into account the existence of treaties in force between the parties.

ARTICLE 91

The Permanent Council shall also:

(a) Carry out those decisions of the General Assembly or of the Meeting of Consultation of Ministers of Foreign Affairs the implementation of which has not been assigned to any other body;

(b) *Watch over the observance of the standards governing the operation of the General Secretariat and, when the General Assembly is not in session, adopt provisions of a regulatory nature that enable the General Secretariat to carry out its administrative functions;*

(c) *Act as the Preparatory Committee of the General Assembly, in accordance with the terms of Article 58 of the Charter, unless the General Assembly should decide otherwise;*

(d) *Prepare, at the request of the Member States and with the cooperation of the appropriate organs of the Organization, draft agreements to promote and facilitate cooperation between the Organization of American States and the United Nations or between the Organization and other American agencies of recognized international standing. These draft agreements shall be submitted to the General Assembly for approval.*

(e) *Submit recommendations to the General Assembly with regard to the functioning of the Organization and the coordination of its subsidiary organs, agencies, and committees;*

(f) *Present to the General Assembly any observations it may have regarding the reports of the Inter-American Juridical Committee and the Inter-American Commission on Human Rights; and*

(g) *Perform the other functions assigned to it in the Charter.*

ARTICLE 92

The Permanent Council and the General Secretariat shall have the same seat.

XV. THE INTER-AMERICAN ECONOMIC AND SOCIAL COUNCIL

ARTICLE 93

The Inter-American Economic and Social Council is composed of one principal representative, of the highest rank, of each Member State, especially appointed by the respective Government.

ARTICLE 94

The purpose of the Inter-American Economic and Social Council is to promote cooperation among the American countries in order to attain accelerated economic and social development, in accordance with the standards set forth in Chapters VII and VIII.

ARTICLE 95

To achieve its purpose the Inter-American Economic and Social Council shall:

(a) *Recommend programs and courses of action and periodically study and evaluate the efforts undertaken by the Member States;*

(b) *Promote and coordinate all economic and social activities of the Organization;*

(c) *Coordinate its activities with those of the other Councils of the Organization;*

(d) *Establish cooperative relations with ths corresponding organs of the United Nations and with other national and international agencies, especially with regard to coordination of inter-American technical assistance programs; and*

(e) *Promote the solution of the cases contemplated in Article 35 of the Charter, establishing the appropriate procedure.*

ARTICLE 96
The Inter-American Economic and Social Council shall hold at least one meeting each year at the ministerial level. It shall also meet when convoked by the General Assembly, the Meeting of Consultation of Ministers of Foreign Affairs, at its own initiative, or for the cases contemplated in Article 35 of the Charter.

ARTICLE 97
The Inter-American Economic and Social Council shall have a Permanent Executive Committee, composed of a Chairman and no less than seven other members, elected by the Council for terms to be established in the statutes of the Council. Each member shall have the right to one vote. The principles of equitable geographic representation and of rotation shall be taken into account, insofar as possible, in the election of members. The Permanent Executive Committee represents all of the Member States of the Organization.

ARTICLE 98
The Permanent Executive Committee shall perform the tasks assigned to it by the Inter-American Economic and Social Council, in accordance with the general standards established by the Council.

XVI. THE INTER-AMERICAN COUNCIL FOR EDUCATION, SCIENCE AND CULTURE

ARTICLE 99
The Inter-American Council for Education, Science, and Culture is composed of one principal representative, of the highest rank, of each Member State, especially appointed by the respective Government.

ARTICLE 100
The purpose of the Inter-American Council for Education, Science, and Culture is to promote friendly relations and mutual understanding be-

tween the peoples of the Americas through educational, scientific, and cultural cooperation and exchange between Member States, in order to raise the cultural level of the peoples, reaffirm their dignity as individuals, prepare them fully for the tasks of progress, and strengthen the devotion to peace, democracy, and social justice that has characterized their evolution.

ARTICLE 101

To accomplish its purpose the Inter-American Council for Education, Science, and Culture shall:

(a) *Promote and coordinate the educational, scientific, and cultural activities of the Organization;*

(b) *Adopt or recommend pertinent measures to give effect to the standards contained in Chapter IX of the Charter;*

(c) *Support individual or collective efforts of the Member States to improve and extend education at all levels, giving special attention to efforts directed toward community development;*

(d) *Recommend and encourage the adoption of special educational programs directed toward integrating all sectors of the population into their respective national cultures;*

(e) *Stimulate and support scientific and technological education and research, especially when these relate to national development plans;*

(f) *Foster the exchange of professors, research workers, technicians, and students, as well as of study materials; and encourage the conclusion of bilateral or multilateral agreements on the progressive coordination of curricula at all educational levels and on the validity and equivalence of certificates and degrees;*

(g) *Promote the education of the American peoples with a view to harmonious international relations and a better understanding of the historical and cultural origins of the Americas, in order to stress and preserve their common values and destiny;*

(h) *Systematically encouage intellectual and artistic creativity, the exchange of cultural works and folklore, as well as the interrelationships of the different cultural regions of the Americas;*

(i) *Foster cooperation and technical assistance for protecting, preserving, and increasing the cultural heritage of the Hemisphere;*

(j) *Coordinate its activities with those of the other Councils. In harmony with the Inter-American Economic and Social Council, encourage the interrelationship of programs for promoting education, science, and culture with national development and regional integration programs;*

(k) *Establish cooperative relations with the corresponding organs of the United Nations and with other national and international bodies;*

(l) *Strengthen the civic conscience of the American peoples, as one of the bases for the effective exercise of democracy and for the observance of the rights and duties of man;*

(m) *Recommend appropriate procedures for intensifying integration of the developing countries of the Hemisphere by means of efforts and programs in the fields of education, science, and culture; and*

(n) *Study and evaluate periodically the efforts made by the Member States in the fields of education, science, and culture.*

ARTICLE 102

The Inter-American Council for Education, Science, and Culture shall hold at least one meeting each year at the ministerial level. It shall also meet when convoked by the General Assembly, by the Meeting of Consultation of Ministers of Foreign Affairs, or at its own initiative.

ARTICLE 103

The Inter-American Council for Education, Science, and Culture shall have a Permanent Executive Committee, composed of a Chairman and no less than seven other members, elected by the Council for terms to be established in the statutes of the Council. Each member shall have the right to one vote. The principles of equitable geographic representation and of rotation shall be taken into account, insofar as possible, in the election of members. The Permanent Executive Committee represents all of the Member States of the Organization.

ARTICLE 104

The Permanent Executive Committee shall perform the tasks assigned to it by the Inter-American Council for Education, Science, and Culture, in accordance with the general standards established by the Council.

XVII. THE INTER-AMERICAN JURIDICAL COMMITTEE

ARTICLE 105

The purpose of the Inter-American Juridical Committee is to serve the Organization as an advisory body on juridical matters; to promote the progressive development and the codification of international law; and to study juridical problems related to the integration of the developing countries of the Hemisphere and, insofar as may appear desirable, the possibility of attaining uniformity in their legislation.

ARTICLE 106

The Inter-American Juridical Committee shall undertake the studies and preparatory work assigned to it by the General Assembly, the Meeting of Consultation of Ministers of Foreign Affairs, or the Councils of the

Organization. It may also, on its own initiative, undertake such studies and preparatory work as it considers advisable, and suggest the holding of specialized juridical conferences.

ARTICLE 107

The Inter-American Juridical Committee shall be composed of eleven jurists, nationals of Member States, elected by the General Assembly for a period of four years from panels of three candidates presented by Member States. In the election, a system shall be used that takes into account partial replacement of membership and, insofar as possible, equitable geographic representation. No two members of the Committee may be nationals of the same State. Vacancies that occur shall be filled in the manner set forth above.

ARTICLE 108

The Inter-American Juridical Committee represents all of the Member States of the Organization, and has the broadest possible technical autonomy.

ARTICLE 109

The Inter-American Juridical Committee shall establish cooperative relations with universities, institutes, and other teaching centers, as well as with national and international committees and entities devoted to study, research, teaching, or dissemination of information on juridical matters of international interest.

ARTICLE 110

The Inter-American Juridical Committee shall draft its statutes, which shall be submitted to the General Assembly for approval.

The Committee shall adopt its own rules of procedure.

ARTICLE 111

The seat of the Inter-American Juridical Committee shall be the city of Rio de Janeiro, but in special cases the Committee may meet at any other place that may be designated, after consultation with the Member State concerned.

XVIII. THE INTER-AMERICAN COMMISSION ON HUMAN RIGHTS

ARTICLE 112

There shall be an Inter-American Commission on Human Rights, whose principal function shall be to promote the observance and protection of human rights and to serve as a consultative organ of the Organization in these matters.

An inter-American convention on human rights shall determine the structure, competence, and procedure of this Commission, as well as those of other organs responsible for these matters.

XIX. The General Secretariat

[1948 Text: Chapter XIII. The Pan American Union]
ARTICLE 113

The General Secretariat is the central and permanent organ of the Organization of American States. It shall perform the functions assigned to it in the Charter, in other inter-American treaties and agreements, and by the General Assembly, and shall carry out the duties entrusted to it by the General Assembly, the Meeting of Consultation of Ministers of Foreign Affairs, or the Councils.

ARTICLE 114

The Secretary General of the Organization shall be elected by the General Assembly for a five-year term and may not be reelected more than once or succeeded by a person of the same nationality. In the event that the office of Secretary General becomes vacant, the Assistant Secretary General shall assume his duties until the General Assembly shall elect a new Secretary General for a full term.

ARTICLE 115

The Secretary General shall direct the General Secretariat, be the legal representative thereof, and, notwithstanding the provisions of Article 91.b, be responsible to the General Assembly for the proper fulfillment of the obligations and functions of the General Secretariat.

ARTICLE 116

The Secretary General, or his representative, participates with voice but without vote in all meetings of the Organization.

ARTICLE 117

The General Secretariat shall promote economic, social, juridical, educational, scientific, and cultural relations among all the Member States of the Organization, in keeping with the actions and policies decided upon by the General Assembly and with the pertinent decisions of the Councils.

ARTICLE 118

The General Secretariat shall also perform the following functions:
(a) Transmit ex officio to the Member States notice of the convocation of the General Assembly, the Meeting of Consultation of Ministers of Foreign Affairs, the Inter-American Economic and Social Council, the

Inter-American Council for Education, Science, and Culture, and the Specialized Conferences;

(b) *Advise the other organs, when appropriate, in the preparation of agenda and rules of procedure;*

(c) *Prepare the proposed program-budget of the Organization on the basis of programs adopted by the Councils, agencies, and entities whose expenses should be included in the program budget and, after consultation with the Councils or their permanent committees, submit it to the Preparatory Committee of the General Assembly and then to the Assembly itself;*

(d) *Provide, on a permanent basis, adequate secretariat services for the General Assembly and the other organs, and carry out their directives and assignments. To the extent of its ability, provide services for the other meetings of the Organization;*

(e) *Serve as custodian of the documents and archives of the Inter-American Conferences, the General Assembly, the Meetings of Consultation of Ministers of Foreign Affairs, the Councils, and the Specialized Conferences;*

(f) *Serve as depository of inter-American treaties and agreements, as well as of the instruments of ratification thereof;*

(g) *Submit to the General Assembly at each regular session an annual report on the activities of the Organization and its financial condition; and*

(h) *Establish relations of cooperation, in accordance with decisions reached by the General Assembly or the Councils, with the Specialized Organizations as well as other national and international organizations.*

ARTICLE 119

The Secretary General shall:

(a) *Establish such offices of the General Secretariat as are necessary to accomplish its purposes; and*

(b) *Determine the number of officers and employees of the General Secretariat, appoint them, regulate their powers and duties, and fix their remuneration. The Secretary General shall exercise this authority in accordance with such general standards and budgetary provisions as may be established by the General Assembly.*

ARTICLE 120

The Assistant Secretary General shall be elected by the General Assembly for a five-year term and may not be reelected more than once or succeeded by a person of the same nationality. In the event that the office of Assistant Secretary General becomes vacant, the Permanent Council shall elect a substitute to hold that office until the General Assembly shall elect a new Assistant Secretary General for a full term.

ARTICLE 121

The Assistant Secretary General shall be the Secretary of the Permanent Council. He shall serve as advisory officer to the Secretary General and shall act as his delegate in all matters that the Secretary General may entrust to him. During the temporary absence or disability of the Secretary General, the Assistant General shall perform his functions.

The Secretary General and the Assistant Secretary General shall be of different nationalities.

ARTICLE 122 [87]

The *General Assembly,* by a two-thirds vote of *the Member States,* may remove the Secretary General or the Assistant Secretary General, *or both,* whenever the proper functioning of the Organization so demands.

ARTICLE 123

The Secretary General shall appoint, with the approval of the respective Council, the Executive Secretary for Economic and Social Affairs and the Executive Secretary for Education, Science, and Culture, who shall also be the secretaries of the respective Councils.

ARTICLE 124 [89]

In the performance of their duties, *the Secretary General and* the personnel *of the Secretariat* shall not seek or receive instructions from any Government or from any authority outside the *Organization, and* shall refrain from any action that *may be incompatible with* their position as international *officers* responsible only to the *Organization.*

ARTICLE 125 [90]

The Member States pledge themselves to respect the exclusively international character of the responsibilities of the Secretary General and the personnel *of the General Secretariat,* and not to seek to influence them in the discharge of their duties.

ARTICLE 126

In selecting the personnel of the General Secretariat, first consideration shall be given to efficiency, competence, and integrity; but at the same time, in the recruitment of personnel of all ranks, importance shall be given to the necessity of obtaining as wide a geographic representation as possible.

ARTICLE 127 [92]

The seat of the *General Secretariat* is the city of Washington.

XX [XIV]. THE SPECIALIZED CONFERENCES
ARTICLE 128
The Specialized Conferences are intergovernmental meetings to deal with special technical matters or to develop specific aspects of inter-American cooperation. They shall be held when either the General Assembly or the Meeting of Consultation of Ministers of Foreign Affairs so decides, on its own initiative or at the request of one of the Councils or Specialized Organizations.

ARTICLE 129
The agenda and rules of procedure of the Specialized Conferences shall be prepared by the Councils or Specialized Organizations concerned and shall be submitted to the Governments of the Member States for consideration.

XXI [XV]. THE SPECIALIZED ORGANIZATIONS
ARTICLE 130 [95]
For the purposes of the present Charter, Inter-American Specialized Organizations are the intergovernmental organizations established by multilateral agreements and having specific functions with respect to technical matters of common interest to the American States.

ARTICLE 131
The General Secretariat shall maintain a register of the organizations that fulfill the conditions set forth in the foregoing Article, as determined by the General Assembly after a report from the Council concerned.

ARTICLE 132 [97]
The Specialized Organizations shall enjoy the fullest technical autonomy, *but they* shall take into account the recommendations of *the General Assembly and of the Councils,* in accordance with the provisions of the Charter.

ARTICLE 133 [98]
The Specialized Organizations shall *transmit to the General Assembly annual* reports on the progress of their work and on their annual budgets and expenses.

ARTICLE 134
Relations that should exist between the Specialized Organizations and the Organization shall be defined by means of agreements concluded between each organization and the Secretary General, with the authorization of the General Assembly.

ARTICLE 135 [100]

The Specialized Organizations shall establish cooperative relations with world agencies of the same character in order to coordinate their activities. In concluding agreements with international agencies of a world-wide character, the Inter-American Specialized Organizations shall preserve their identity and their status as integral parts of the Organization of American States, even when they perform regional functions of international agencies.

ARTICLE 136

In determining the location of the Specialized Organizations consideration shall be given to the interest of all of the Member States and to the desirability of selecting the seats of these organizations on the basis of a geographic representation as equitable as possible.

PART THREE

XXII [VI]. THE UNITED NATIONS

ARTICLE 137 [102]

None of the provisions of this Charter shall be construed as impairing the rights and obligations of the Member States under the Charter of the United Nations.

XXIII [XVII]. MISCELLANEOUS PROVISIONS

ARTICLE 138

Attendance at meetings of the permanent organs of the Organization of American States or at the conferences and meetings provided for in the Charter, or held under the auspices of the Organization, shall be in accordance with the multilateral character of the aforesaid organs, conferences, and meetings and shall not depend on the bilateral relations between the Government of any Member State and the Government of the host country.

ARTICLE 139 [103]

The Organization of American States shall enjoy in the territory of each Member such legal capacity, privileges and immunities as are necessary for the exercise of its functions and the accomplishment of its purposes.

ARTICLE 140

The representatives of the Member States on the organs of the Organization, the personnel of their delegations, as well as the Secretary

General and the Assistant Secretary General shall enjoy the privileges and immunities corresponding to their positions and necessary for the independent performance of their duties.

ARTICLE 141

The juridical status of the specialized Organizations and the privileges and immunities that should be granted to them and to their personnel, as well as to the officials of the General Secretariat, shall be determined in a multilateral agreement. The foregoing shall not preclude when it is considered necessary, the concluding of bilateral agreements.

ARTICLE 142 [106]

Correspondence of the Organization of American States, including printed matter and parcels, bearing the frank thereof, shall be carried free of charge in the mails of the Member States.

ARTICLE 143

The Organization of American States does not allow any restriction based on race, creed, or sex, with respect to eligibility to participate in the activities of the Organization and to hold positions therein.

XXIV [XVIII]. RATIFICATION AND ENTRY INTO FORCE

ARTICLE 144 [108]

The present Charter shall remain open for signature by the American States and shall be ratified in accordance with their respective constitutional procedures. The original instrument, the Spanish, English, Portuguese and French texts of which are equally authentic, shall be deposited with the *General Secretariat,* which shall transmit certified copies thereof to the Governments for purposes of ratification. The instruments of ratification shall be dposited with the *General Secretariat,* which shall notify the signatory States of such deposit.

ARTICLE 145 [109]

The present Charter shall enter into force among the ratifying States when two-thirds of the signatory States have deposited their ratifications. It shall enter into force with respect to the remaining States in the order in which they deposit their ratifications.

ARTICLE 146 [110]

The present Charter shall be registered with the Secretariat of the United Nations through the *General Secretariat.*

ARTICLE 147 [111]

Amendments to the present Charter may be adopted only at *a General Assembly* convened for that purpose. Amendments shall enter into force in accordance with the terms and the procedure set forth in Article 145.

ARTICLE 148 [112]

The present Charter shall remain in force indefinitely, but may be denounced by any Member State upon written notification to the *General Secretariat,* which shall communicate to all the other each notice of denunciation received. After two years from the date on which the *General Secretariat* receives a notice of denunciation, the present Charter shall cease to be in force with respect to the denouncing State, which shall cease to belong to the Organization after it has fulfilled the obligation arising from the present Charter.

XXV. TRANSITORY PROVISIONS

ARTICLE 149

The Inter-American Committee on the Alliance for Progress shall act as the permanent executive committee of the Inter-American Economic and Social Council as long as the Alliance is in operation.

ARTICLE 150

Until the inter-American convention on human rights, referred to in Chapter XVIII, enters into force, the present Inter-American Commission on Human Rights shall keep vigilance over the observance of human rights.

NOTE. The following declarations were made at the time of the signing of the 1967 Protocol:

1. "The Delegation of *Ecuador,* drawing its inspiration from the devotion of the people and the Government of Ecuador to peace and law, states for the record that the provisions approved with respect to peaceful settlement of disputes do not carry out the purpose of Resolution XIII of the Second Special Inter-American Conference, and that the Permanent Council has not been given sufficient powers to aid the Member States effectively in the peaceful settlement of their disputes.

"The Delegation of Ecuador signs this Protocol of Amendment to the Charter of the Organization of American States in the understanding that none of its provisions in any way limits the right of the Member States to take their disputes, whatever their nature and the subject they deal with, to the Organization, so that it may assist the parties and recommend the suitable procedures for peaceful settlement thereof."

2. "The Delegation of *Panama,* upon signing the Protocol of Amendment to the Charter of the Organization of American States, states that it does so in the understanding that none of its provisions limits or in any way impedes the right of Panama to bring before the Organization any conflict or dispute that may have arisen with another Member State to which a just solution has not been given within a reasonable period after applying, without positive results, any of the procedures for peaceful settlement set forth in Article 21 of the present Charter."

3. "On signing the present Protocol, the *Argentine Republic* reiterates its firm conviction that the amendments introduced in the Charter of the OAS do not duly cover the requirements of the Organization, inasmuch as its basic instrument should contain, in addition to the organic, economic, social, and cultural standards, the essential provisions that would make the security system of the Hemisphere effective."

Appendix

28. Covenant of the League of Nations

Adopted by the Paris Peace Conference on June 28, 1919, and incorporated as Part I of the Treaty of Versailles and of other Peace Treaties, the Covenant came into force on January 10, 1920. Amendments are printed in italics.

The High Contracting Parties,

In order to promote international cooperation and to achieve international peace and security

by the acceptance of obligations not to resort to war,

by the prescription of open, just and honourable relations between nations,

by the firm establishment of the understandings of international law as the actual rule of conduct among Governments, and

by the maintenance of justice and a scrupulous respect for all treaty obligations in the dealings of organised peoples with one another,

Agree to this Covenant of the League of Nations.

ARTICLE 1

1. The original Members of the League of Nations shall be those of the Signatories which are named in the Annex to this Covenant and also such of those other States named in the Annex as shall accede without reservation to this Covenant. Such accession shall be effected by a Declaration deposited with the Secretariat within two months of the coming into force of the Covenant. Notice thereof shall be sent to all other Members of the League.

2. Any fully self-governing State, Dominion or Colony not named in the Annex may become a Member of the League of its admission is agreed to by two-thirds of the Assembly, provided that it shall give effective guarantees of its sincere intention to observe its international obligations, and shall accept such regulations as may be prescribed by the League in regard to its military, naval and air forces and armaments.

3. Any Member of the League may, after two years' notice of its intention so to do, withdraw from the League, provided that all the international obligations and all its obligations under this Covenant shall have been fulfilled at the time of its withdrawal.

ARTICLE 2

The action of the League under this Covenant shall be effected through the instrumentality of an Assembly and of a Council, with a permanent Secretariat.

ARTICLE 3.

1. The Assembly shall consist of Representatives of the Members of the League.

2. The Assembly shall meet at stated intervals and from time to time as occasion may require at the Seat of the League or at such other place as may be decided upon.

3. The Assembly may deal at its meetings with any matter within the sphere of action of the League or affecting the peace of the world.

4. At meetings of the Assembly, each Member of the League shall have one vote, and may have not more than three Representatives.

ARTICLE 4.

1. The Council shall consist of Representatives of the Principal Allied and Associated Powers, together with Representatives of four other Members of the League. These four Members of the League shall be selected by the Assembly from time to time in its discretion. Until the appointment of the Representatives of the four Members of the League first selected by the Assembly, Representatives of Belgium, Brazil, Spain, and Greece shall be members of the Council.

2. With the approval of the majority of the Assembly, the Council may name additional Members of the League whose Representatives shall always be members of the Council; the Council with like approval may increase the number of Members of the League to be selected by the Assembly for representation on the Council.

2 bis. The assembly shall fix by a two-thirds majority the rules dealing with the election of the nonpermanent members of the Council, and particularly such regulations as relate to their term of office and the conditions of reeligibility.

3. The Council shall meet from time to time as occasion may require, and at least once a year, at the Seat of the League, or at such other place as may be decided upon.

4. The Council may deal at its meetings with any matter within the sphere of action of the League or affecting the peace of the world.

5. Any Member of the League not represented on the Council shall be invited to send a Representative to sit as a member at any meeting of the Council during the consideration of matters specially affecting the interests of that Member of the League.

6. At meetings of the Council, each Member of the League represented on the Council shall have one vote, and may have not more than one Representative.

ARTICLE 5

1. Except where otherwise expressly provided in this Covenant or by the terms of the present Treaty, decisions at any meeting of the Assembly or of the Council shall require the agreement of all the Members of the League represented at the meeting.

2. All matters of procedure at meetings of the Assembly or of the Council, including the appointment of Committees to investigate particular matters, shall be regulated by the Assembly or by the Council and may be decided by a majority of the Members of the League represented at the meeting.

3. The first meeting of the Assembly and the first meeting of the Council shall be summoned by the President of the United States of America.

ARTICLE 6

1. The permanent Secretariat shall be established at the Seat of the League. The Secretariat shall comprise a Secretary-General and such secretaries and staff as may be required.

2. The first Secretary-General shall be the person named in the Annex; thereafter the Secretary-General shall be appointed by the Council with the approval of the majority of the Assembly.

3. The secretaries and staff of the Secretariat shall be appointed by the Secretary-General with the approval of the Council.

4. The Secretary-General shall act in that capacity at all meetings of the Assembly and of the Council.

5. *The expenses of the League shall be borne by the Members of the League in the proportion decided by the Assembly.*

ARTICLE 7

1. The Seat of the-League is established at Geneva.

2. The Council may at any time decide that the Seat of the League shall be established elsewhere.

3. All positions under or in connection with the League, including the Secretariat, shall be open equally to men and women.

4. Representatives of the Members of the League and officials of the League when engaged on the business of the League shall enjoy diplomatic privileges and immunities.

5. The buildings and other property occupied by the League or its officials or by Representatives attending its meetings shall be inviolable.

ARTICLE 8

1. The Members of the League recognise that the maintenance of peace requires the reduction of national armaments to the lowest point consistent with national safety and the enforcement by common action of international obligations.

2. The Council, taking account of the geographical situation and circumstances of each State, shall formulate plans for such reduction for the consideration and action of the several Governments.

3. Such plans shall be subject to reconsideration and revision at least every ten years.

4. After these plans shall have been adopted by the several Governments, the limits of armaments therein fixed shall not be exceeded without the concurrence of the Council.

5. The Members of the League agree that the manufacture by private enterprise of munitions and implements of war is open to grave objections. The Council shall advise how the evil effects attendant upon such manufacture can be prevented, due regard being had to the necessities of those Members of the League which are not able to manufacture the munitions and implements of war necessary for their safety.

6. The Members of the League undertake to interchange full and frank information as to the scale of their armaments, their military, naval and air programmes and the condition of such of their industries as are adaptable to warlike purposes.

ARTICLE 9

A permanent commission shall be constituted to advise the Council on the execution of the provisions of Articles 1 and 8 and on military, naval and air questions generally.

ARTICLE 10

The Members of the League undertake to respect and preserve as against external aggression the territorial integrity and existing political independence of all Members of the League. In case of any such aggression or in case of any threat or danger of such aggression the Council shall advise upon the means by which this obligation shall be fulfilled.

ARTICLE 11

1. Any war or threat of war, whether immediately affecting any of the Members of the League or not, is hereby declared a matter of concern to the whole League, and the League shall take any action that may be deemed wise and effectual to safeguard the peace of nations. In case any such emergency should arise, the Secretary-General shall on the request of any Member of the League forthwith summon a meeting of the Council.

2. It is also declared to be the friendly right of each Member of the League to bring to the attention of the Assembly or of the Council any circumstance whatever affecting international relations which threatens to disturb international peace or the good understanding between nations upon which peace depends.

ARTICLE 12

1. The Members of the League agree that if there should arise between them any dispute likely to lead to a rupture, they will submit the matter either to arbitration *or judicial settlement* or to inquiry by the Council, and they agree in no case to resort to war until three months after the award by the arbitrators *or the judicial decision* or the report by the Council.

2. In any case under this Article the award of the arbitrators *or the judicial decision* shall be made within a reasonable time, and the report of the Council shall be made within six months after the submission of the dispute.

ARTICLE 13

1. The Members of the League agree that whenever any dispute shall arise between them which they recognize to be suitable for submission to arbitration *or judicial settlement,* and which cannot be satisfactorily settled by diplomacy, they will submit the whole subject-matter to arbitration *or judicial settlement.*

2. Disputes as to the interpretation of a teaty, as to any question of international law, as to the existence of any fact which if established would constitute a breach of any international obligation, or as to the extent and nature of the reparation to be made for any such breach, are declared to be among those which are generally suitable for submission to arbitration *or judicial settlement.*

3. *For the consideration of any such dispute, the court to which the case is referred shall be the Permanent Court of International Justice, established in accordance with Article 14, or any tribunal agreed on by the parties to the dispute or stipulated in any convention existing between them.*

4. The Members of the League agree that they will carry out in full good faith any award *or decision* that may be rendered, and that they will not resort to war against a Member of the League which complies therewith. In the event of any failure to carry out such an award *or decision,* the Council shall propose what steps should be taken to give effect thereto.

ARTICLE 14

The Council shall formulate and submit to the Members of the League for adoption plans for the establishment of a Permanent Court of International Justice. The Court shall be competent to hear and determine any dispute of an international character which the parties thereto submit to it. The Court may also give an advisory opinion upon any dispute or question referred to it by the Council or by the Assembly.

ARTICLE 15

1. If there should arise between Members of the League any dispute likely to lead to a rupture, which is not submitted to arbitration *or judicial settlement* in accordance with Article 13, the Members of the League agree that they will submit the matter to the Council. Any party to the dispute may effect such submission by giving notice of the existence of the dispute to the Secretary-General, who will make all necessary arrangements for a full investigation and consideration thereof.

2. For this purpose the parties to the dispute will communicate to the Secretary-General, as promptly as possible, statements of their case with all the relevant facts and papers, and the Council may forthwith direct the publication thereof.

3. The Council shall endeavour to effect a settlement of the dispute, and if such efforts are successful, a statement shall be made public giving such facts and explanations regarding the dispute and the terms of settlement thereof as the Council may deem appropriate.

4. If the dispute is not thus settled, the Council either unanimously or by a majority vote shall make and publish a report containing a statement of the facts of the dispute and the recommendations which are deemed just and proper in regard thereto.

5. Any Member of the League represented on the Council may make public a statement of the facts of the dispute and of its conclusions regarding the same.

6. If a report by the Council is unanimously agreed to by the members thereof other than the Representatives of one or more of the parites to the dispute, the Members of the League agree that they will not go to war with any party to the dispute which complies with the recommendations of the report.

7. If the Council fails to reach a report which is unanimously agreed to by the members thereof, other than the Representatives of one or more of the parties to the dispute, the Members of the League reserve to themselves the right to take such action as they shall consider necessary for the maintenance of right and justice.

8. If the dispute between the parties is claimed by one of them, and is found by the Council, to arise out of a matter which by international law is solely within the domestic jurisdiction of that party, the Council shall so report, and shall make no recommendation as to its settlement.

9. The Council may in any case under this Article refer the dispute to the Assembly. The dispute shall be so referred at the request of either party

to the dispute, provided that such request be made within fourteen days after the submission of the dispute to the Council.

10. In any case referred to the Assembly, all the provisions of this Article and of Article 12 relating to the action and powers of the Council shall apply to the action and powers of the Assembly, provided that a report made by the Assembly, if concurred in by the Representatives of those Members of the League represented on the Council and of a majority of the other Members of the League, exclusive in each case of the Representatives of the parties to the dispute, shall have the same force as a report by the Council concurred in by all the members thereof other than the Representatives of one or more of the parties to the dispute.

ARTICLE 16

1. Should any Member of the League resort to war in disregard of its covenants under Articles 12, 13, or 15, it shall *ipso facto* be demmed to have committed an act of war against all other Members of the League, which hereby undertake immediately to subject it to the severance of all trade or financial relations, the prohibition of all intercourse between their nationals and the nationals of the covenant-breaking State, and the prevention of all financial, commercial or personal intercourse between the nationals of the covenant-breaking State and the nationals of any other State, whether a Member of the League or not.

2. It shall be the duty of the Council in such case to recommend to the several Governments concerned what effective military, naval or air force the Members of the League shall severally contribute to the armed forces to be used to protect the covenants of the League.

3. The Members of the League agree, further, that they will mutually support one another in the fianancial and economic measures which are taken under this Article, in order to minimize the loss and inconvenience resulting from the above measures, and that they will mutually support one another in resisting any special measures aimed at one of their number by the covenant-breaking State, and that they will take the necessary steps to afford passage through their territory to the forces of any of the Members of the League which are cooperating to protect the covenants of the League.

4. Any Member of the League which has violated any covenant of the League may be declared to be no longer a Member of the League by a vote of the Council concurred in by the Representatives of all the other Members of the League represented thereon.

ARTICLE 17

1. In the event of a dispute between a Member of the League and a State which is not a member of the League, or between States not members of the League, the State or States not members of the League shall be in-

vited to accept the obligations of membership in the League for the purposes of such dispute, upon such conditions as the Council may deem just. If such invitation is accepted, the provisions of Articles 12 to 16 inclusive shall be applied with such modifications as may be deemed necessary by the Council.

2. Upon such invitation being given the Council shall immediately institute an inquiry into the circumstances of the dispute and recommend such action as may seem best and most effectual in the circumstances.

3. If a State so invited shall refuse to accept the obligations of membership in the League for the purposes of such dispute, and shall resort to war against a Member of the League, the provisions of Article 16 shall be applicable as against the State taking such actions.

4. If both parties to the dispute when so invited refuse to accept the obligations of membership in the League for the purposes of such dispute, the Council may take such measures and make such recommendations as will prevent hostilities and will result in the settlement of the dispute.

ARTICLE 18

Every treaty or international engagement entered into hereafter by any Member of the League shall be forthwith registered with the Secretariat and shall as soon as possible be published by it. No such treaty or international engagement shall be binding until so registered.

ARTICLE 19

The Assembly may from time to time advise the reconsideration by Members of the League of treaties which have become inapplicable and the consideration of international conditions whose continuance might endanger the peace of the world.

ARTICLE 20

1. The Members of the League severally agree that this Covenant is accepted as abrogating all obligations or understandings *inter se* which are inconsistent with the terms thereof, and solemnly undertake that they will not hereafter enter into any engagements inconsistent with the terms thereof.

2. In case any Member of the League shall, before becoming a Member of the League, have undertaken any obligations inconsistent with the terms of this Covenant, it shall be the duty of such Member to take immediate steps to procure its release from such obligations.

ARTICLE 21

Nothing in this Covenant shall be deemed to affect the validity of international engagements, such as treaties of arbitration or regional understandings like the Monroe doctrine, for securing the maintenance of peace.

ARTICLE 22

1. To those colonies and territories which as a consequence of the late war have ceased to be under the sovereignty of the States which formerly governed them and which are inhabited by peoples not yet able to stand by themselves under the strenuous conditions of the modern world, there should be applied the principle that the well-being and development of such peoples form a sacred trust of civilization and that securities for the performance of this trust should be embodied in this Covenant.

2. The best method of giving practical effect to this principle is that the tutelage of such peoples should be entrusted to advanced nations who by reason of their resources, their experience or their geographical position can best undertake this responsibility, and who are willing to accept it, and that this tutelage should be exercised by them as Mandatories on behalf of the League.

3. The character of the mandate must differ according to the stage of the development of the people, the geographical situation of the territory, its economic conditions and other similar circumstances.

4. Certain communities formerly belonging to the Turkish Empire have reached a stage of development where their existence as independent nations can be provisionally recognized subject to the rendering of administrative advice and assistance by a Mandatory until such time as they are able to stand alone. The wishes of these communities must be a principal consideration in the selection of the Mandatory.

5. Other peoples, especially those of Central Africa, are at such a stage that the Mandatory must be responsible for the administration of the territory under conditions which will guarantee freedom of conscience and religion, subject only to the maintenance of public order and morals, the prohibition of abuses such as the slave trade, the arms traffic and the liquor traffic, and the prevention of the establishment of fortifications or military and naval bases and of military training of the natives for other than police purposes and the defence of territory, and will also secure equal opportunities for the trade and commerce of other Members of the League.

6. There are territories, such as South West Africa and certain of the South Pacific Islands, which, owing to the sparseness of their population, or their small size, or their remoteness from the centres of civilization, or their geographical contiguity to the territory of the Mandatory, and other circumstances, can be best administered under the laws of the Mandatory as integral portions of its territory, subject to the safeguards above mentioned in the interests of the indigenous population.

7. In every case of mandate, the Mandatory shall render to the Council an annual report in reference to the territory committed to its charge.

8. The degree of authority, control, or administration to be exercised by the Mandatory shall, if not previously agreed upon by the Members of the League, be explicitly defined in each case by the Council.

9. A permanent Commission shall be constituted to receive and examine the annual reports of the Mandatories and to advise the Council on all matters relating to the observance of the mandates.

ARTICLE 23

Subject to and in accordance with the provisions of international conventions existing or hereafter to be agreed upon, the Members of the League:

(a) will endeavour to secure and maintain fair and humane conditions of labour for men, women, and children, both in their own countries and in all countries to which their commercial and industrial relations extend, and for that purpose will establish and maintain the necessary international organizations;

(b) undertake to secure just treatment of the native inhabitants of territories under their control;

(c) will entrust the League with the general supervision over the execution of agreements with regard to the traffic in women and children, and the traffic in opium and other dangerous drugs;

(d) will entrust the League with the general supervision of the trade in arms and ammunition with the countries in which the control of this traffic is necessary in the common interest;

(e) will make provision to secure and maintain freedom of communication and of transit and equitable treatment for the commerce of all Members of the League. In this connection, the special necessities of the regions devastated during the war of 1914–1918 shall be borne in mind;

(f) will endeavour to take steps in matters of international concern for the prevention and control of disease.

ARTICLE 24

1. There shall be placed under the direction of the League international bureaux already established by general treaties if the parties to such treaties consent. All such international bureaux and all commissions for the regulation of matters of international interest hereafter constituted shall be placed under the direction of the League.

2. In all matters of international interest which are regulated by general conventions but which are not placed under the control of international bureaux or commissions, the Secretariat of the League shall, subject to the consent of the Council and if desired by the parties, collect and distribute all relevant information and shall render any other assistance which may be necessary or desirable.

3. The Council may include as part of the expenses of the Secretariat the expenses of any bureau or commission which is placed under the direction of the League.

ARTICLE 25

The Members of the League agree to encourage and promote the establishment and cooperation of duly authorized voluntary national Red Cross organizations having as purposes the improvement of health, the prevention of disease and the mitigation of suffering throughout the world.

ARTICLE 26

1. Amendments to this Covenant will take effect when ratified by the Members of the League whose Representatives compose the Council and by a majority of the Members of the League whose Representatives compose the Assembly.

2. No such amendment shall bind any Member of the League which signifies its dissent therefrom, but in that case it shall cease to be a Member of the League.

ANNEX TO THE COVENANT

I. *Original Members of the League of Nations, Signatories of the Treaty of Peace*

United States of America	Haiti
Belgium	Hejaz
Bolivia	Honduras
Brazil	Italy
British Empire	Japan
Canda	Liberia
Australia	Nicaragua
South Africa	Panama
New Zealand	Peru
India	Poland
China	Portugal
Cuba	Rumania
Ecuador	Serb-Croat-Slovene State
France	Siam
Greece	Czechoslovakia
Guatemala	Uruguay

States Invited to Accede to the Covenant

Argentine Republic	Persia
Chile	Salvador
Colombia	Spain
Denmark	Sweden
Netherlands	Switzerland
Norway	Venezuela
Paraguay	

II. *First Secretary-General of the League of Nations. The Hon. Sir James Eric Drummond, K.C.M.G., C.B.*